FINNTOPIA

"Among the world's countries, Finland ranks at or near the top in air quality, education, equality, happiness, honest government, milk consumption, opportunities for children, preparedness, safety, trust in its police, and many other things. Eighty years ago, most of those things were not true. How did Finland become so successful, so quickly, across such a broad spectrum? How can other countries achieve Finland's happiness? Read this wonderful book, and learn the answers!"

JARED DIAMOND, Professor of Geography, UCLA and Pulitzer-Prize-winning author of *Guns, Germs, and Steel*

"As inequality reaches eye-watering levels around the world, this book contains some fascinating and important lessons on how policies like progressive taxation and investing in public services can lead to more equal – and happier – societies."

DANNY SRISKANDARAJAH, chief executive, Oxfam GB

"Finland is one of the fairest, most inclusive and dynamic countries to live in. This is not because it is small or culturally homogeneous, or enjoys a great deal of oil wealth. As Danny Dorling and Annika Koljonen show us in this marvellous book, it is because of what Finns have learned about 'caring for each other more and more cleverly' over recent decades. We would do well to follow their example."

SIMON REID-HENRY, Reader in Geography, Queen Mary University of London, and Senior Researcher at the Peace Research Institute in Oslo

"Good enough to be true – just like the story of Finland."

ANNA SIEVÄLÄ, journalist, Joensuu

"An absorbing, insightful and scholarly book, grounded in emancipatory hope and humility, that captures the very essence of why Finland has become one of the most equitable countries in a highly unequal world."

PAUL STEPNEY, Adjunct Professor of Social Work,
Tampere University, Finland

"*Finntopia* is the remarkable story of a country on Europe's perceived fringes that should instead be in the centre of our view for creating a better society. Dorling and Koljonen provide a compelling picture of why Finland may not be the Utopia that it sometimes is portrayed as, but can still teach us many lessons about a different kind of politics, one that has the interest of people at its heart."

BENJAMIN HENNIG, Professor of Geography, University of Iceland

". . . in simple terms, the image of Finland I see in
your book is precisely how I see things."

MARKKU LÖYTÖNEN, Professor of Geography, University of Helsinki

"A fascinating book which reads like a detective story. It makes one wonder if the secret behind the happiness of Finns is their ignorance of their own happiness. There is much to learn from *Finntopia*, even for a native Finn."

JUHA KAAKINEN, chief executive of the Y-Foundation
(that has built 6500 homes for the homeless in Finland)

"Danny Dorling and Annika Koljonen's portrait of Finland's socio-political system and history is a thought-provoking read. They convincingly demonstrate that the most profitable investment any institution or country can make is to invest in the well-being, education, and capabilities of its people."

MIKKO WECKROTH, postdoctoral researcher,
Helsinki Institute of Sustainability Science

FINNTOPIA

FINNTOPIA

*What we can learn from
the world's happiest country*

DANNY DORLING
AND
ANNIKA KOLJONEN

agenda
publishing

First published in 2020 by Agenda Publishing

Reprinted 2020

First published in paperback 2022

Agenda Publishing Limited
The Core
Bath Lane
Newcastle Helix
Newcastle upon Tyne
NE4 5TF

www.agendapub.com

ISBN 978-1-78821-215-1 (hardcover)
ISBN 978-1-78821-216-8 (paperback)

British Library Cataloguing-in-Publication Data
A catalogue record for this book is available from the British Library

Typeset in Nocturne by Patty Rennie

Printed and bound in the UK by TJ Books Ltd

To our grandmothers
Leena Asikainen and Ritva Koljonen (née Viiala)
Mary Charlesworth (née Kershaw) and Phyllis Dorling (née Bing)

Contents

Acknowledgements

In 2017 in the city of Cambridge in the UK, a local group known as the Cambridge Commons launched "Imagine 2027", a series of 15 public talks on different aspects of inequality and strategies to create a more equal society within ten years. Then, as now, Cambridge was the most unequal city by income in England (Rae & Nyanzu 2019), England the most unequal country in the UK, and the UK the most unequal large country in the European Union (OECD 2019a). The Cambridge Commons is affiliated to the Equality Trust, whose founders, a decade earlier, wrote a book called *The Spirit Level: Why More Equal Societies Almost Always Do Better*.

Annika Koljonen, originally from Helsinki and studying politics and international relations at the University of Cambridge, was a volunteer at Imagine 2027. Danny Dorling gave the second Imagine 2027 talk in the autumn of 2017, titled "Education, Equality and Everything Else: A Fairer England in 2027". It was there that we met. Just over two years later we had finished writing this book.

So why Finntopia? The answer was that even before it had been declared the happiest country in the world in 2018, 2019 and 2020 by the United Nations, Finland already stood out (Yle Uutiset 2019a). In his Imagine 2027 talk, Danny showed slide after slide about what was so wrong in the UK, along with data showing how public spending in European nations was highest in Finland and dramatically lower in England and the United States, and that Finnish students excelled while the British and Americans appeared to be dullards. To most of the audience in Cambridge, that renowned city of learning, all of this was news. But not to Annika.

Thanks to a suggestion from Alastair Breward, the main organizer of Imagine 2027, we then worked together in the summer of 2018 on a comparison of Finland and England, hoping to understand why statistics about Finland's education, healthcare and political system were beginning to be mentioned so frequently in discussions about equality, especially when it came to better ways to build a functioning welfare (or well-being) state.

A six-week summer project, however, was not nearly long enough to explore all the history leading up to, and the social policy implications of, greater equality. What were the factors behind Finland's success and how, once greater equality had been won, had it been defended? Later that year, we wrote an article for a UK newspaper about how public health was improving in Finland and worsening across all of the UK (Koljonen & Dorling 2018). But there is only so much you can say in one newspaper article – and there is so much more that needs to be learned from Finland.

We approached Alison Howson, who is now our editor at Agenda Publishing. Danny had helped international relations scholar Robbie Shilliam with a few statistics for a book that he was writing for Agenda (Shilliam 2018). Agenda is a publisher interested in new ideas – and by now we had a lot of very new ideas. Instead of writing yet again about what is so wrong with the world's most unequal affluent countries, we thought, why not take a detailed look at one of the world's most equitable countries, and along the way try to work out how its people had created it and how they benefited from it?

In writing this book we needed a great deal of help. In particular we would like to mention Eero Suominen, who in his last year as the Ambassador of Finland in South and North Korea helped us to better understand Finnish politics. We are also very grateful to Anthony Caira-Carnell for helping us unravel the Finnglishness of trying to write about Finland in English; to David Dorling, especially for help with understanding the geology; and to Bill Kerry, who tested how clear we were being (suggesting many useful clarifications), and Jakki Stewart, Paul Stepney, Anna Sievälä, and Benjamin Hennig who all kindly commented on the book and suggested a few changes. We are especially grateful to Karen Shook who helped add a more radical edge and checked every line for sense. Many thanks are due to Stacy Hewitt for helping with the English to deftly make what we thought made sense, make sense; to Mikko Weckroth for commenting on the proposal at an early stage and Salla

Jokela and Hannu Linkola for advice about the images we used; to Salla for commenting on a draft alongside Simon Reid-Henry and Jorma Sipilä, both of whom were ever so generous with their comments.

Most importantly we are grateful to Alison Howson and Steven Gerrard of Agenda for being so receptive to the idea of us writing this book and for encouraging us to change our initial approach to something more useful, and for her later careful and copious editing of the final manuscript; and for his brilliant copyediting and meticulous checking of the final text; to Claire Hann for sterling research assistance throughout and reading the final copy to help identify errors; to Ailsa Allen for drawing up all the figures so carefully; to Jyri Lehtonen, grandson of Aukusti Tuhka, for letting us use Aukusti Tuhka's designs; to Paul Stepney who works as an academic in both Finland and England and very kindly agreed to share his perspective about what was different and what was similar and who also commented in detail on a draft of the manuscript; to Jussi Salonen, deputy mayor of Tuusula, for agreeing to be interviewed to provide background material for the book; and to the geographer Markku Löytönen who was also ever so helpful in reading a later draft of the manuscript, providing sources and pointers of where next to look and for giving a passionate explanation of why Finland had managed to get to where it is today. Markku also introduced us to Arttu Paarlahti, the GIS wizard of Helsinki who helped us access the files that Ben Hennig so kindly turned into the cartogram of voting in Finland that is included in this book. Ben and Tina Gotthardt also kindly made the website that accompanies this book: www.dannydorling.org/finntopia.

Finally, thanks too to Maria Sjovik, who was extremely helpful and gave us a huge amount of advice and references. She works for the agency SEK, which recently helped Visit Finland launch its "Rent a Finn" promotional campaign that encourages Finns to volunteer as happiness guides for foreigners! Finally, special thanks are due, too, to Juliette Powell for introducing us to Maria – and thinking that this book was a good idea too at the point when we needed to know that it was!

DANNY DORLING (Oxford)

ANNIKA KOLJONEN (Helsinki)

Preface – Onnen maa
(The land of happiness)

In a little over half a century, Finland has become one of the most equitable countries in the world. It is the country with the best life chances for children, and the happiest people. What makes Finland so successful? To what extent is bold social policy key to that success? Or is it because of the growth of a shared belief in the well-being of everyone – and, if so, what role has its recent history played in the rise of that belief? Finland is just as subject to the vicissitudes of globalization and environmental threats as other affluent countries, but today it often confronts these problems better than almost all others and appears to be incredibly robust. We believe that it is time to take a close look at what other countries can learn from Finland.

What drawbacks might there be from so much equality? What are the downsides, if any, to Finntopia? Why haven't more countries achieved what Finland has achieved, and how many have done nearly as well as (or even better than) Finland on one or more aspects of equality – and why? If there are no great disadvantages to the Finnish system, then why don't more people move there or more countries emulate it? Why are there still far-right political parties in a country where life looks – in comparison to the reality for so many people in Britain or the United States – like paradise?

This book begins by acknowledging what almost everyone first mentions: the Finnish winters. And indeed, for many months of the year in Finland, it is very cold. We show that it is not this fact, nor the small size and high homogeneity of Finland's population, that are the underlying reasons for the social equality that exists in Finland today. In the pages that follow, using a huge range of statistics and sources, we explain why it is not Finland's climate, its demographics or its ethnicity that matter. None of those factors made everything that transpired inevitable. In fact, in many cases these factors have been a hindrance to Finland's economic, social and political development.

Along the way, we hope to debunk several myths about Finland, a country whose history may well surprise our readers. For one thing, its transition to an egalitarian society is relatively recent. Until the very end of the 1960s, its education system was deeply unequal. Greater equality in its schools was only very gradually won after fierce political debates, with a significant number of powerful elected politicians arguing that selectivity and competition were essential to an effective school system and a prosperous society. Finland's overhaul of its formerly elitist educational structure demonstrates that nationwide reforms to some of society's most important institutions are possible. With creative thinking, movement-building and a lot of stubborn perseverance, changes such as these can happen.

From education to housing, political will and perseverance have been crucial in almost all of Finland's milestones in equity, although it is worth noting that even in a country that in parts appears to be utopian, no accomplishments can be taken for granted. The Finnish healthcare system has fallen behind Finland's other achievements and nationwide reform has been ongoing since 2006 (Strömberg 2019). As the chapters to come will show, Finnish society is remarkable for its determination to keep innovating and adapting for the future, even if some attempts produce disappointing outcomes, such as the initial results of a universal basic income experiment carried out in very recent years. Of course, Finland is not utopia – but its people have worked to build a better world with far more rigour and determination than any other nation on the planet.

Most recently, first in 2018, then again in 2019 and 2020, and now again in 2021, Finland has been proclaimed the happiest nation in the world (Helliwell *et al.* 2019; Martela *et al.* 2020). Interestingly, however, whenever rankings such as these are published, or any of the more than 100 league tables listed in the appendix of this book in which Finland ranks first, second or third out of roughly 200 competitors, many Finns try to explain why Finland doesn't deserve these top spots, and instead highlight the rankings in which it does not perform especially well. The problems of alcoholism, gambling, depression, and security for women are frequently cited as rebuttals to the argument that there is nothing left for the country to improve. It is clear that Finns still want their nation to become even better, and – more importantly – they believe that it is possible. Finns are also – quietly and remarkably reservedly – very proud any time Finland is mentioned abroad (unless they have just won the Ice Hockey World Championships, when they are neither quiet nor reserved in expressing their pride).

The older generation of Finns, those born during the Second World War, have lived through the immense changes that Finland has experienced as it went from being one of the least developed European countries to eventually becoming one of the most stable and most admired. This change was only possible because the Finnish state invested in its people. When you benefit from being part of the state from birth through childhood, with parents who can take parental leave and afford childcare, and in youth and adulthood you receive free education and universal healthcare, and have the security of knowing you will never have to sleep rough, and in old age you receive a decent state pension upon retirement, you appreciate the true value of the tax taken off your salary.

Finland should be proud of its achievements, but the final third of this book explains that it must not let complacency win. Finns must not let the praise their country now receives go to their heads. Like the rest of the world, Finland must confront the climate emergency, manage the needs of an ageing population, and address the rising inequality within parts of its society. It must also grapple with the challenge of integrating immigrants into its society and the apparently concomitant (but surely not inevitable) rise of right-wing populism.

As an example of how much a single nation can get right, Finland's work toward ending inequality makes it too important to fail, and hopefully it is now too far ahead to flounder. Although there are many other states in the world that are nearly as equal, it is Finland that has travelled the furthest and fastest, despite limited natural resources beyond forests and some minerals, and with no chance event that might have thrust equality upon it. Finland is a beacon for those who think that another world is possible. It allows us to put aside fantasies of what could be built, and look instead at what has actually been created. Go to Finland and see for yourself, or better still, save the carbon pollution and the airfare, and read the pages that follow.

We did not write this book for people in Finland, although we have talked to a great many Finns and read the works of many more. This is a book for people elsewhere in the world. It is for people who may not believe that what has happened in Finland could also happen in their country. It is especially for British and American readers, whose nations are in the grip of the dire harm that high inequality brings, and the hopelessness that is perhaps the most dangerous economic-inequality outcome of all.

We say little about the 2020 COVID-19 pandemic in this book because, as we write, it is still unfolding. Readers can judge for themselves the extent to which they think Finland was better prepared than almost all of the rest of Europe for when the pandemic struck, and how that contrasts with the preparedness and behaviour of politicians and officials in those afflu- ent countries least like Finland. The Finns are not naturally sheltered from pandemics by their geographical isolation. The influenza pandemic of 1918 ravaged the country, and was one of a series of such past tragedies, as Figure 8.1 in this book illustrates.

Just a century ago, Finns had it worse than almost all other people in Europe. Their success is not a story of having access to resources and using those well, or even of a triumph out of adversity. Finland's achievements were the result of a long, patient slog, and the people of Finland are testament to what can be achieved if and where and when there is the will. Finland offers us an example of what bold policies can produce: policies that put the equal- ity of individuals at their heart, with the aim of building a fairer, happier, more prosperous society. The story of Finland shows that anything is possible.

Preface to the paperback edition
– Finland and the pandemic

Despite the times not everything was dark in early 2021 in Finland. Finns were fortunate to see a proper winter that year, considering 2020 saw barely any snow in the south of the country. Snow, helping light up dark winter days, also helped lighten minds exhausted by the enduring pandemic that had so severely restricted many people's lives around the world since early 2020.

At the time of us beginning to write this preface, in March 2021, the Finnish government had once again declared a state of emergency, just as it had a year earlier in March 2020. This was hardly a surprising turn given the rather relaxed restrictions of its earlier "hybrid strategy" that were seen as inadequate in the face of the more infectious variant of the disease that was then spreading across Europe. In March 2021, Finland's death rate per 10,000 was 1.4, as compared to 18 per 10,000 in the United Kingdom and 16 per 10,000 in the United States. Fewer than 800 people had died of the disease in 12 months in Finland. Less than died on many single days elsewhere.

We are making the final changes to these words in September 2021 following what has been a long and very hot summer in Finland. Cases of the disease fell to be very low by early June, but rose again later that month and throughout July after Finnish football fans returning from Russia brought the disease back with them, although the Delta-variant was already spreading in Finland (Ministry of Social Affairs and Health 2021). However, in the six months to September 2021 fewer than 300 people died of the disease and by

September cases were decreasing again. Deaths were still only just 1,000 in total since the pandemic began.

Internationally, Finland has been used as an example of a pandemic success story. The leading party in the coalition government, the Social Democratic Party, led by Prime Minister Sanna Marin, had also maintained great popularity throughout the year, at times polling better than the largest opposition party, the Finns Party. It is still too soon to make many conclusions, and there is also no denying that there was a fair amount of luck involved as well. Finland is a sparsely populated country, not located at a global crossroads, and even Helsinki does not necessarily count as a big city. Finland's borders are much easier to control than those of a country in, say, central Europe. It has a well-functioning healthcare system, a very effective welfare state, less inequality, automatic economic stabilizers (automatically increasing general government expenditure alongside reducing tax revenues in an economic downturn), is highly digitalized, and there is generally a high level of trust in authorities that helps promote compliance to both formal rules and informal general advice.

The Finnish government was able to enact strict restrictions from mid-March to mid-June 2020 using an Emergency Powers Act. No Act of this type had been used since the Second World War. Decrees issued on the basis of this Act must be immediately submitted to parliament, which can decide whether they need to be amended or rescinded. So, enacting these emergency powers in Finland only transfers legislative powers to the executive branch in a rather limited way. The most important body for parliamentary scrutiny in these matters is the Constitutional Law Committee, which Finland has in lieu of a constitutional court. The decrees were repealed in June 2020, and Finns were able to enjoy a relatively normal summer, although not the usual music festivals and holidays abroad, with very few daily cases of the disease being reported and negligible deaths. Thereafter the government carried on with its "hybrid" strategy of testing, tracing, (primarily voluntary) quarantine, working from home when possible, income support for people in quarantine, reduction of all travel across international borders, and limitations on public gatherings.

Like elsewhere in Europe, the autumn of 2020 saw a rise in cases in Finland. What is perceived as high and low in terms of infections and deaths varies dramatically between countries. Across Europe, Iceland, Norway and Finland suffered rates of disease and mortality ten times lower than much of the rest of Europe – but still ten times higher than those experienced in much of South East Asia. People in each country were far more likely to make comparisons with places with much *lower* rates than much *higher*. By the end of 2020 the mortality rate in Iceland was 16 times higher than in Singapore, the rate in Germany was 14 times higher than in Japan, Norway was 20 times higher than New Zealand, and Finland has seen seven times more people die due to the pandemic (per person) than South Korea. In fact, in Europe, the only countries that had slightly fewer deaths per person than Finland were Norway, Iceland and the Faroe Islands.

For someone reading this in the UK or United States it may be somewhat surprising to know just how seriously the pandemic was taken in Finland despite fewer than 800 people having died of the disease in its first year, and less than 300 more in the next six months. In the US and the UK, deaths per capita have been 11 and 13 times higher respectively. The main reason for this was that the disease spread so much more easily after arriving in the UK and US as compared to what happened when it arrived in Finland. In Finland, the precautions taken largely held it at bay, and they were taken because even a relatively small rise was seen as very concerning. Rates of disease that would have been deemed low enough for children to return to school and for university students to sit in lecture theatres elsewhere – were deemed high enough to instigate remote learning in Finland!

In November 2020 high school students in municipalities in Finland with above-average rates of infection returned to remote learning. University education had continued mainly by distance learning since March 2020. While cases rose towards the end of November, the much-feared rise in cases after Christmas and the New Year did not occur. Restaurants, cafes and bars were able to remain open until 9 March 2021. After the decrees issued on the basis of the Emergency Powers Act were repealed in June 2020, the government tried to control the epidemic within the bounds of normal legislation. Despite the Communicable Diseases Act being amended throughout the pandemic to achieve this, the government still had to enforce the closure of bars and restaurants by enacting the Emergency Powers Act. The Communicable Diseases Act is also limited in emergencies as it works by delegating decision-making powers to what are largely semi-autonomous Regional State Administrative Agencies, as well as municipalities and doctors specializing in infectious diseases (Scheinin 2021). These limitations were counterbalanced by the general concern to control the disease. What was seen as a significant rise in cases during February and early March also led to the postponing of the local elections to 13 June from 18 April. These local elections faced their lowest voter turnout in 70 years, falling to 55.1 per cent, 3.8 per cent less than in the previous elections in 2017.

Within Finland the political discourse on restrictions has largely been framed in legal jargon concerning basic rights and liberties protected by the constitution, such as the freedom of movement and the freedom to engage in commercial activity, and the division of executive and legislative powers. This has contributed to what have been viewed internally as quite mild restrictions on, for instance, restaurants, and the preference for recommendations (for example on face masks) over decrees enforced by legal penalties. These legal complexities were also the result of decentralized decision-making that allowed for differing interpretations when new laws were indistinct as well as political decisions made to not amend normal legislation to allow for greater restrictions on basic rights and liberties. The current government is also wary about setting a precedent that would allow for any future government to restrict basic rights at a lower threshold. It is worth noting that Finland also has not faced national emergencies such as widespread terrorist attacks in recent decades that might have required the government to swiftly restrict basic rights before (Luukka 2021).

The media has largely not been allowed inside hospitals to cover Covid-19 wards, although as of March 2021, the healthcare system has nowhere yet been overwhelmed by the pandemic. The number of inpatients in Finland with Covid-19 peaked in April and May 2020 at around 150, with about half in intensive care. It peaked again in December at around 250, but with only a fifth in intensive care by then, reaching similar figures in early March.

As for how Finland's economy has weathered the crisis, the projected economic costs of the pandemic have become smaller than what was feared in mid-2020. Finland was to receive €3.2 billion in the EU Recovery Plan, but in the light of the new economic projections made later, this was decreased by €500 million in January 2021. Finland will also have retained the monies that

Finns travelling abroad in the winter would have spent in other countries. Conversely, the local tourist industry has lost out. Savings increased amongst those who could save.

Sales have increased for grocery and hardware stores. The manufacturing industry has avoided a sharp fall in its turnover, and the construction and IT sectors have remained stable (Hartikainen 2021). Construction and manufacturing were not shut down in 2020. Predictably, tourism, hospitality and catering, the arts, entertainment, and transport are among the services most affected by the pandemic. Among the significantly affected companies is also the state-owned company Veikkaus, a gambling monopoly, as slot machines and gaming arcades have been periodically closed off from the public. Compared to 2019, Veikkaus suffered a loss of €300 million in 2020. It is important to recall that profits from gambling in Finland are used to fund the arts, science, social work and various other public interests. Thus the decrease in gambling profits has forced the public discourse into an uncomfortable reflection on this contradiction, as the state-owned gambling industry's profits come largely from gambling addicts and the disadvantaged.

The employment rate (the proportion of employed persons between the ages of 15 and 64) was 69.9 per cent in January 2021, while in January 2020 this stood at 71.9 per cent (Statistics Finland 2021). Jobs lost were concentrated in hospitality and food services, wholesale and retail, as well as human health and social work activities. This increase in unemployment is not a relatively high number in comparison to the millions of additional people now unemployed in the United States or unemployed or put on furlough in the UK. In August 2021, however, the employment rate was 73.4 per cent, 3.3 per cent higher than in August 2020.

In contrast to the situation in many other countries, in Finland a bankruptcy wave was prevented throughout 2020 thanks to restrictions on the right of creditors to petition for bankruptcy. This ended in February 2021 so relatively more bankruptcies are anticipated in 2021. However, in early 2021 various pension-insurance providers indicated that they were not at risk (Mäntylä 2021). It appeared that most businesses and banks in Finland could see the light at the end of the pandemic tunnel. Support packages have focused more on supporting businesses rather than households, which already benefited from progressive taxation and redistribution, for example from generous unemployment benefits, in part compensating for lost income. However, some temporary measures were introduced to accommodate Covid-19-related furloughs for both businesses and those laid-off.

Some of the most significant domestic economic shocks during the crisis have been observed in the forestry sector. In August 2020, forest industry giant UPM announced it planned to close its paper mill in Kaipola, where 450 people worked, as it was no longer competitive compared to UPM's paper mills in Germany and Austria, attributing this to higher wages and taxes as well as higher transport costs given Finland's distance from other countries. This sparked fierce political and social media debate about the social responsibility of companies in a pandemic but also about a world where countries and companies compete for lower taxes and wages to boost their profits. Internationally, office paper demand has fallen during the pandemic, although (often recycled) cardboard demand has increased due to the rise in online sales.

In late 2020 Neste, a large oil, gas and chemical company, announced they would begin "co-operation negotiations", a requirement of the Co-operation Act. Co-operation negotiations are talks between the employer and employees preceding major decisions, often foreshadowing lay-offs. In this case, around 370 jobs were lost. However, in February 2021 a large forestry company, Metsä Group, announced the largest investment in the history of forestry in Finland, a bioproduct mill (producing non-fossil-fuel electricity as well as wood products) in Kemi costing €1.6 billion. Time will tell, but economically Finland appears to have weathered the pandemic storm relatively well.

In 2019 Finland's debt-to-GDP ratio was close to 60 per cent, which rose towards 70 per cent during 2020. The increasing debt-to-GDP ratio caused concern despite the international trends (encouraged by many economists) to take on debt now to improve recovery. Finland maintains a fiscally cautious approach to debt and making structural reforms to improve productivity remains high on the governmental agenda. Among other planned reforms, the cabinet decided to gradually repeal the "pension pipeline" by 2025, which allowed unemployed people close to retirement age to claim higher income-linked jobless benefits for some time before being eligible for their pensions.

Like the UK, Finland also had a scandal over personal protective equipment (PPE) at the beginning of the pandemic. The National Emergency Supply Agency (NESA) rushed through purchases of masks at the end of March 2020 involving millions of euros. In early April journalists discovered and reported that some of these deals were dodgy. The head of NESA promptly resigned and two officials were fired. The procurements were investigated by the independent international consultancy firm Deloitte, which published its report on the shortcomings in June 2020. It found that NESA was not properly prepared for procurement at speed on this scale and was unable to function cohesively. In July one company involved was ordered by an Estonian court to repay an advanced payment received for products that it failed to deliver on time. End of story. In contrast, the UK government just denied that there was any procurement scandal despite its scandal being many orders of magnitude larger.

So, why did Finland weather the first year and a half of the Covid-19 pandemic so much better than elsewhere, and without any draconian measures? Part of the reason will be luck – the first case was confirmed on 29 January, in a Chinese woman from Wuhan, making the diagnosis probable, and putting Finland on the alert. Fourteen contacts were quarantined and there was no spread. The next case was not until a month later, a Finnish woman returning from Italy. During March there were 1,346 cases recorded. The first wave peaked on 10 April 2020, and ended in early June 2020, there having been 7,000 cases and 320 deaths in all by then. In the next year a further three peaks in cases were recorded in winter, spring and summer and 120,000 more cases, but few deaths as the elderly were by now very well protected (not least by vaccines). As we say above, part of the reason why Finland has had so few deaths will be geographical – isolation and relatively low population density. Part of the reason will be social – good social security and healthcare systems and a stable economy. A part will be history and better politics and democratic support for the government's strategy. We do not yet know the final outcome of the pandemic, but this book is about how and why Finland got to where it is now; how it was so well prepared economically, socially and politically for dealing with emergencies such as this as compared to elsewhere; and thus about how a better, safer and more caring world is possible almost anywhere.

Tables and figures

PART I

The context

In the following three chapters, we look at the context of Finland's achievements. The first chapter focuses on geography and climate, which are issues that invariably arise early on in any conversation about the country. Finland is often described as remote, but remoteness is relative. It very much depends on where you are looking from, and how much more easily (for the affluent at least) everywhere is now connected to everywhere else as compared to how difficult travel was even in the recent past. We begin the chapter with a map that puts Finland at its centre, showing how a large part of the world's surface looks from that vantage point.

Chapter 1 continues by showing just how warm the summers are in Finland and how cold it can be in winter, but also how clear the skies can be and how clean the air is. Outsiders are rarely aware of the large geographical variations in climate across the country. We end our introductory chapter by describing how ancient Finland is, geologically speaking, and how its landscape of lakes and forest includes places where rare elements are found in abundance. Although Finland is one of the places where the effects of global warming are likely to be the least adverse, it is also one of the countries at the forefront of initiatives to reduce, mitigate and adapt to climate change – including, controversially, the building of new nuclear power plants that are due to begin operation in 2020 (Reuters 2019).

The second chapter in this section considers the history of Finland amid the empires that surrounded it and dominated it for so long. We chart how for centuries it was the poorest of nations, and show how its towns and cities grew along with the development of transportation routes between its countless lakes; we detail its many border changes, and speculate on the impact of Finland's past as a colony on the outlook of Finns today.

Our third and final chapter in Part I gives a brief overview of the economy and the welfare system that Finland is so famous for. We document the economic woes and successes of Finland in recent decades; we chart how its current (and increasingly green) economic growth surpasses that of Norway, Sweden, Denmark, Germany, France, the Netherlands and many other similar countries; we show how people in Finland now have the second-lowest risk of poverty in the European Union; and we discuss why all this came about and how it has helped make Finland the happiest country in the world today.

Travel to Lapland (*c*.1935) by graphic designer Aukusti Tuhka (1895–1973), who worked for the Erva-Latvala Advertising Agency. Copyright ownership of the Archive of Aukusti Tuhka, held by Jyri Lehtonen. Reproduced with kind permission.

1

Geography and climate

"I'm considering applying for a scholarship to study in Finland. My only hesitation is the six months of darkness. I wonder how that would affect my ability to study, because I tend to think and work better in the early morning when I can watch the sun rise. Given the number of reasons I have to live in Finland, I'm quite surprised at my reaction to the idea of lack of light when it comes to the practicality of living there."

American woman living in
New York City, July 2019

"Honestly, I don't find New York City winters that different from ours. The period from October to December is usually very agreeable: sauna, mulled wine, hot chocolate, woolly socks, Christmassy fairy lights, pre-Christmas parties and gift-wrapping. The only taxing bit is January, which is also almost always the coldest month, too. In February the sun begins to shine again, at least for a few hours per day, and reflects off the white snow. In March we start to realize that it's time to wash the windows again and we start looking forward to spring. If you decide to come here, I will buy you a light therapy lamp for a welcoming present; I haven't needed one myself, but many people who find the darkness too dense consider it a useful delight."

Reply from her friend in
Helsinki, August 2019

A long way from anywhere

Finland is far away. Unless you are in Finland, in which case it is – very prob-ably – home. Everywhere is a long way from most places. And everywhere is home to someone.

To the east of Finland lies Russia, endless Russia, Russia as far as the mind can imagine and as far as a car or a train can travel in a day, or two, or three (Figure 1.1). It feels as if it has always been Russia over there.

To the south is the rest of Europe, country after country, sea after sea, peoples and languages, so many languages all just needing to be learned and used in the places just waiting to be visited. And no more meaningful borders. Finland is in the European Union and the eurozone. With a voter turnout of 74 per cent, 56.9 per cent of Finns voted for EU membership in an advisory referendum held in 1994 (Ministry for Foreign Affairs 2019a).

To the west are Sweden and Norway, and then Iceland and Greenland, and even further west are Canada and the United States – all places to escape to when times are too hard. Places where so many of the siblings of the Finns' forefathers started their new lives and from where they never returned.

To the north is Lapland, and the Sámi, and the beautiful county of Finn-marc (a part of Norway), and then sea, ice and the top of the world. North are the lights that dance in the sky, north is Svalbard, the pole, the East Siberian Sea, and then, along the same meridian, the Siberian wilderness. Keep travel-ling on that great arc and to your right is idyllic Sapporo in Japan, and lonely Wake Island lies next to your left. You pass over the Solomon Sea, and past island atolls now slowly sinking under the Pacific. You swoop past the Gold Coast of Australia, over the Tasman Sea, and to your left glimpse New Zea-land before flying over the Antarctic, hitting land at Port Elizabeth, travelling across most of Africa and then all of Europe before you are home again.

So why is the nearest thing to Utopia found here, in the cold extremes of northern Europe; when there are so many other places it could have been built?

Finns and the cold

What comes to mind when you think of Finland? Many people's first thought is of the cold, and the dark, inhospitable winters. Somehow Finland has

Figure 1.1: A Finland-centred map

Source: Finland and its surrounds on an Azimuth map projection, made using the website http://fldx.org/site/azimuth-map.php and redrawn by Ailsa Allen. The sea monsters are taken from a map of Iceland that appeared in the atlas *Theatrvm Orbis Terrarvm* [Theatre of the World], drawn by Abraham Ortelius and published in 1592. Many of the mythical creatures were derived from actual sightings. The Ziphius, described as "a horrible sea monster that swallows a black seal in one bite" was probably an Orca.
For the illustrations see: https://www.canadiangeographic.ca/article/toronto-exhibition-celebrates-maps-works-art.

become a successful, equitable, sustainable, innovative country, despite its famously harsh climate. It is true that Finns have been able to adapt to extremes of temperature, and even to exploit them. But it is also very easy to overstate the negative impact of cold weather, the lack of light in winter, the geographical isolation, and the snow.

It is often suggested that the rigours of the climate have shaped the Finnish character. Because of the weather and rugged landscape, it is said, Finns became industrious, and developed great tenacity and resilience. This way of thinking is called "environmental determinism" and is wrong. It is wrong because what happens to peoples in the world is almost always largely due to what happens to other peoples. Western Europe did not become rich after 1492 because of its rivers and mountains and climate, but because of its boats landing in the Americas and bringing lethal diseases with them. The inhabitants of so many Pacific Islands are not poor because they live on those islands, but because of how those islands now fit into a world economy.

So if it is not the harsh climate and rugged landscape that has contributed to the success of Finland as a nation, we will have to think again about what did. Today Finland is a far more hospitable place to live than it once was, thanks to central heating and triple-glazing in almost every Finnish building. Environmental determinism is not the secret of Finnish success, because many countries have climates and environments just as harsh as Finland's – just as cold, or instead very hot – and yet they do not rank number one in so many measures of happiness, innovation, equitable prosperity and education. Now that we know that the secret to Finland's success isn't the cold, it's still worth considering why so many people, including our American friend from New York City, worry about its long dark winters.

The long winter

The long winter does have some advantages: "In Finland, officials sometimes visit parks just after a snowfall to see where they should place new paths – the paths people have made through the newly fallen snow are then incorporated into park planning" – Tweet posted by the BBC television show *QI*, 6 October 2019 (BBC 2019a).

Finland's seasonal variations have captured the imagination of countless writers. Generations of travellers, traders and sailors from western Europe wrote vivid accounts of the wonders and harshness of the Finnish winter. The Winter War of 1939–40 between Finland and the Soviet Union became famous as much for the physical conditions in which the battles took place as for the military engagements themselves. During this particularly harsh winter, the Finns turned the stark conditions to their advantage – for instance, using white camouflage to blend into the snow-covered countryside (Mead & Smeds 1967).

Winter in Finland starts in November, with the first snowfall usually coming in December. January tends to be the darkest, bleakest month: inhabitants of the far north of Finland spend up to eight weeks without any daylight, although in the south of the country the sun can be seen briefly even in mid-winter. However, it is November that Finns complain about the most – a depressing, dark and rainy month after their lovely summers with the longest (together with Iceland) sunny days in the world.

On crystal clear days and moonlit nights, winter in Finland can be beautiful. Although the sun doesn't rise over the horizon, "its presence is reflected in a sunset glow that burns on the horizon" for several hours (Nickels 1965). The darkness is tempered by the whiteness of the snow, and the sudden, frequent appearances of the Northern Lights, known in Finnish as *revontulet*, or "fires of the fox". In Lapland, there can be as many as 200 displays of the Northern Lights a year (Norum & Proctor 2010).

Days begin to lengthen in February, and by March in the south (and April in the north) there are 11–14 hours of daylight each day. The thaw starts in April, and by the end of May the snow has gone. Spring's "glorious delicate greenness takes on a special significance after the long, white winter" (Nickels 1965: 59). Although those words were written over half a century ago, as yet global warming has not had too large an effect on Finland's seasons; but better living standards have had a huge effect on Finns' experience of them. What does worry people is that southern Finland has been experiencing significantly less snow in recent years. This affects peoples' hobbies, and the lack of snow makes winters even darker – possibly contributing to seasonal affective disorder.

Declining influence of the seasons

Over the course of the twentieth century, life in Finland was affected less and less by the changing seasons. Rising affluence and technological improvements have made it easier for Finns to adapt to winter conditions. Despite widely fluctuating temperatures outside, homes and industrial buildings maintain a constant temperature throughout the year. Furthermore, the cold makes highly efficient heating and insulation a cost-effective necessity.

In the 1960s – a time when central heating was seen as something of a luxury in countries such as Britain – it had long been accepted as essential in Finland. What's more, the Finns' superior insulation and triple-glazing has meant that, for the past several decades, less energy is consumed during the coldest parts of the Finnish winter than in the coldest spells in other affluent countries (Hatzfield-Rea 1969).

In the past, travel and trade were often disrupted for weeks during the winter, with negative impacts on the Finnish economy. For centuries, the freezing of the Baltic Sea brought the seasonal closure of ports and the interruption of trade. These patterns were altered for the better thanks to the technological advancements of the twentieth century, including icebreakers and other steel-plated ships, as well as telegraphic and radio communications that facilitated the rapid and accurate forecasting of ice and weather conditions (Mead & Smeds 1967).

In tandem with Canada, Finland also led innovation in a number of aspects of aviation technology in the early twentieth century, including float- and ski-modified aircraft, and short take-off and landing (STOL) technology. Often by modifying German designs, Junkers F13 and G24 in particular, Finns designed and built aircraft that could land on frozen lakes, on ice, and on snow and water, in order to distribute medicine and supplies, mail and trade goods.

Today, Finland keeps all 78,000km of its public roads open throughout the year by municipal snow ploughs that operate from early morning (5am in the city of Tampere). By law, winter tyres must be used between November and April. Traditional methods such as the use of salt and sand are still deployed, but the system works so well because Finnish (state provided) road-maintenance lorries can simultaneously plough, scrape and add salt or sand to road surfaces (Rankola 1997). Compressed air is used to thaw ice so that inland ferries can navigate lakes in winter, and the under-runway heating at Helsinki Airport has been there for a very long time (Mead & Smeds 1967).

Winter used to be a period of under- and unemployment for many Finns, particularly for the many people who worked in farming and forestry. The growth of manufacturing has led to fewer seasonal variations in labour requirements, and thus also in local patterns of both consumption and output. It has become more common for building construction to continue throughout the winter, thanks in large part to innovations such as cement that hardens quickly even at very low temperatures, and the use of insulating cocoons of plastic around buildings under construction. Many construction workers are now employed in factories during the winter making prefabricated "flat-pack" houses for assembly in the summer. Half of all new homes in Scandinavia are built this way, and they are also gaining in popularity abroad (Scandinavian Homes 2019).

In the past, food shortages were commonplace at the end of the Finnish winter, at a time of year when demand for energy from people and animals was greatest, but today's seasonal and regional variations in food supply are much smaller, because of a revolution in fodder production for livestock and improvements in transportation and importation. Nevertheless, the tradition of conserving food in summer for winter use continues, with many Finnish households still bottling berries, preserving mushrooms, pickling cucumbers and salting and smoking meat and fish. More and more this is done to keep traditions alive, rather than out of necessity.

Winter opportunities

Finns have always had to make the most of the opportunities presented by the winter season, and they have done this with no small success. Skiing is an integral part of life for a nation of people who, we are told, are virtually born on skis. With the exception of those living in central Helsinki, people almost anywhere in the country can ski away from their front door, and as late as the 1950s many children in the countryside skied to school (Mead & Smeds 1967: 109). Fewer children do so today, and school buses are now ubiquitous in the countryside; but Finns still walk more than many other Europeans. Finns do complain about the weather, but it doesn't stop them from doing things.

Cross-country skiing is a popular sport. Ski-jumping is not quite as popular as it used to be when Finns had great international success in competitions; nevertheless Finland still has some of the highest ski jumps in the world. But it is pesäpallo (Finnish baseball) that is the national sport and a novelty for any tourist to Finland who seeks it out.

Tourism has grown in recent decades, and in 2016 it contributed €4.5 billion, or 2.5 per cent, to the country's GDP (Visit Finland 2019). Foreign visitors spent some 6.8 million nights in Finland in 2018; during December of that year, half of visitor nights were spent in Lapland (Statistics Finland 2018a), either for skiing or to visit Santa Claus (who also has another home at the North Pole, with the Canadian postal code H0H 0H0).

Someone in Finland managed to appropriate the myth of Santa and placed him and his elves in its north. While this might be good for tourist income, it is hardly good for the environment. And most children today know where toys are actually made, because it is stamped on them: China.

Finland experiences a huge range of temperatures during the year, varying from an average of over 20°C in July across the parts of the country where the majority of people live, to frequently dropping below −20°C in the north and always below zero even in the warmest corners of the south in January (Figure 1.2).

The Finns have used snow and ice to their economic advantage in many ways, becoming expert manufacturers and exporters of icebreakers, of sports- and ski-clothing, and wood products. Coniferous forests cover 70 per cent of Finland's land area, and almost all of them are managed for timber production. Thanks to the size of the country, and the ability to carry out logging in winter, Finland is the largest wood-pulp producer in the EU (Norum & Proctor 2010).

Winter has gone from being a season to be survived to a time for Finns to value and appreciate the beauty of the landscape, its colours and changing light conditions. It is now more a season of recreation than a period of hardship and shortage. That said, Finns haven't entirely conquered winter, and in recent years unusually mild or cold winters have still affected the country advantageously or detrimentally, both economically and socially.

Figure 1.2: The Climate of Finland (maximum and minimum temperatures) 1971–2000

Maximum and minimum temperatures: (averages, °C):

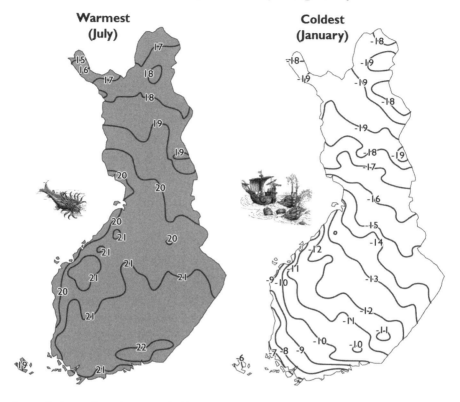

Source: Redrawn from data provided by the Finnish Meteorological Institute and published on-line in 2019 by "This is Finland"; https://finland.fi/life-society/finlands-weather-and-light/.

The winter of 2007–08, for example, was anomalously mild in Finland, with temperatures 3–6°C higher than normal for February. Conversely, in 2010–11 the winter was unusually cold, with February temperatures up to 6°C cooler than normal. There were financial advantages to that milder winter in 2007–08, with total icebreaker costs in Finnish waters dropping to just €22 million and train punctuality hitting 89 per cent; in 2010–11, icebreaker costs soared to €90 million, and trains were on schedule just 70 per cent of the time. However, the lack of frost and its associated hard ground made harvesting logs more difficult in 2007–08, and ski-lift ticket sales in southern Finland dropped to €7.5 million, compared to €12 million in 2010–11 (Ilkka, Heikki & Väinö 2012).

Winter behaviour

The Finns have coined the phrase "winter behaviour", which refers to ways in which the climate influences everyday interactions. Because of the extremely low temperatures, Finns who meet outdoors often don't stop and chat for more than a few seconds, if at all. There is little or no smiling and laughing out of doors. As one commentator observed: "A broad American smile at 15°C below in Eastern Helsinki makes one's front teeth ache" (Lewis 2005: 19). The cold wind that whips people's faces means that Finns often speak outdoors with narrowed eyes or limited eye contact.

It is sometimes said that this outdoor behaviour has been extended to indoor communications too, where economy of expression and an ability to summarize are commonplace, and facts and figures are favoured over gossip. This preference for action over discussion is, it is often speculated, one of the secrets of Finnish success. For all we know, of course, this could be as much a Finnish myth as the notion that the topography of the country plays a key role in Finland's fortunes, with its extensive wetlands, forests and thin soils atop glacially abraded bedrock forcing Finns over many generations to develop resilience, self-reliance and industriousness (Lewis 2005). If such environmental determinism was all that mattered, then the inhabitants of the Tibetan plateau would have a higher GDP per capita and more autonomy.

Neither is geography completely inconsequential. Cold winters make homelessness a more critical issue, for example, given the increased risk of death due to hypothermia (Zhang *et al.* 2019). It is also an issue for the US and the UK, but (unlike Finland) those states have not yet developed effective national strategies to tackle homelessness. We will return to Finland's approach to homelessness in a later chapter. For now, it is worth noting that a 2015 international review of Finland's strategy highlighted the importance of coordination between different sectors and realistic goal-setting. That report noted that there was a collective will to continue with these initiatives beyond the then Centre Party government of Matti Vanhanen (2003–10) that introduced Finland's current "Housing First" homelessness policy (Pleace *et al.* 2015).

Geography has played a role in Finland's development, but it is far from the only factor that matters. For an example of climate's importance to Finnish society, Finland's extreme winter conditions, coupled with its sparse population, directly influenced the country's early adoption of mobile phone networks and internet usage. In 1981, Finland, together with Sweden and Norway, formed the first international mobile phone network. The aim was to address the prohibitive costs of providing traditional telephony in sparsely populated countries, and to permit people to summon help when driving in harsh weather or living in a remote house during long, dark days and nights.

By 1994, up to 12 per cent of people in the Nordic countries owned a mobile phone, compared with just 7 per cent in the US (*The Economist* 1994: 76). By 2000, Finland had the highest mobile phone usage per head of population in the world and, proportionally, the world's largest online-banking population: better to log on remotely than to venture out in winter weather (*The Economist* 2000).

To summarize, while the winter cold has presented Finns with many challenges, these can hardly be said to have been a disadvantage. None of the environmental difficulties that Finland faced were ones that could not be overcome, and some of them could be said to have encouraged tenacity and innovativeness – qualities which have contributed directly to Finland becoming a world leader in business, competitiveness and social welfare.

The physical geography of Finland

Finland is large. With a total land area of 338,000km, it is almost 30 per cent larger than Great Britain's 245,000km. In the US, only four states – Alaska, Texas, California and Montana – are larger. Finland is twice the size of Florida, three times as big as Virginia, and four times as large as South Carolina (This is Finland 2019).

The Finnish landscape is striking: the picture-postcard image of innumerable lakes fringed with rocky shores covered in conifers is what springs to most people's minds when they think of Finland. However, there is so much more to its landscape, memorably described in the 1950s by the travel writer Wendy Hall as being one of eternity and yet great variety. Eternity in the shape of lakes, moorlands and forests that stretch as far as the eye can see, with a stillness that allows people to hear subtle variations of sound, and variety in terms of its varied geology, many latitudes, and the great differences between the seasons. The Finns have a very rich language to describe their landscape and environment, with different words for the wind that sighs in the birch trees (*humista*) and wind in the conifer trees (*kohista*) (Hall 1953).

The rocks of Finland are old, extremely old (Figure 1.3). To the north and in the middle of the country, the bedrock is up to 3 billion years old, and was already there when the planet was less than half the age it is today. In the south it is younger, nearer 2 billion years old, and occasionally there are sediments that are just 500 million years old. After the last ice age, additional glacial scrapings were left as more recent deposits; but essentially Finland is a solid plate of rock that has been worn so flat from erosion and so smooth over time that it is now riddled with thousands of rivers and tens of thousands of lakes. Furthermore, because of the great age of its rocks, rare earth elements are found in abundance in some places (a few are shown on Figure 1.3). Most of these have not yet been mined, but some are very likely to be in the near future.

The idea of the eternity of the Finnish landscape also refers to the fact that even under human occupation it has remained largely unchanged through the millennia. The land was shaped by glaciation and the subsequent retreat of the glaciers – again and again and again. The ancient bedrock of granite and gneiss is overlain by large-scale glacial deposits, clays along the coastal plain, and sands and gravels in the interior of the country.

Finland is studded with glacial moraines, drumlins and eskers – long ridges of earth and stones that can stretch for several kilometres (Martineau 1980). The overall effect of the many ice ages was to smooth and soften the contours of the land "as though a giant hand had passed over it to remove its furrows and give it an underlying serenity" (Hall 1953: 32). The only mountainous part of the country is in Lapland, where Finland's highest mountain – Mount Halti, 1,328 metres high – can be found near to the Norwegian border (Martineau 1953).

The landscape

As the images used on both the cover of this book and at that start of this chapter make clear, the most notable feature of Finland is its lakes. Often referred to as "the land of a thousand lakes", Finland in fact has more than 56,000 of them, mostly fairly shallow and containing countless islands (Martineau 1953). Many Finns holiday on the islands in summer, when they are full of lush green foliage and the surrounding waters are warm.

The largest lake in Finland is Lake Saimaa (4,400km² in area – larger than Rhode Island). Rivers flow between the lakes, their course occasionally interrupted by rapids and waterfalls. There are five main river systems in Finland, with the longest river being the Kemi, at 550km, which flows into the Gulf of Bothnia. Finland is also the most densely forested country in Europe, with trees covering nearly two thirds of its surface.

The apparent stability and serenity of the Finnish landscape belies the great variations among the different parts of the country. North, south, east and west each have their own distinctive character, shaped in part by the climate and in part by the underlying geology. The south and south-west of Finland is comparable to the English landscape, with gently rolling hills and lakes fringed by birch trees. The climate is milder and a little wetter here, with average winter temperatures between −2°C and −5°C.

The growing season is longer in the south, at 180 days, than Lapland's 110 days and 130 in central Finland (Martineau 1980). Deciduous trees such as birch, hazel and aspen are found only in the south. In central and eastern Finland the landscape is dominated by lakes and islands separated by sharp lines of pine forests; to the west lie wide, flat plains and marshland.

Lapland

Lapland, to the north, has the starkest landscape in all of Finland, with fewer lakes and trees, wider and faster rivers, and fewer settlements, and great extremes of temperature and light between the seasons. Although Finland is the most northerly country in Europe along with Iceland, the proximity of the Arctic Ocean and the Gulf Stream mean that its climate is milder than that of other regions at the same latitude. Summer temperatures can reach

Figure 1.3: The ancient bedrock of Finland

KEY for the map opposite and the diagram below

Ancient – 0.5 billion years old
1. Caledonian Rocks. The youngest bedrock in Finland, marine sedimentary rocks created at the start of the closure of the Iapetus Ocean and pushed over Archean Rocks.

Very ancient – 1.6 to 0.7 billion years old
2. Sedimentary rocks (Neo- and Meso-proterozoic). Sandstone, siltstone, arkose, shale and conglomerates. When not laid down under sea, often red.
3. Igneous rocks (Meso-proterozoic). Rapakivi granites. An uncommon highly textured granite used as polished slabs.

Very, very ancient – 2.5 to 1.6 billion years old
4. Igneous rocks (Paleo-proterozoic). Formed by the melting of the lower crust of the mantle or by intrusions.
5. Metamorphic rocks (Paleo-proterozoic). Schists formed from mudstone and shale by compression and heat.

Very, very very ancient – Over 2.5 billion years old (Archean)
6. Granite and Gneiss. The roots of very ancient mountains, having lost tens of kilometres of overlying rock from erosion.

Recent Geology Timeline

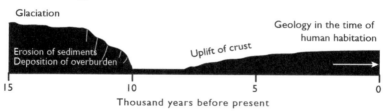

Glaciation

Geology in the time of human habitation

Erosion of sediments
Deposition of overburden

Uplift of crust

15   10   5   0

Thousand years before present

Ancient Geology Timeline

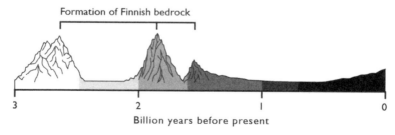

Formation of Finnish bedrock

3   2   1   0

Billion years before present

Sources: Geological timeline redrawn from an original in Nenonen & Portaankorva (2009); map redrawn from an original first published in Sarapää *et al.* (2013).

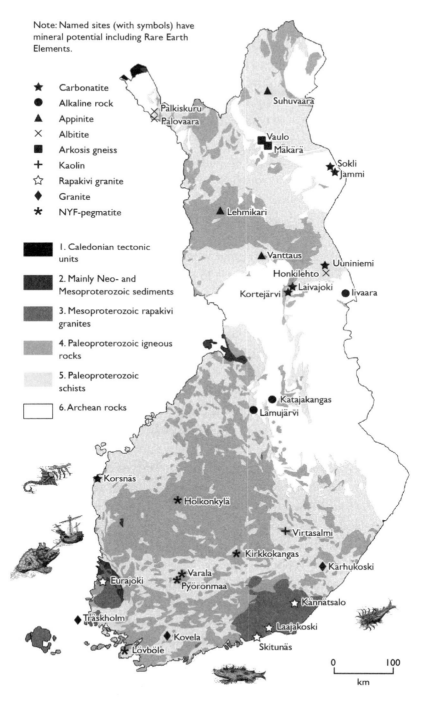

Note: Named sites (with symbols) have
mineral potential including Rare Earth
Elements.

★   Carbonatite
●   Alkaline rock
▲   Appinite
✕   Albitite
■   Arkosis gneiss
＋   Kaolin
☆   Rapakivi granite
◆   Granite
✳   NYF-pegmatite

1. Caledonian tectonic units

2. Mainly Neo- and Mesoproterozoic sediments

3. Mesoproterozoic rapakivi granites

4. Paleoproterozoic igneous rocks

5. Paleoproterozoic schists

6. Archean rocks

Suhuvaara

✕ Pälkiskuru
✕ Palovaara

Vaulo
Mäkärä

Sokli
Jammi

Lehmikari

Vanttaus

Uuniniemi
Honkilehto ✕
Laivajoki
Kortejärvi
Iivaara

Katajakangas
Lamujärvi

Korsnäs

Holkonkylä

Virtasalmi

Kirkkokangas

Karhukoski

Varala
Pyörönmaa
Eurajoki

Kännätsalo

Träskholm

Kovela
Laajakoski
Lövböle
Skitunäs

0   100
km

19

27°C in Lapland, but during the long winter they may drop as low as −30°C. Similarly, while in the summer it's possible to see the sun at midnight in Lapland, the winter days are long and dark. Often the sky turns as grey-white as the land, and the horizon almost disappears.

Finland is beautiful, and yet its future beauty is not assured, especially in the north. Currently 100,000 tourists visit Rovaniemi, the capital of Lapland, each December, more than a fifth of them British. They come to see the Northern Lights, the lakes, and Lapland's pristine nature – but depending on how they behave, or even through sheer numbers alone, they may become a threat to all that is unspoilt.

The greatest threat of all is an increasingly contentious proposal by the government in Helsinki and mining companies with a vested interest to build a railway through Europe's last great wilderness and the home of the Sámi, the only surviving indigenous people in Europe. As Tiina Sanila-Aikio, president of the Sámi parliament, explains: "First, they took the religion, then they broke the Siida [local community plus reindeer district] system, then they took the lands and the language. And now they want to build a railroad." (Wall 2019). All is not necessarily well in this winter-icy and summer-warm paradise, and whether or not the railway plans are defeated, treasure hunters (mining company prospectors) looking for rare earth elements may be the next invaders to threaten the area (Yle Uutiset 2018a).

An international research team of Finns, Danes and Swedes working on the issue of threats to the environment of Lapland explain it thus: "underlying those immediate concerns there are also more fundamental issues of conflicting worldviews and modes of perceiving and engaging with the environment" (Herva 2018). Elsewhere in the world, in Northern Canada, across almost all of the USA, elsewhere in Europe and in Russia environmental threats such as these would be taken less seriously. Not so in Finland.

Although Finland is not a Utopia, it is arguably the nearest thing to Utopia in the world today; or at least in the statistical world of social facts and the physical world of remote beauty. Oscar Wilde once remarked (before he was sent to prison for being in love), "A map of the world that does not include Utopia is not worth even glancing at, for it leaves out the one country at which Humanity is always landing. And when Humanity lands there, it looks out, and, seeing a better country, sets sail. Progress is the realisation of Utopias." (Wilde 1891). If Finns have the collective will to prevent the environmental destruction of Lapland, it would be the realization of one small part of one further voyage towards Utopia.

What looks as if it were just as nature had made it, never is. The Sámi have herded reindeer over the northlands ever since the ice retreated from the last Ice Age. Prior to that, the reindeer would have been less numerous, because there were no humans in Lapland to protect them from other predators and herd them from pasture to pasture to maximize their numbers. What vegetation would have grown on the land before there were people would have been quite different from what is there today.

Conclusion: the rocks, the ice and the thaw

Long ago the climate was very different. The rocks that make up Finland today are very old and have moved from much warmer climes as the plates they constitute shifted over time. And yet still we often think that Finland has always looked like this, especially during the Finnish winter, when rivers and lakes remain frozen for almost half the year, from November to the end of April.

In some years the sea also freezes over, and it is possible to cross from Finland to Sweden on sea ice. Every year the rivers freeze. There are records all the way back to 1693 of the date in spring when the ice broke up on the River Torne on the Swedish/Finnish border. These data are a key part of an international set of ancient records that give us a sense of long-term trends in global warming in Europe (Dorling 2017: 160). Much later in this book, we look at how Finland is doing more than other countries to combat climate change.

One third of the precipitation in Finland falls as sleet or snow, which typically covers the country like a blanket from mid-November until sometimes as late as May; although as we finished writing this chapter in late 2019, the snow has come especially late. The planet is now warming faster than ever before. Nevertheless, with so much change between winter and summer in Finland, it can be hard to detect the gradual changes in climate as a whole.

In Finland, the same landscape can look dramatically different in winter and summer: "Green turns to white overnight with the first fall of

21

snow ... Skies that hang leaden grey for months clear to sparkling blue within an hour" (Hall 1953: 31). But underneath the seasonal changes – winter snow, spring rains, summer greenery – there is an underlying stability and serenity. More and more, throughout all its seasons and more strongly with each year that passes today, Finland looks like a place of safety and a beacon of hope in an uncertain world.

Viipuri (Vyborg) is the former capital of Karelia and was one of the largest towns in Finland. Karelia was home to over 400,000 people, who were relocated when the area was ceded to Russia after the Winter War of 1939–40. Permission to use this image has kindly been provided by the museum of Etelä-Karjala (Etelä-Karjalan museo).

2

History amid empires

"Only after World War II did the nation experience reconciliation to such an extent that political and ideological debate could be conducted without threat to democracy or fear of retribution. The national healing had progressed sufficiently to accept diversity as a sign of a healthy nation."

Börje Vähämäki, translator's note, in
"Under the North Star 3" (Linna 2003: xii)

The land between the powers

To the outside world Finland may not appear particularly diverse, but its own people see things rather differently, particularly when looking at the complex history and shifting politics in the years up to the Second World War. Writing in October 1939, one American media mogul claimed "Stalin is treading on dangerous ground when he attacks Finland [...] Finland is the most upright and honest nation in Europe. She is the one nation that has recently paid its duly contracted debts to us. She is the one nation whose word of honor is worth a centime or a farthing. She is the one nation that the United States has reason to respect" (Hearst 1939). It may well have been William Randolph Hearst, the model for the protagonist of Orson Welles' film *Citizen Kane*, who helped create the myth of the steadfast, independent-minded, stubborn yet diplomatic character of the Finns.

From the early twelfth century until 1945, Finns were caught in the middle of larger nations' ambitions and empires: Sweden in the west, Russia in the east, Germany to the south, and with the cold relentlessly sweeping down from the north to add to the drama. Finland was, in effect, controlled by Denmark in the form of the Kalmar Union of Scandinavia aristocracy from 1397 to 1523, ending with Sweden's rebellion. Sweden then ruled Finland more or less uninterrupted until 1809, although at the end of the Great Northern War (1700–21) its grip was perilously weak. From 1809, Russia dominated Finland, invading at times, ruling at others, until independence day, 6 December 1917. During the period 1941–44, Finland was – despite not being run by Nazis – an ally of Germany and reliant on it for imports of food, fuel and armaments. In 1944, however, the Finns turned on Germany, in the Lapland War (September 1944 to April 1945).

How Finns dealt with this balancing act, and with what was often so completely out of their control, and how they now tell their story, defines the history of their nation. At different points in the past 500 years, Finland was a colony of Sweden, dominated by Germany, and controlled by both Denmark and Russia, before it finally declared independence in 1917. It was then almost immediately plunged into a bitter, if short-lived, civil war and what became known as the Terror.

The four-month conflict, which pitted urban, socialist Reds against reactionary Whites composed of rural and northern elites and peasants, could have resulted in a longer term deeply divided nation. It could have resulted in a communist state. Almost 40,000 people died in the Terror. Following a shoot-on-sight declaration made on 25 February 1918 by Baron Carl Gustaf Emil Mannerheim, military leader of the Whites, some 10,000 mainly working-class Reds would be executed or massacred, or met violent ends in other ways.

Only 1,000 Whites perished; had the Whites not been victorious, perhaps more would have been killed. Eighty thousand Reds were imprisoned, including hundreds of children. Different sources give slightly different figures (Balkelis 2015), with the fighting and cover-up of atrocities being so terrible that no decent records were kept. And yet somehow the country, so utterly riven a century ago, has come to be seen today as a model of solidarity. Opinion remains divided in Finland over the Terror (Yle Uutiset 2018b), a civil war whose official end was never declared, signed or ratified. In 1918, when the defeat of the Reds had led to a de facto end of the conflict, Helsinki was controlled by German troops, and it remained occupied until the fall of the Kaiser in November of that year (Donner 2017).

The civil war was far from the end of Finland's formational struggles. The Second World War took a heavy toll on the country, not only in terms of loss of life, but also loss of land and people's livelihoods, and in the wake of the Moscow Armistice of 1944 and the requirement to pay heavy reparations to Russia. Yet the country emerged from these dark years as an economically successful and well-respected player in global affairs, known within the United Nations as the "Super Peacekeeper" (Lewis 2005). Former President Martti Ahtisaari won the Nobel Peace Prize in 2008 "...for his important efforts, on several continents and over more than three decades, to resolve international conflicts." So, in the few pages that we have below, we will try to tell a short story of how Finland found itself where it is today.

Early history

The earliest traces of human occupation in what is now known as Finland have been dated to between 7,000 and 8,000 BCE. After the very last Ice Age receded, hunter-gatherers began to enter the land of many lakes. In the big picture of human expansion across the planet, these were the people at the very ends of the earth. Only a very few other places on the planet – remote islands such as Madagascar and, much later, New Zealand – would become inhabited by humans as late as Finland.

In many ways the people who first settled around the lakes of Finland were not unlike those who, thousands of years earlier, crossed the Bering Strait land bridge and then moved southward through the Americas. The original Finns may have been superseded by groups migrating up and across from central and northern Asia. The current main Finnish language, which is part of the Uralic group of languages along with Estonian and Hungarian, is thought to have reached Finland about 5,000 years ago (Branch 2019). In future decades it is very likely that genetic and linguistic research will tell a more comprehensive story of who first came to Finland, who supplanted and mixed with them and much else that will have happened before anyone began to write it down.

The first recorded reference to the Finnish people was in Alfred the Great's "Geography", written in the ninth century AD. The early Finns settled in three areas: Suomi in the south-west, Häme in the mid-west and Karelia in the east. These three tribes each had their own laws, social structures and defence systems (Nickels 1977). The language used by each also evolved from the one that they brought with them. During the Viking era, the Finns pushed further north to reach the salmon rivers and game-rich lands of the Lapps and forced the Lapps to pay tribute to them (Nicol 1975).

The Swedish era, 1155–1809

There is a myth that in the middle of the twelfth century, King Eric of Sweden, under the direction of the Pope, carried out a series of crusades in which Finland was conquered and its inhabitants converted to Christianity. In reality Swedes just gradually colonized the south-west of Finland. Swedish legal and social institutions were gradually assimilated rather than being arbitrarily imposed, and Sweden served as a conduit for Finland's cultural and trading contact with the West. Swedish is still one of the two official languages of Finland, with a small minority of Finns speaking Swedish as their first language.

The main effect of the Swedish incursions appears to have been an increase in the cost of living. Almost everyone in Finland farmed, and a few hunted. Grain could often be in short supply. In the fourteenth century, legends tell of a loaf of bread costing as much as a cow, and a slice of bread being exchanged for a bull calf (Nicol 1975: 23). It was at this time that Margaret I of Denmark (1353–1412) secured Danish rule over the foreign affairs of Sweden, and hence also of Finland. This continued until 1523 when the Swedes rebelled.

Finland was a lesser-developed part of a backwater, Sweden, which was itself only peripheral in Scandinavia, which was (in turn) one of the less-developed areas of Europe. Until 1492, Europe was on the edge of the known world and a very long way away from the great civilizations of India and China. At the end of the seventeenth century, a severe famine killed nearly a third of the Finnish population (Lewis 2005). Life at the edges of the earth was frequently tough. Paying tribute to overseas rulers made it tougher.

By the year 1600, Finland's average GDP per head was equivalent to around (US) $812 a year, or $2.22 a day – in other words, at the subsistence poverty level (See Figure 2.1). Across Europe, GDP per person was only lower in what is now Germany. People in Spain, and in Flanders and the Low

Countries (now Belgium), were on average twice as well off. By 1700, Finnish GDP per head, when converted to today's money, had risen only to $907 a year, or 26 cents more a day. By 1800, Finns were getting by on even less, $827 a year, which was much less than half of what people living in the US enjoyed. And by 1850, people in the UK were almost three times wealthier on average than Finns, although of course the UK was at the heart of a huge empire, and in contrast Finland was a country surrounded and dominated by empires.

Figure 2.1: GDP per capita 1600–1850 (US$)

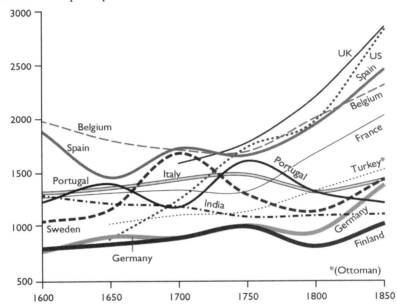

Source: Maddison Project Database, version 2018; Bolt *et al.* (2018).

Over time the Finns grew weary of their ties to Sweden. They disapproved of the extravagances of the Swedes' court in Turku, and with Finland a buffer state between warring Sweden and Russia, they were tired of their country serving as an almost constant battleground for east–west conflict. Between 1713 and 1721, for example, Finland was occupied by Russia – a period known as the Great Wrath, which became "synonymous with all that's wretched and brutal" (Nicol 1975: 24). There was also growing concern that Swedish influence was "slowly stifling any potential of a purely Finnish character and culture" (Nickels 1977: 89). The Finnish language was seen by the country's elites as little more than a peasant tongue. Those who wanted to progress were expected to learn Swedish, and almost all posts in the upper echelons of Finnish society were occupied by Swedes.

Just as satisfaction with Sweden and its dominance was waning, the strategic value of Finland to Russia grew during the eighteenth century. The new city of St Petersburg, which when completed in 1703 was already the largest city in northern Europe, was built on what was then Swedish land, among Finnish-speaking people (see Figure 2.2). While Sweden held power over Finland, St Petersburg's geographical position was precarious for Russia (Lewis 2005). An attempt by Finnish separatists in the mid-eighteenth century to gain independence from Sweden, with the help of Russia's Empress Elizabeth, was unsuccessful. However, in February 1808 Russia and Denmark attacked Finnish Sweden, with the war culminating in the Treaty of Fredrikshamn (Hamina in Finnish) in September 1809, whereby Sweden was compelled to cede Finland to Russia (Nickels 1977: 89).

The Russian era, 1809–1917

During the period of Russian rule, Finland demonstrated loyalty to Russia while simultaneously pursuing its own national interests, as defined by the Finnish elite. Violent protests by prospective civil servants against an attempt to impose a prerequisite examination in the Russian language in 1812 exacerbated the language barrier between Finnish and Russian authorities (Meinander 2013: 82). Nevertheless, the beginnings of Russian rule, under Tsar Alexander I, were not disadvantageous to Finland, which gained control of its own affairs, and its own legislation.

The legal code established in 1734 remained in force. Finland was recognized as a Grand Duchy and a self-governing province of the Russian Empire, with its own ruling body, the Senate, composed of elite Finns. However, it was still ruled by a governor-general representing the Tsar. Arguably, Russia allowing a degree of autonomy via government structures, including the ability to enact local legislation, led to a nurturing of Finnish values. This was in part a way for the Russians to ensure that Finland further distanced itself from Sweden and the West (Lewis 2005).

Figure 2.2: The lakes, rivers and towns of Finland

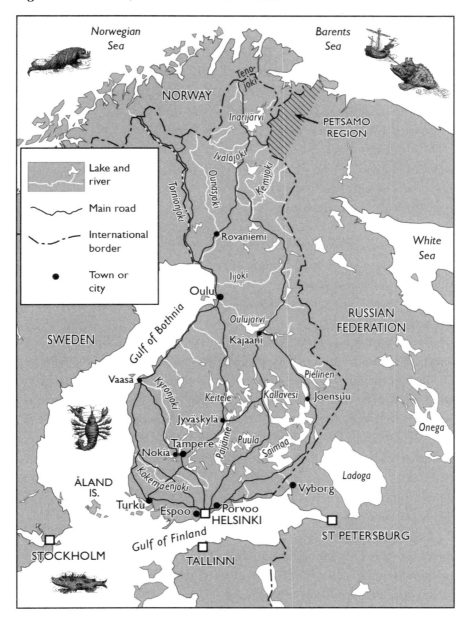

Source: Drawn by the authors and Ailsa Allen from a wide range of sources.

In 1812, the capital of the Grand Duchy of Finland was moved from Turku, on the western coast, to Helsinki. Finland's main university did likewise (see Figure 2.2 for locations). Officially, Finland has only had a capital city since 1809, with Turku holding that designation for just three years, although it had been a much bigger administrative centre than Helsinki for several centuries. Soon, however, that was to change. Moving the capital was yet another part of the strategic decision to strengthen ties with Russia at the expense of those with Sweden (Zetterberg & Pulma 2003: 387–8).

Much of the nineteenth century was a period of political stability and peace in Finland, during which its economic and cultural life developed and prospered. Moving from the rule of a more developed Sweden to a less developed Russia brought advantages, as some Finnish industries gained access to the Russian market without significant competition (Poropudas 1996: 353). Exports to Russia from the metalworking and textile industries grew, and new techniques for the manufacture of paper from wood pulp gave a boost to the timber industry. As sea-borne trade grew in importance, Finland built a large merchant shipping fleet, although much of it would be destroyed in the Crimean War of 1854–56.

The construction of the first railway in 1857 helped to address the challenges of transportation in such a sparsely populated lake-filled country by facilitating the movement of heavy raw material from northern Finland to southern Finland even in the three to four months a year when winter ice prevented travel by sea (Myllyntaus 2016: 35). Rail connections between Helsinki and other cities also helped boost its economy, and in the last four decades of the nineteenth century its population grew from 32,000 to 136,000 (Meinander 2010: 155). As the city grew, so did the number of Helsinki residents whose mother tongue was Finnish, rising from 10 per cent in 1857 to over 50 per cent in 1900.

Although Finland's late industrialization in the latter half of the nineteenth century brought better transport and an increasingly Finnish culture to its capital, the era was not without its setbacks. In the 1866–68 famine, an estimated 120,000 people, or 8 per cent of the Finnish population, lost their lives. In its wake came a shift in agricultural policy towards livestock and away from cereal farming (Meinander 2011: 105).

The rise of nationalism

A nationalist revival (Fennomania) in Finland during the nineteenth century, fostered by groups of intellectuals and the Finnish Literature Society (founded in 1831), was given further impetus by the 1835 publication of the *Kalevala*, a compendium of Finnish folklore collected and edited by Elias Lönnrot. Around the same time, J. L. Runeberg published a series of patriotic poems idealizing Finnish rural life. As with many proto-independent countries in the nineteenth century, Finland's history – part myth and part reality – and the notion of its "people" were being constructed. Later, that history would be adapted and altered to suit the interests of those who wanted a particular future.

J. V. Snellman, a Finnish intellectual with anti-Russian and pro-Finnish views, had been blocked from a professorship at the University of Helsinki by the Russian Tsar, Nicholas I. But the emperor's death in 1855 enabled Snellman to come to Helsinki and eventually serve as a senator (Utti 2006). In that role, he was able to pass a language decree that gave the Finnish language equal status to Swedish in government.

Tsar Nicholas I's successor, Alexander II (1818–81), was more liberal than his predecessor, and more accepting of Finnish autonomy. Alexander's wife was Maria Feodorovna, empress-consort of Russia and the second daughter of Christian IX of Denmark. Her older sister was Alexandra of Denmark, the wife of Queen Victoria's eldest son, Edward, who would accede the British throne as Edward VIII in 1901.

Alexander II was sympathetic to the Finnish nationalist cause, and helped to ensure that Finland acquired many of the institutions of a modern state. A separate Finnish currency, the markka, was established in the 1860s, and Finland was given the right to maintain its own national army from 1878. It also had a state railway network, a national Bank of Finland, and a national anthem. However, much of that nation-state-building was later undone by Tsar Alexander III, who ruled from 1881 to 1894 and adopted a policy of Russification. The Finnish postal system was abolished, and it became compulsory to use Russian in all official correspondence.

Alexander III's successor, Nicholas II (1868–1918), absorbed the Finnish army into Russian forces, removed some key administrative functions from the Finnish Senate, entirely abolished the use of Finnish in the administration of the country, and flooded the Finnish market with Russian products. This approach was not dissimilar to that favoured by the UK in its dealings with colonies and de facto colonies, including Ireland. Indeed, in matters of history, language and policy, the relationship between Ireland and Great Britain was in many ways similar to that between Finland and Russia.

Nevertheless, Finnish nationalism continued to grow. New literary figures continued to spread ideas of statehood. Zacharias Topelius' 1875 work *The Book About Our Country*, written in Finnish for use in elementary schools, was highly influential. A few years earlier, Aleksis Kivi's *Seven Brothers* (published in 1871) had depicted "the confrontation between Finnish peasant culture and modern civilization". Its popularity rose significantly some two decades later when, according to historian Henrik Meinander (2013: 113), "a specifically Finnish culture had become more established and there was scope for national self-irony".

Nicholas II's actions culminated in the virtual nullification of the Finnish Constitution in 1899, which drew condemnation from leaders across Europe. An early revolutionary rising in Russia (before the main events to come) allowed a brief respite for Finland, and a new constitution was drawn up in 1906. It introduced a single-chamber parliament and universal suffrage, making Finnish women the first in Europe to have the vote. But following the outcome of a national election in 1907, the Finns found themselves, despite having had a vote, living under an oppressive Russian police regime for the next and final decade of subjugation (Nickels 1977).

Once the First World War began Russia turned its attention elsewhere, and for a time the Finns found themselves with no government, including no police. Then came privately organized police groups, sometimes organized by more conservative-leaning intelligentsia and landowners. Next, two separate police forces emerged, which became the two main militias known as the Whites and Reds, and – with them – the Terror.

Paradoxically, it was the Terror that would finally bring freedom to Finland. The Great War had been expected to be over in a few weeks or months, but instead it lasted years, and the map of Europe was changed forever. Russia was plunged into revolution, Britain began to lose Ireland (and later many of its other colonies), and far away the United States began to grow in power.

The Bolshevik revolution in Russia in October 1917 prompted deep concern amongst the bourgeois majority in the Finnish Parliament. They lost no time in proclaiming Parliament the supreme authority in Finland and appointing a new Senate in a bid to prevent the spread of the revolutionary wave that began in St Petersburg (Lewis 2005). Amongst the major powers, only Britain and the US took some time to deliberate before recognizing the newly independent nation. Thus, on 6 December 1917 the independent republic of Finland was born; but it was not a happy birth (Nickels 1977).

Consolidating the new state: 1917–39

Immediately after independence, civil war broke out in Finland between the Red Army composed of Finnish socialists, with the support of 70,000 Russian troops still stationed in Finland, and the White Army, which was led by minor members of the aristocracy but consisted largely of peasants under orders, and land-owning farmers who had a particular fear of the possibility of communism. The White Army was backed by German forces under the command of the formidable officer and Finnish statesman Baron Carl Gustav Emil Mannerheim, who, although critical of Nazism, would attend hunting trips with Hermann Göring in the 1930s (Donner 2017).

Within three months, the White Army had defeated the Reds. Although the Germans then tried to take control of Finland, Germany's defeat by the Allies in 1918 prevented the planned accession of a German prince to the Finnish throne and, in 1919, Finland adopted a republican constitution. In this constitution, the president was given six years in office and strong authority in order to promote unity, tame radicalism, and maintain the power of the bourgeois members in the new government. Presidential powers were only restricted much later in 1991, in 2000 when a revised constitutional law was passed, and furthermore in 2012 (Meinander 2013: 130).

In 1920 Finland signed a peace treaty with the Russians which acknowledged Finnish independence and gave Finland access to the Arctic Ocean via the ice-free port of Petsamo (Martineau 1980). The reconciliation of Finnish Reds and Whites took much longer. At first the Reds were painted as being on the wrong side of history, and uniquely vicious and cruel. Slowly, however, the facts of the civil war emerged. For every man, woman or child who died in the conflict or was executed in atrocities committed by the Reds, some ten had been slaughtered by the Whites. Furthermore, the Whites were unremittingly harsh in their imprisonment and treatment of their defeated opponents. Today the island of Suomenlinna is a Unesco World Heritage site, much frequented by tourists who take the short boat trip there from Helsinki. A century ago, however, it was a mass prison where many hundreds of Finns starved to death, the victims of food shortages and the callousness of their captors, the Whites.

Despite the legacy of civil war, in its first 20 years as an independent country Finland made great progress culturally, economically and politically. Although the 1919 constitution had given very wide-ranging powers to the president, the Finns remained committed to democratic party rule. As an example, an Act of Amnesty was passed in 1920, pardoning those Red leaders in the civil war who had not already been executed, and allowing electoral participation by the left-wing Social Democrats, who went on to form a government in 1926–27. The 1920s also saw the introduction of compulsory education and conscripted military service. In the 1930s, new industries were established, and more land brought into cultivation. A great variety of clubs, societies and associations were founded, and new scientific discoveries were made.

A great deal of mistrust remained between the Social Democrats and the conservative parties, even after the Communists broke away from being a faction within the Social Democrats (Meinander 2013:132). The 1920s would see the formation of 13 coalition governments, testimony to a lack of willingness to compromise and respect legal decisions, which one historian, Meinander (2013: 134) suggested was "a reluctance to comply with the rules of parliamentary democracy". In 1929, Finland saw Communist demonstrations and strikes and the rise of the reactionary right-wing Lapua movement, which steadily became more radical leading up to an abortive coup d'état in 1932 that finished off the movement. Extreme right-wing politics in Finland then moved into the parliamentary sphere and later, in 1932, the Patriotic People's Movement was formed (Koivulaakso *et al.* 2012: 70). Nevertheless, Finland's parliamentary democracy endured, and working-class citizens continued to support the Social Democrats and, importantly, the nation-state.

Quite why the divisions created by Finland's 1918 civil war were overcome relatively quickly, in contrast to what happened in the wake of civil war in most other countries, is unclear. A variety of hypotheses have been advanced. Did it have something to do with Finland's past as a colonized country? Centuries of being invaded or ruled by neighbours creates a certain kind of solidarity. If you can trust no country around you, maybe you have to start trusting each other? Equally significant are the country's social and economic circumstances: it was a place that continuously lost many of its children, not just to high infant mortality but also to emigration to the United States and Canada.

As a land relatively poor in resources in an era when iron, steel, rubber, cotton, tea, coffee and later oil were key global goods, there was less to fight over and a pressing need to try to create conditions that could stem depopulation. Furthermore, a land reform, which had been under debate prior to the civil war, was approved by the new government in 1918 (Jakobson 1987: 85). This diversified land ownership to smallholders by allowing the rural proletariat composed of landless labourers and tenant farmers to purchase (the legal term being "redeem") ownership of land at reduced prices, strengthening national unity. Initially, immediately after the war, the parliament had agreed that those convicted and then given at least ten years of imprisonment or sentenced to death would not be eligible. The clause limiting the right to redeem land had targeted the defeated Reds. However, in 1919, that clause was abolished (Rasila 1970: 369).

The Second World War and its aftermath

Russia was keen to stop Hitler expanding his influence in Europe following Germany's invasion of Czechoslovakia in 1938, so the Russians offered Finland large areas of land in Karelia in exchange for the southern parts of the Karelian Isthmus. Juho Kusti Paasikivi, who would later become president but at the time was a minister without portfolio in the cabinet of Risto Ryti, and Mannerheim (who was once again commander of the Finnish forces) were keen to consider this offer. The Finnish government declined, however, as it wished to maintain its contacts in the West. The result was the so-called Winter War between Russia and Finland, which began in November 1939 and was over by March 1940. Finland was forced to cede a large area of Karelia in the south and some territories in the north to the Soviet Union. Russia gained

10 per cent of Finnish territory and "Finland learned the lesson that in war she had to go it alone and that she lived next door to a neighbour she was unlikely ever to vanquish" (Lewis 2005: 37).

In June 1941 Finland attacked the Soviet Union with assistance from Nazi Germany, regaining its previously lost territory and becoming the northern flank of the siege of Leningrad (St Petersburg). This was called the Continuation War. In 1944, when things turned against Germany, the Soviet Union regained most of its former territories in the region, including Karelia.

In the run-up to the Winter War, Finland had naïvely trusted that the Western powers or Sweden would come to its aid. By the second war against Russia, however, it had learned to rely instead on *realpolitik*. In an attempt to regain the land taken from it by the Soviet Union, Finland joined Germany in attacking Russia. However, after the Moscow Armistice between Finland and the USSR and the UK in 1944, Russia asked Finland to drive out the German troops, which it did. This was a tactical move by Mannerheim, who wanted to free Finland from Russian control whilst remaining in favour with the Allies who would dictate the peace terms, and who would be important partners for Finland in the longer term.

The Continuation War, as it is now known, ended after three years in a truce in September 1944, the terms of which were confirmed in the Paris Peace Treaties signed in 1947. Finland had suffered huge losses and continued to suffer after the war. In postwar trials headed by the Allies, eight members of the Finnish government were imprisoned, including former President Risto Ryti, who was given the longest (ten year) sentence, but who was freed early in May 1949 on grounds of ill-health. Nevertheless, these were much lighter sentences than those handed down in the Tokyo and Nuremberg trials (Meinander 2013: 160).

The toll on the country as a whole was high. During the course of the Second World War, some 65,000 Finnish troops had been killed and 158,000 wounded. Finland was obliged to cede its northernmost Petsamo region to the Soviet Union, which meant giving up its only corridor to the Arctic Ocean. It also lost 62 per cent of its shipping fleet during the war, with another 7 per cent claimed by Russia, worth some $300 million at the time – which, rising with inflation, ended up nearer $600 million (Sletholt 1951). Whilst these reparations took a heavy toll, ultimately the build-up of industry that Finland undertook in order to pay off its debts contributed to the country's success as an independent nation.

Immediately following the war, Finland persuaded the Soviet Union that it was in the USSR's interest for Finnish defence forces to remain at a reasonable strength, in order to prevent the use of Finland as a base for attack (on the USSR) by a third party. The result was the Treaty of Friendship, Co-operation and Mutual Assistance, signed by Finland and the USSR in 1948, which would become the cornerstone of Finnish foreign policy for the duration of the Cold War. Although the treaty was viewed as an act of appeasement by the West, Finland succeeded in remaining much further outside the scope of Soviet domination than the Eastern Bloc nations did.

In 1944, anti-communist laws were repealed and the communist Finnish People's Demographic League (SKDL) was formed. Between 1945 and 1966 it won between 21 per cent and 24 per cent of the vote in parliamentary elections, with its support declining in subsequent years until it became part of the new Left Alliance in 1990. Finland's communists were not essential to maintaining relations with the Soviet Union (Meinander 2013: 162–3). Finns whose sympathies might have normally been with communism worked instead on improving social democracy. Finland strengthened its political, economic and cultural ties with the West, particularly its Nordic neighbours, whilst maintaining good relations with the Soviet Union – yet another empire abutting Finland, along its longest and by far most porous border.

For a country to end up leading on so many positive social indicators in 2020, a great number of things had to go the right way for Finland. In hindsight, one key factor was being on the losing side in the Second World War. As with Germany and Japan, which both prospered greatly some decades after losing the war, Finland ultimately benefited from being a defeated country. Some members of the ruling elite were removed from power as a result of the war trials, but key figures from its past, Mannerheim and Paasikivi, would go on to become president and prime minister respectively (Jakobson 1987: 58).

Even political insiders during the war who were tried and imprisoned, such as Väinö Tanner, would return to politics in the 1950s. Following the war trials, however, there was no new constitution, and the political landscape was relatively turbulent with 16 governments from 1948 to 1963 (Parliament of Finland 2019a). It took decades to rebuild the public's trust in government

(Meinander 2013:14) and Finland still grappled with Soviet influence and threat.

Many European countries were rebuilt after the Second World War with assistance received through the US Marshall Plan, but despite initial interest Finland declined such aid, owing to Soviet pressure over the political strings attached. It later received interest-bearing loans from the US instead (Hallberg & Martikainen 2018a).

New industries were set up to supply the products demanded by the USSR as part of the war reparations, two thirds of which were to be goods from the metal industry, including ships and cable products (Sletholt 1951). These industries would flourish in the years to come, with Finland exporting to the rest of Europe and the West. Indeed, even in the twenty-first century, the Russian Federation is dependent on a number of Finnish products for its own industries (Lewis 2005).

In the postwar period, Finland would demonstrate great competence in diplomacy, managing to maintain good relations with the Soviet Union whilst not being subject to the same level of control over its affairs as countries on the other side of the Iron Curtain. Juho Kusti Paasikivi, mentioned earlier for his role in the Second World War, became president in 1946 and successfully steered Finland's independence along the knife-edge of East–West relations – a policy which became known as the Paasikivi Line – and a policy that was still followed carefully decades later at the height of the Cold War (Nickels 1977). Today, more than a lifetime later, Finland continues to achieve that balancing act with what appears to be ever greater ease.

Conclusion: 1950s and beyond

In 1951, Finland's future was pessimistically described by one commentator as likely to remain "grey and dreary", as the economic repercussions of the war and its aftermath continued to affect day-to-day life, including the resettlement of populations in the wake of readjusted borders, rising prices, shortages of goods, and numerous strikes by hungry workers. At the time it was said: "Before Finland can settle down to a peaceful and well-regulated life, she has a long way to go" (Sletholt 1951: 126). But Finland's future was much brighter than this assessment indicated, as it was entering a period of political stability, economic progress and diplomatic success.

Figure 2.3: Finland's changing border and capital cities

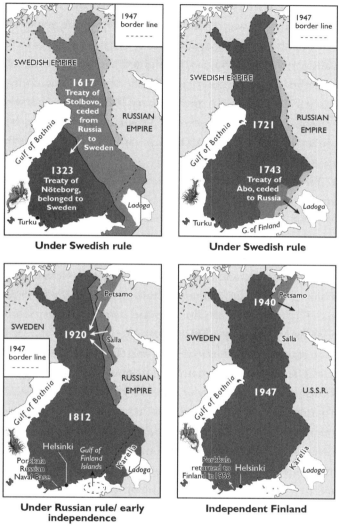

Under Swedish rule

Under Swedish rule

Under Russian rule/ early independence

Independent Finland

Source: Drawn from a wide variety of sources including https://finland.fi/life-society/tracing-finlands-eastern-border/ and https://en.wikipedia.org/wiki/Finland–Russia_border.

After the heavy losses, exhaustion and negotiation of international crises that characterized Finnish history in the first half of the twentieth century, the second half of the century was "pay-off time" (Lewis 2005: 198), an era when Finland's international standing gradually strengthened and the country secured its place as a respected diplomatic player on the world stage. The Olympic Games were staged in Helsinki in 1952, the same year that the last of Finland's war reparations were sent to the Soviet Union. Finland was the only country to pay its Second World War debts in full and on time (Elovainio 1999). In 1955, Finland joined the Nordic Council and was accepted into the United Nations. Urho Kekkonen was elected Finnish president in March 1956 and served until January 1982. His powers were greater than those afforded to his successors. Throughout this time, he pursued an active policy of neutrality, with the aim of increasing Finland's room to manoeuvre in international affairs.

In 2007 Finland was named the fourth most stable state in the world, or a little more accurately, the 175th least fragile out of the 178 countries assessed. In 2008 it became the third most stable. In 2011 it became the second most stable, and in 2013 it was named the most stable worldwide. It has held that position ever since (Fragile States Index 2019a). Today Norway is second, Switzerland third and Denmark fourth; all are assessed as such using a complex basket of indicators (Fragile States Index 2019b; and see Table 9.1 in this book). Finland began its climb toward its present position during the 1980s and 1990s; by the early 2000s, it was essentially top ranked.

Unlike the equivalent bodies in the UK and the US, the Finnish Parliament is unicameral (there is only one chamber, one house, one sovereign authority). The constitution states that power is held by the people; legislative power is held by parliament, which represents the people; executive power is held by government and the president who are to be trusted by parliament; and judicial power is held by independent courts, with the highest courts being the Supreme Court and the Supreme Administrative Court (Finlex 1999). An amendment to a constitutional law requires the approval of two-thirds of parliament, and that two consecutive parliaments adopt these amendments.

At the turn of the millennium, Finland's constitution was revised, with the most significant change relating to the restriction of presidential powers to foreign policy, making it largely a ceremonial role and so strengthening parliamentary democracy (Raunio 2005: 473). In 1991 presidential powers were restricted so that they may serve a maximum of two consecutive terms, and no longer hold an unrestricted right to dissolve parliament and call for new elections. The president also merely formally appoints the prime minister and other cabinet ministers, but ministerial appointments are decided, in effect, by the prime minister during negotiations on the formation of the government following elections. The prime minister is typically the chair of the largest party and must be ratified by an absolute majority in parliament, which is made up of 200 MPs.

The seismic changes in the late 1980s that led to the collapse of the Soviet Union and the end of the division of Europe were echoed in Finland as the nation became more assertive and began to take new foreign policy initiatives. In 1989, it became a member of the Council of Europe and in 1995 joined the European Union, following a successful referendum. Finland was then seen as an ideal negotiator between the EU and Russia and the Baltic States, given its geographical position and history of close contact with Russia over two centuries.

During Finland's successful EU presidency in 1999, the Finns showed their even-handedness and competence in international negotiations. In 2019 the Finns again held the presidency, ironically at the same time that the UK was trying to leave the EU after a controversial referendum, and the possibility that Scotland might regain independence and try to become Scandinavian. Northern Ireland, too, looked insecure in its relationship with the UK following the Brexit vote and ensuing negotiations. Its border with the rest of Ireland is, in effect, a border with Finland as well, given how solidly Finland is now a member of the EU.

After spending the twentieth century managing a delicate political balancing act between East and West, Finland, "having been menaced by the East and let down by the West . . . is now in a position to get the best from both sides" (Lewis 2005: 201). Finland is a respected member of the EU and stands out as the lone example of continuous foreign policy success with Russia, having kept on good terms with its former ruler and aggressor. Finland's relationships with Sweden and Germany, too, are more than cordial. Headteachers from around the world visit to learn how to run schools. Industrialists arrive to try to understand how such a small country could have created Nokia, at one point one of the world's most successful telecommunications companies. Politicians and academic researchers come to study what it takes to create a country of solidarity, and just how important lessons we take from history can be in that process.

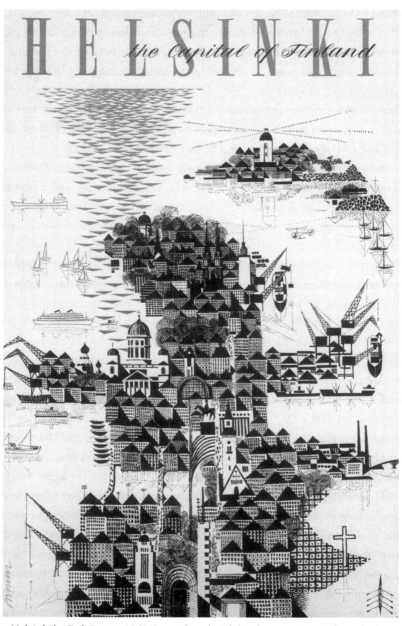

Helsinki by Erik Brunn, 1962. Reproduced with kind permission. Erik studied at the Institute of Industrial Arts (1944–49) and his art has become: "part of Finland's cultural heritage" (Londen, Enegren & Simons 2008: 238). This picture shows Helsinki viewed from above from the north, looking to the south and the sea.

3

Economy and welfare

"The idea that a contemporary Nordic society is anything like socialism is absurd. Over the past 70 years what the experience of the Nordic
nations actually suggests is that even the United States, with its already
very impressive commitments to freedom, might actually be able to
learn a few things from us about freedom and free-market capitalism."

Anu Partanen (2018) – author of *The Nordic Theory*
of Everything: In Search of a Better Life.

Challenger ecosystem

In 2020 Finland is performing remarkably well in numerous global economic
and social rankings and has been for some time. Two years earlier, the World
Economic Forum's Global Competitiveness Report (World Economic Forum
2018) ranked Finland eleventh in competitiveness, and first for the sound-
ness of its banks. In 2019 the World Economic Forum named Greater Helsinki
as one of its 12 "Challenger Ecosystems", cities close behind the top ten globally leading start-up hubs (Penzel 2019). Finland is also ranked as the most
politically stable country in the world, with some of the highest levels of press
freedom, and has been proclaimed the happiest place to live (see Parkkinen
2019). In many ways it has achieved what many idealists in the past dreamt
of – the winning of freedoms – rather than merely a superficial commitment
to the idea of freedom.

Statistics released shortly after the turn of the century led the United

Nations to rank Finland as the thirteenth most developed country in the world in its Human Development Report of 2004, twelfth by 2009 and twelfth again by 2019. At the time, few people noticed how quickly it had risen up the ranks, not least because its Nordic neighbours, Norway and Sweden, over-shadowed it in their even more rapid rise. However, what is remarkable about Finland is that it has achieved this without the oil advantages of Norway or the historic imperial advantages of Sweden.

Instead, Finland made use of what it had – forests. The forest industry pro-vided material for exports that supported its economic growth throughout the twentieth century when demand was high (Poropudas 1996: 352). Instead of an important land-owning aristocracy or gentry Finland had a significant class of peasant proprietors, or *talonpojat* (Häkkinen & Forsberg 2015: 101). Instead of rewards being concentrated in the hands of an elite likely to use the money in unproductive ways, such as buying luxury goods from abroad, the rewards were spread more evenly and benefited the domestic economy. This supported the growth of domestic industries and the local production and consumption of consumer goods. Inequality between the landless (the rural proletariat, as discussed in Chapter 2) and the landowners (including *talonpojat*) did grow during the nineteenth century as the population grew dramatically, but land reforms helped remedy this after the civil war.

Finland's vast forests have been a pillar of the country's economic devel-opment and its exports, accounting at times for around 20 per cent of export revenue. Hundreds of thousands of Finns are forest owners who depend on the forestry sector, and also invest in its management and sustainability (Ministry of Agriculture and Forestry 2019). Although Finland's forests are largely privately owned, its citizens, like their counterparts in other Nor-dic countries, have the right to roam all forests, lakes and fields free of any charges, and berry and mushroom foraging is open to all. That old commit-ment to the commons is now very carefully protected – as a freedom.

The country's particular economic path and arrangement is partly the result of chance over both resources and its *talonpojat* historic social struc-ture. Importantly, wood as a raw material is not as valuable a natural resource as petroleum. Finland does, however, have a strong oil refinery business even though the country has no natural oil resources of its own. The Finnish com-pany Neste's profits were derived mainly from oil refining, but by 2018 it diversified and biofuels made chiefly of wood became the main source of its profits (Parviala 2019). Its business leaders tend to think further ahead, more carefully and more sustainably than do those running businesses elsewhere. The chemical industry's share in Finnish exports has also increased as that industry has become more sophisticated.

Table 3.1 shows the ranking of countries by the 2004 Human Development Index (HDI), which tends to be volatile year on year, and is made up of a mixture of GDP per capita, life expectancy and the proportion of children who are well educated, or at least attend school for a large number of years. The HDI takes no account of quality of education, or distribution of income, so the US ranks highly even though only a small minority of Americans enjoy anything like its mean average income, and even fewer are well-off.

By 2009 Finland ranked above the UK, in part because the UK had been so badly affected by the financial crash. By 2014 Finland had dropped to 24th place because national income had grown more slowly than it had in other countries, and because Finnish children formally start school later, which reduces Finland's mean years of schooling. (This does not mean, however, that Finnish children are less well educated; a subject we will return to in Chapters 4 and 5). By 2019, and despite that disadvantage, the country once again ranked twelfth, three places above both the UK and US.

In addition to the strengths that contribute to its high placement in the Human Development Index rankings, Finland is also endowed with a strong welfare state and comparatively good wealth equality and income equality. Many valid criticisms can be made of HDI as a measure, and more sustainable alternatives have been suggested (Hickel 2020). Ranking by HDI (arguably inadvertently) rewards states for socially, economically or environmentally unjust policies; it is worth noting that Finland's high score, unlike that of some other states, owes little to such detrimental factors.

For an example of how the use of HDI can be misleading, Singapore now ranks ninth, above Finland, but the life expectancy component of its HDI is high in part because poorer women who are not citizens, almost all working as servants in Singapore, are pregnancy-tested every three months and usually leave the country if pregnant. This serves to reduce Singapore's infant mortality rates, artificially raising life expectancy and the country's HDI rank in that category. Singapore also suffers from one of the highest income

Table 3.1: The twenty "most developed" states in the world in 2004–19 (HDI)

HDI rank 2004	HDI = Human Development Index	HDI rank 2009	HDI rank 2014	HDI rank 2019
1	Norway	1	1	1
2	Sweden	7	12	8
3	Australia	2	2	6=
4	Canada	4	8	13
5	Netherlands	6	4	10
6	Belgium	17	21=	17
7	Iceland	3	13	6=
8	United States	13	5	15=
9	Japan	10	17	19
10	Ireland	5	11	3
11	Switzerland	9	3	2
12	United Kingdom	21	14	15=
13	**Finland**	**12**	**24**	**12**
14	Austria	14	21=	20
15	Luxembourg	11	21=	21
16	France	8	20	26
17	Denmark	16	10	11
18	New Zealand	20	7	14
19	Germany	22	6	4=
20	Spain	15	27	25

Source: UNDP, Human Development Reports (2004, table 1; 2009, table A; 2014, table 1; and 2019).

Note: countries in the top 20 in 2019 not in the top 20 in 2004 included Hong Kong China (=4th), Singapore (9th) and Liechtenstein (18th). There is very little real movement over long periods of time.

inequality rates amongst top ranking countries, so few of its citizens enjoy the economic freedoms that its GDP per capita implies.

Norway consistently ranks highest on the HDI index partly because of the boost to its GDP from oil. Australia now ranks sixth, in part because of revenues from fossil fuel exports and also because so many of its young people attend university, albeit at a very high cost under its privatized university system. In contrast, Finland's high HDI standing reflects many of the things for which it is known and admired: a high-quality education system (including publicly funded universities that are not distracted by the need to seek profits), a strong welfare state, and comparatively good wealth equality and income equality – although there were slight rises in levels of income inequality in 2014 when Finland ranked less well on HDI. These were noted at that time by commentators such as Thomas Piketty (Wall 2014).

Over the course of the twentieth century, Finland rose from being one of the poorest European countries to one that managed to compete effectively in the global economy without creating social inequalities and leaving the disadvantaged in Finnish society behind. While it is not the only country in the world to have become wealthier while simultaneously building a strong welfare state, Finland has done so in the face of unique geopolitical constraints. In a way its Nordic neighbours have never had to, Finland has always had to balance its relationship with the Soviet Union and subsequently with the Russian Federation, alongside its aim of integrating with the West (Vartiainen 2011: 58). One reason Finland has been less successful than its Western neighbours in trading with international consumer and service markets is that it was able to rely on the Soviet Union as a trading partner for so long throughout the twentieth century (Böckerman & Kiander 2006: 141).

State intervention played a crucial role in the reorganization of Finland's postwar economy and in the country's ability to pay its war debts, and state participation in the capital of corporations remains comparatively high compared with other countries in the EU, exceeding about 40 per cent in 2016 (European Commission 2016). One of the most controversial state-owned enterprises is Veikkaus, a gambling monopoly formed from the 2017 merger of three firms, each holding separate Finnish gambling licences (European Casino Association 2019). Monopolies on gambling are permissible under EU law as long as they are established in order to address gambling's associated risks, which was the case in Finland. In 2018, Veikkaus's turnover was €3.15 billion and its gross gaming revenue was €1.76 billion. In its annual report that year, Veikkaus' CEO (Olli Sarekoski) reported that digital gaming limits imposed by the government had reduced its yearly revenue by around €21 million (Veikkaus 2019). Finland has just one casino on the mainland and another one in Åland (FATF 2019: 30), so the majority of high stakes gambling is done online. Casino Tampere, however, will open in 2021.

Despite the risks associated with gambling, the tax revenue that Veikkaus generates and the percentage of its profits channelled into charities has given the industry an unusually positive and nationalist connotation (Gillin 2018c). While the incidence of money laundering is low in Finnish gambling, as there is a smaller chance for criminal groups to infiltrate or own gambling companies when they are exclusively under state control (FATF 2019: 121), the social consequences of easy access to gambling through any of the 18,500 slot machines found in many shops or kiosks are increasingly attracting scrutiny (Yle Uutiset 2019b). According to a survey by the National Institute of Health and Welfare, 3.3 per cent of the population has a gambling problem, and one in five Finns has a relative or close friend who has (Järvinen-Tassopoulos 2017).

Beyond Veikkaus and the issues of what it actually promotes, the Finnish economy has had other problems. Finnish banks and corporations are not scandal-free, and some were mentioned in the 2016 Panama Papers data leak. Nordea, one of the largest Nordic banking groups, which is headquartered in Helsinki, was implicated in recent years in money-laundering scandals (Milne 2019).

Postwar economy

After the Second World War, Finnish exports experienced a long period of decline (Honkapohja & Vihriälä 2019: 126). The USSR exacted an "indemnity" (another term for the war reparations detailed above) for eight years in recompense for Finland's role as a German ally, and Finland's wartime leaders were tried in court by the Allied powers. This proved economically fortunate as it swept away much of the old hierarchies and led to the emergence of a new elite in Finland, and later the election of centre-left governments that balanced cooperation with business and banks while maintaining close links to an increasingly active labour movement (Vartiainen 2011: 58).

Centre-left governments were dominant following the Second World War. A government formed in 1958 which included the National Coalition Party and the Social Democratic Party was forced to resign in early 1959 because

50

the Soviet Union disapproved of their Western leanings. After a parliamentary defeat in 1966, the National Coalition Party remained in opposition until 1987 (Hallberg & Martikainen 2018b). Following this electoral loss, the National Coalition Party grew quieter in its calls for dismantling the welfare state (Jacobson 1987: 81).

Finland's final total war repayments to the Soviet Union were equivalent to over US $5 billion today. Paying war debts required the country to increase exports and hence employment. In effect, losing the war acted as a spur to both basic industry and entrepreneurship. The Finnish postwar growth regime was characterized by a high rate of state-led investment in key manufacturing industries such as paper, wood pulp and metalworking, a high rate of foreign capital accumulation, and low interest rates (Vartiainen 2011: 59). Enhancing industrialization was also a way of providing employment for returning military service personnel and Finnish citizens who had been displaced during the war. State intervention also played an important role in resettling Karelian refugees who made up an eighth of Finland's population in 1940 (see Chapter 2, above).

In 1948 the US' European Recovery Program, popularly known as the Marshall Plan, contributed the equivalent of US$100 billion, mostly in grants, to Western Europe for its rebuilding efforts. It is worth reiterating the point made in Chapter 2 that it was Soviet pressure that dissuaded Finland from accepting Marshall Plan money, although it did later secure separate loans from the US without the political requirements attached to Marshall Plan aid. Its economy and social recovery, and its ability to pay reparations, were all made possible by a great increase in exports both of wood and from its newly developing industries.

Finland's economic recovery could hardly be said to have been guaranteed, given the unique impediments it faced. Although the Soviet Union was a valuable trading partner, it was reluctant to allow Finland to engage in Western trade (Honkapohja & Vihriälä 2019: 20). Nevertheless, in 1961 Finland signed a free trade agreement with the European Free Trade Association (EFTA) and in 1973 joined the European Economic Community (EEC).

A balance of protectionist policies and inclusion in free-trade agreements was essential for the growth of Finland's export trade. Integration into the strengthening economic cooperation of Western Europe was also important as a means for political integration and for establishing greater distance from the USSR (Vartiainen 2011: 62). Finland participated in GATT (anti-protectionist) negotiations and later became part of the World Trade Organisation (WTO). Although the Finnish economy was beginning to liberalize and free-trade agreements were valued, protectionist measures remained in force through to the 1980s, mainly in agriculture. Finland's achievements did not come by allowing untrammelled free trade.

In the 1950s, Finland's economy was almost exclusively forestry and agriculture-based (Halme *et al*. 2014: 1). Nevertheless, it was able to benefit greatly from the second wave of globalization following the Second World War, as evident from its average of 3.8 per cent GDP-per-capita growth between 1961 and 1979. This figure exceeded the growth in Sweden, the US, and the global average, which were 3.6 per cent, 2.9 per cent, and 3 per cent respectively. In recent years, the ground its economy has made up has continued to grow, albeit at a slower pace. The average annual GDP growth per annum in Finland was 2.5 per cent, 2.8 per cent and 1.5 per cent in 2016, 2017 and 2018 – as compared to 1.4 per cent, 0.7 per cent and 1.1 per cent in neighbouring Sweden for the same years (World Bank 2019a).

Part of Finland's economic story, therefore, is about it slowly (but surely) catching up with its far more powerful neighbours. Figure 3.1 illustrates how GDP growth in Finland continues to exceed that of countries in Europe that tend to be richer than it is, in the most recent three years for which we have data. Noteworthy is the fact that it is not just growing more strongly than Sweden and Norway; but also more than Germany, France, Italy and the UK. This gaining of ground is not merely attributable to Finland's having started from a lower base. More importantly, as we explain in Chapter 8, an increasing proportion of this growth is green growth.

Although the period from the 1960s through to the early 1970s in the West is often seen as the golden era of capitalism tempered by John Maynard Keynes' theories of demand management, in Finland it was a fiscally conservative time, with budgetary policy dominated by monetarist principles, and much less of a focus on full employment. Even today, employment levels in Finland remain lower than in Norway and Sweden, states that followed a more clearly Keynesian path in the postwar era (Uusitalo 1984: 40). Successive Finnish governments' reluctance to take steps to raise employment

Figure 3.1: Average GDP/capita growth 2016–18 (%), high-income European countries

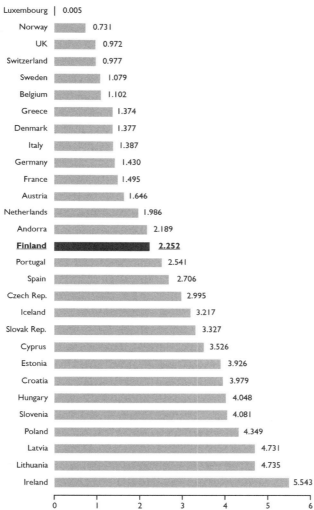

Source: World Bank and analysis by authors

Note: The Channel Islands, Faroe Islands, Gibraltar, Greenland, Isle of Man, Liechtenstein, Monaco and San Marino are not included as their reports to the World Bank were all late at the time of accessing this data. Data is annual percentage growth rate of GDP per capita based on constant local currency for high-income countries ("high" as defined by the World Bank): calculated without making deductions for depreciation of fabricated assets or for depletion and degradation of natural resources, data series: NY.GDP.PCAP.KD.ZG; https://datacatalog.worldbank.org/.

levels were, arguably, influenced by the more corporatist involvement of its business community encouraging governments in the prioritization of the export sector (Vartiainen 2011: 60).

The 1960s and 1970s was an age in which Finland's approach to free markets was careful and controlled. When credit rationing was in force from the 1940s through to the late 1970s, business loans were prioritized, and household loans were limited to mortgages (Vartiainen 2011: 62). Yet despite Finland's generally monetarist approach at this time, its social welfare provisions were not dissimilar to those of other Nordic countries. The Social Democratic Party and its particular progressive history was key (Uusitalo 1984: 44). This was balanced by Finland's Central Bank (the fourth oldest in Europe, established in 1811) which played a rather stronger (and more conservative) role in national fiscal policy in comparison to those in other European countries (Bank of Finland 2019a).

In Finland's postwar economy, the government and Central Bank were both highly involved in what they deemed to be strategic industries, which were at the receiving-end of bank credit flow. The Finnish state's significant control of foreign investment (Chang 2008: 60) is a long-standing one. In the 1930s, a series of laws classified enterprises "with more than 20% foreign ownership as dangerous" (Chang 2008: 84). Decades later, between 1971 and 1985, the country had one of the lowest ratios, outside the Eastern Bloc, of foreign direct investment in total fixed capital formation – in the long-term assets typically described under the designation "property, plant and equipment" – at just 0.6 per cent (Chang 2008: 239).

It was not until 1987 that Finland relaxed its foreign investment legislation and the foreign ownership ceiling for ownership of a company was raised to 40 per cent, but such investors still had to be approved by the Ministry of Trade and Industry (Chang 2008: 85). According to Ha-Joon Chang (2002: 101), foreign direct investment is beneficial for economic development, but only when implemented once a country has developed sufficient productive capabilities to offer prosperous investment locations, with strong productive inputs such as skilled workers and infrastructure. In 2018, Finland attracted the most foreign direct investment of all Nordic countries, and its particular strength has been identified as offering diversity, with investments made in software, social and health services, corporate and expert services and machinery industry (Heiskanen 2019). Fortuitously for Finland, general liberalization took place in the 1990s in preparation for European Union membership. Each country's history is also partly a matter of luck.

According to a study by Oxford Economics (2019), Finland has received around €31.7 billion of inward foreign direct investment since it joined the EU in 1995, and its net contribution to the EU's coffers is relatively small, at 0.04 per cent of its GDP, when weighed against total EU expenditure in Finland. Of the €8.3 billion allocated to Finland by the EU for 2014–20 (European Commission 2017), €2.3 billion has flowed to its rural development budget. The EU also provided additional funds to the Finnish farmers most affected by the 2014 Russian ban on agricultural imports from the EU: €8.9 million in 2015, and €7.5 million in 2016.

In aggregate, the numbers clearly show, and Eurobarometer surveys confirm, that Finland is a net beneficiary of the EU. Membership was an important step in the process of integration into Western Europe as an advanced market economy, not least by reducing Finland's dependence on its Eastern neighbour with which it has had a long and often difficult relationship. EU membership has brought in 40,000 more jobs, an increase in GDP per capita of 1.2–1.7 per cent, and a rise in total international trade from 9 to 26 per cent (Oxford Economics 2019). Finland has one of the lowest electoral participation rates in European Parliament elections, with 2019's fairly modest turnout of 40.8 per cent being the highest so far. Most Finns are now very positive towards the EU and consider immigration and climate change to be Finland's greatest challenges, although Eurobarometer results should be taken with a grain of salt as Finland's response rate is notoriously low and in 2018 was 14 per cent (Bennike 2018). Across Europe, support for the euro hovers at an average of 62 per cent, whereas 80 per cent of Finns support economic and monetary union and hence the euro.

Development of the welfare state and incomes policy

Finland's welfare state was largely built in the 1960s. However, as Kettunen (2001: 26) points out, more generous social security benefits and more extensive public services were introduced only in the 1970s, as it began catching up with the world's most affluent economies (Vartiainen 2011: 53; Kokkinen

2011). Paradoxically, Finland's state provision was growing just as the welfare state was beginning to retreat or decline in much of the rest of the Western world.

From the 1960s onwards, one of the country's most significant policy shifts was to an increased focus on its educational system, with growth in size, quality and the years of schooling offered. In 1968 there was a political consensus to transform the parallel segregated school system to a comprehensive school system (Risku 2014). It had been a long time coming, with unsuccessful reform attempts in 1932, 1948, 1957, 1959 and 1965. The 1968 initiative aimed to raise educational standards and lessen the impact of students' family background and location on their educational achievement (see Chapter 4). Vocational schools were also established, and by the end of the 1960s, Finland's higher education sector numbered 15 institutions from the lone university it had boasted at the turn of the century (Lemola 2014: 29).

Commentators such as Vartiainen (2011: 68–9) have suggested that Finland's programme of education and welfare service improvements was aimed at gaining acceptance of wage moderation and the structural reforms that were deployed postwar with the aim of promoting economic growth, but which yielded both winners and losers. Broader safety nets would, it was hoped, catch the losers.

A major plank of the Finnish welfare state was the incomes policy that was introduced in the late 1960s, in which tripartite agreements were reached among the government, trade unions, and employers from the public and private sector and agricultural producers (Kettunen 2001: 26). This policy aimed to tie wage increases to greater macroeconomic objectives (Vartiainen 2011: 56, 66). Income settlements reached as part of this policy, along with currency devaluations in 1949, 1957, 1967 and 1977–80, contributed to meeting Finland's postwar goal of rapid capital accumulation, with wage growth restricted only for two to three years in this period to retain the benefits of the devaluation for profitability. Harmonious labour relations, rising wages, more stable employment and broad national support for these income settlements were all dependent on rising external competitiveness.

Although informal income policy agreements between the Finnish government and employers began in the 1950s, the first official agreement on incomes policy, known as the Liinamaa Agreement, was made in 1969 (Hassel

2006: 206). Whereas growing labour discontent with previous attempts to restrict wage growth with limited consultation had culminated in a 1956 General Strike, the new tripartite social contracts were designed to achieve buy-in from increasingly powerful trade unions (Vartiainen 2011: 67).

The government actively encouraged unionization, which reached its height between 1965 and 1975 (Vartiainen 2011: 67), to build a social consensus for Finland's economic policy during the Cold War. Following the Liinamaa Agreement, national wage coordination was conducted via tripartite package deals, although the decisions were not binding for all member unions of the Central Organisation of Finnish Trade Unions (SAK), which could also opt to negotiate sectorally. Such sector negotiations frequently challenged the corporatist tripartite wage restraint (Hassel 2006: 229; SAK 2019a).

From the standpoint of workers, the fairest wage agreements were reached in years when the Social Democratic Party was in government and especially when those governments were facing serious electoral challenges (Hassel 2006: 210). Notably, no tripartite agreement was reached between 1991 and 1995, years when the country had its first conservative-led government since 1964.

1980s and 1990s: prelude to Finland's worst economic depression

Credit controls and international capital movements were heavily regulated in Finland until the 1980s. During this decade, however, domestic lending rates and private foreign borrowing were freed from earlier controls. This deregulation and its corresponding uncontrolled capital flows would unleash excessive credit expansion and growth in inflated nominal demand (Vartiainen 2011: 70).

Between 1986 and 1989, private investment and private consumption contributed some 5–7 per cent of GDP growth. An overvalued currency fuelled imports, while net exports and the current account decreased, with these conditions exacerbated by a series of uncoordinated government policy decisions. The road to Finland's financial stability, economic success and high-income equity has at times been rocky along the way.

In the 1980s the relatively autonomous Bank of Finland adopted low interest rates – which typically (in the past, although less so recently) have been catalysts for financial bubbles. The Bank made these moves to support a new exchange rate target. To add fuel to the fire, the mortgage deduction allowances that had been in place to accommodate credit rationing were now in an environment free of credit controls. Finnish commercial and high-street banks, which had long enjoyed relatively light supervision, marketed excessively generous loans.

On the fiscal side, as Keynesian control of aggregate demand had never been implemented in a concerted way in Finland, it was a difficult sell in an era of financial liberalization. The coalition government of Social Democrats, the Centre Party, and the conservative National Coalition Party that took office in 1987 was unwilling to impose restraint on an overheating economy. Although external events such as the collapse of the USSR would also contribute to the economic upheaval that followed, it was primarily driven by domestic issues.

It was Finland's late-1980s foray into what later become known as *kasinotalous* (casino capitalism), characterized by credit and financial market liberalization, that would see it plunge into its deepest postwar depression. Karl-Oskar Lingdren (2011: 47) argues that the financial shocks suffered in this period were comparable in magnitude to the 1930s Great Depression, and Heikkinen and Kuusterä (2001) characterize it as a "deregulation crisis" similar to that experienced by East Asian economies in the 1990s following sudden inflows of capital. Easy credit makes buying foreign goods easier and, with that, wealth flows out of the domestic market.

Depression, 1991–94

In 1991, Finland's GDP growth dropped from around +5 per cent to −6.5 per cent and would not return to positive growth until 1994 (Vartiainen 2011: 73). Unemployment skyrocketed, incomes declined, and housing prices crashed, causing household savings to increase as people stopped buying. Only one large bank managed to avoid bankruptcy. The Finnish markka collapsed.

Finnish unemployment soared from 3 per cent in 1990 to almost 17 per cent in 1994, the second highest rate in the OECD. Intra-elite trust also suffered greatly as those with significant assets began to mistrust each other (Lingdren 2011: 57). All the while, the outside world ignored Finland and its unprecedented financial crisis. But just over a dozen years later, the world would be taught the bitter lessons that Finland had already learned about the consequences of financial deregulation, as the global economic crash began to take shape and banks from Iceland to Alabama and England to Kazakhstan began to fail.

When the centre-right coalition led by Esko Aho came to power in 1991, it did not follow the example of Sweden, in the grip of a similar financial crisis, in deploying counter-cyclical fiscal policy (Vartiainen 2011: 75). Although austerity measures were enacted in response to the depression, production and labour markets were further (but not excessively) deregulated. However, some employment policy proposals (including some put forth via the traditional tripartite process) were contested and overruled by trade unions, whose membership numbers grew in the wake of the 1990s crisis. For example, labour opposition defeated a proposal to reduce unemployment benefits, and taxes were increased instead (Lingdren 2011: 51). Like many EU countries, Finland has product market regulations that carefully circumvent certain EU free-trade policies, but some were relaxed and privatizations did take place (Lingdren 2011: 53). Employment protection legislation, however, remained largely unchanged.

Recovery and growth

After the depression in the early 1990s, the Finnish government began the process of transitioning to a knowledge economy, which would be partly reflected in Finland's apparently sudden success in the OECD's PISA assessments of secondary school students' attainment (Honkapohja & Vihriälä 2019: 22). However educational advances had been made long before they were picked up in these assessments and made the economic transformation possible. The economy also became reliant once again on export-led growth. The 1990s was a period when net immigration began to exceed emigration, possibly for the first time in many generations (see Chapter 8) and Finland joined the eurozone.

Long before today's economic success, Finland's yearly average GDP growth rate in the second half of the 1990s was 4.6 per cent (Lingdren 2011: 57). However, the employment rate did not recover as quickly following the economic crisis, and for a time remained lower than in other Nordic countries (Honkapohja & Vihriälä 2019: 22). Unemployment remained at around 10 per cent well into the early 2000s (See Figure 3.2).

The Social Democrats returned to power in a new coalition in the mid-1990s and by the end of the decade the government, then led by Paavo Lipponen, placed an even stronger emphasis on particular aspects of the welfare state, such as education and research (Liukas 2017). However, this occurred at the same time as unemployment benefits were restricted, policies to encourage taking paid work were implemented, home care allowances were reduced, and basic social security was not adjusted for inflation (Sipilä 2011: 361). Although there was no drastic change in economic policy from the previous centre-right government, the new "rainbow government" was more cooperative with trade unions and coordinated wage bargaining was restored, because it helped to stabilize both the economy and labour relations (Lingdren 2011: 57). Better trade union relations were also necessary to contain labour cost growth to meet the EU's Economic and Monetary Union (EMU) eligibility criteria, which dominated Finnish economic policy after the depression. Finland needed sound public finances and an appropriate inflation rate (Vartiainen 2011: 76). Euro membership requires the sacrifice of control over monetary policy, including the use of central bank interest rates to contain wage increases and to stimulate the economy.

The loss of that particular wage-control mechanism meant that successful pay bargaining by the Lipponen government was essential in bringing the rate of nominal wage increases under control. Spending cuts, a short-term austerity, made in the 1990s were redressed in the early 2000s by increases in state pensions, the restoration of a minimum allowance in sickness insurance benefits and increases in earnings-related unemployment allowance. The stock market and equity markets grew rapidly. Trade union membership has fallen since the 1990s, although it remains comparatively high in global terms (Lingdren 2011: 62–4).

In 2007, Finland's long-standing incomes policy fell into abeyance when the main national employers' organization, the Confederation of Finnish Industries (CFI), chose not to participate in a tripartite incomes policy

Figure 3.2: Average youth unemployment 2018 (%), high-income European countries

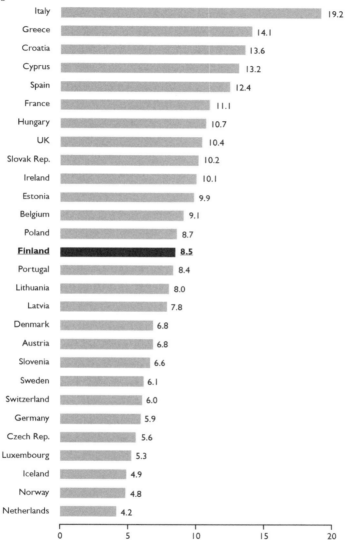

Source: World Bank (2019b) and analysis by authors.

Note: Andorra, Channel Islands, Faroe Islands, Gibraltar, Greenland, Isle of Man, Liechtenstein, Monaco and San Marino are not included as reports were all late at the time of accessing this data: Share of youth not in education, employment or training, total (per cent of youth population aged 15–24 or 15–29): SL.UEM.NEET.ZS; http://databank. worldbank.org/data/reports.aspx?source=&series=SL.UEM.NEET.ZS.

agreement and settlements took place at a sectoral level instead (Vartiainen 2011: 56). Centralized wage agreements resumed in 2011 and 2013, but as of 2016 the Confederation of Finnish Industries stopped taking part in tripartite settlements, meaning that collective bargaining cannot continue as it used to.

The OECD (2019b: 230) views collective bargaining as beneficial, in particular in addressing demographic and technological changes. At the same time, trade union participation and collective bargaining coverage have suffered across OECD countries, which have been associated with increased economic inequality (OECD 2019b: 68). Union participation in Finland as in many other countries worldwide has declined, especially with the growth of part-time work, non-conventional self-employment and zero-hour contracts. Trade union membership in Finland in 2018 was 60.3 per cent, down from 78.4 per cent in 1998 (OECD.Stat 2019a), and is lowest in the service sector, while it remains high in the manufacturing and public sector (Jonker-Hoffrén 2019). In Sweden, Denmark, and Iceland, union membership is at 65.6 per cent (data for 2017), 66.5 per cent, and 91.8 per cent respectively (OECD.Stat 2019b). In the UK it is 23.4 per cent, in the US 10.1 per cent, and in France 8.8 per cent.

Finland has one of the highest reported rates of trust in trade unions amongst the general population, at 65 per cent. Jonker-Hoffrén (2019: 205) attributes high union membership significantly to 1946 legislation that consolidated unions' role in collective bargaining, and the "Ghent-system of unemployment fund management" – which makes trade unions partly responsible for unemployment funds. Some 38 per cent of unemployment benefits are financed by the state, 5.5 per cent by the unemployment insurance fund, and 55.5 per cent by the employment fund (previously the TVR) to which both employers and employees have contributed since the 1990s' crisis. In addition, there is also a General Unemployment Fund that a fifth of Finnish wage earners subscribe to (YTK) and Böckerman and Kiander (2006: 161) have attributed part of the reason for declining trade union membership to the growth of this provision.

While the tripartite agreements have broken down, employers' federations and trade unions still negotiate collective agreements to determine wages in a system of industry-level pattern bargaining, as a minimum wage is not otherwise written into law. Collective bargaining coverage increased from 85 per cent in 2000 to 91 per cent in 2016 (Jonker-Hoffrén 2019: 198). Regardless of membership of the trade union or employers' federation, which negotiate the collective agreement, it still applies to the entire industry. The prevalence of strikes in late 2019, during negotiations, indicated a lack of willingness on the part of employers to compromise before their employees had to resort to strike action. Legally, strikes are not allowed when a collective agreement is active, but are allowed to take place during their negotiations.

Striking is easier when unemployment is relatively low, as it is today in Finland. It is especially so for younger people in Finland, when Finland's unemployment rates are lower than those in other European countries. The recent fall in unemployment rates for young people is arguably attributable to a combination of the end of the 2008 Great Recession in Finland, and the ever decreasing numbers of young people, due to the drop in birth rates two decades ago (which continue to fall today). Figure 3.2 shows youth unemployment rates in Finland in 2018 and how they compare to other European countries. This is the share of young people not in education, employment or training as a proportion of the corresponding age group: youth (ages 15–24), or persons aged 15–29, depending on the convention in each country.

In recent decades services have become more important for the economy and the service sector now contributes over two thirds of Finland's GDP (EK 2018) and almost certainly a higher proportion of its growth. The Finnish economy grew at the turn of the millennium, largely thanks to the short-lived success of Nokia, which developed on the back of a strong information and communication technology (ICT) sector that had been quietly growing, aided by educational reforms in the 1960s and 1970s. Recovery from the 1990s depression was primarily driven by exports. Nokia was early in the adoption of a new technology: efficient mobile phones with low battery consumption and a high-quality keypad. However, it failed to adapt quickly enough (Lemola 2014: 33).

Nokia created products for a world economy and also benefited from a cheap labour force in the former Eastern Bloc and China (Honkapohja & Vihriälä 2019: 130). In contrast with overall European growth, which was in slowdown after 1990, Finland, along with Sweden, grew faster than the US in the 1990s, as those Scandinavian countries' larger welfare budgets were not a constraint to growth (Chang 2012). Even after Nokia went into rapid decline and Microsoft purchased its mobile business in 2013, Finland was not damaged economically as badly as other countries. It weathered the global economic crash of 2008 by raising public spending up to 56.2 per cent of GDP in 2012 – a rate of spending that the government plans to continue to 2022 with only modest reductions, by which time it will have the projected highest public spending in the affluent world (see Table 3.2).

The financial crash and eurozone crisis: Finland's "lost decade"

As a eurozone member, Finland has had to tough out both the 2007–08 global financial crash as well as the subsequent eurozone sovereign debt crisis, which started in 2009 and peaked in 2010 and 2012. In 2009 Finland's GDP per capita shrank to levels that had not been seen since 1918. Despite a brief period of growth, GDP per capita fell again after 2011 (Heikkinen 2017: 306).

From the mid-1980s to the onset of these crises, Finland had experienced a slight increase in income inequality, with the gap between the bottom and top 10 per cent widening slightly, by 1.3 per cent (Matthijs 2015: 4). Finns keep a close eye on inequality, which is one reason why it is so low in their country. An increase in income inequality between the mid-1980s and 2008 was also large enough to be easily measurable by the Gini coefficient (a measure of inequality that takes into account the entire distribution under study), but by this measurement there was also a decrease in income inequality more recently, between 2008 and 2012 (Matthijs 2015: 5). By this point, and largely as a result of low inequality, Finland had the second lowest poverty and social exclusion rate in all of Europe by 2017 (Figure 3.3).

Among the eurozone countries, Finland is part of the northern European core of members that have pushed for EU-wide austerity measures and maintained a strict stance towards southern "debtors" such as Greece. Interestingly, however, even as Finland preached prudence, it actually increased the proportion of its own GDP spent on public services between 2008 and 2014, in contrast to almost every other country in Europe (see Figure 6.2 in Chapter 6). In joining the eurozone, Finland sacrificed the policy option of currency devaluation to increase competitiveness. The economic constraints of eurozone membership have been politicized in public debate and related

Table 3.2: Proportion of GDP spending on public services 2002, 2012, and projected in 2022

% of GDP	2002	2012	2022
Finland	47.5	56.2	52.2
Belgium	49.5	55.9	51.9
France	52.3	56.8	51.7
Denmark	53.2	58.0	50.8
Austria	52.5	51.5	50.3
Norway	45.8	42.2	49.4
Sweden	53.3	50.6	48.3
Italy	46.8	50.8	47.6
Greece	45.8	52.4	45.5
Germany	47.3	44.3	44.4
Portugal	43.7	48.5	43.9
Netherlands	43.9	47.1	43.0
Canada	40.5	41.0	40.0
Spain	38.6	48.1	39.8
United Kingdom	35.8	43.7	37.6
United States	33.6	37.3	36.7
Australia	35.0	36.7	35.3
Japan	35.7	38.7	35.2
New Zealand	33.2	35.9	32.0

Source: Updated January 2018 using October 2017 IMF release: http://www.imf.org/external/pubs/ft/weo/2017/02/weodata/index.aspx.

Note: Data for Ireland are excluded as its GDP in recent years has been artificially inflated by US companies locating their European headquarters there to gain from very low tax rates. The 2012 data include public spending to bail out the banks which was then occurring.

to broader national socio-economic issues of distribution, in particular by the far-right Finns Party (Salo & Rygdren 2018; Soini 2015).

As a eurozone member, Finnish economic policymaking is subject to EU scrutiny, and shortly before the Covid-19 pandemic, the European

Figure 3.3: At risk of poverty or social exclusion rate, 2017 (EU countries at that time)

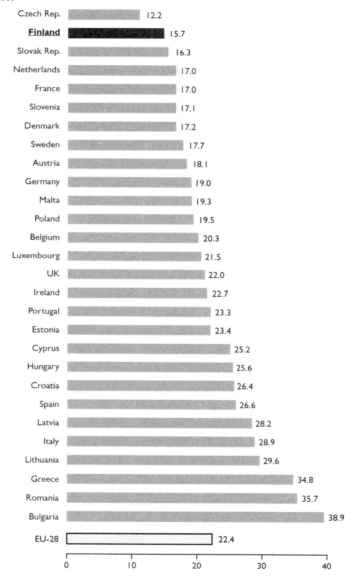

Source: Based on data provided by Eurostat (2018d).

Note: Switzerland, Norway, Iceland, Turkey, North Macedonia are represented by 2016 data instead of 2017.

Commission (EC) raised concerns over Finland's latest budget proposal. Given the added spending the budget proposed, the EC wanted to know how it would be balanced (Muhonen & Sajari 2019). Finland's Ministry of Finance clarified that the budget deficit to GDP ratio would be only 1 per cent in 2020, still below the maximum of 3 per cent allowed within the eurozone, effectively countering European Commission concerns of being a case of "significant" non-compliance. The European Commission (2019) still responded by saying it was "of the opinion that the Draft Budgetary Plan of Finland is at risk of non-compliance with the provisions of the Stability and Growth Pact", albeit not at risk of "significant" non-compliance. Similar warnings were issued to Belgium, Spain, France, Italy, Portugal, Slovenia and Slovakia.

Finland justified its deviation from the provisions of the Stability and Growth Pact by emphasizing that its fiscal expansion during the upcoming widely predicted global economic slowdown was future-oriented, that these were temporary increases in expenditure, and that general government finances would be balanced by 2023 if desired employment levels were reached (Saarenheimo 2019). The government further emphasized that its relatively low debt ratio would remain so, despite expenditure increases due to the sale of central government assets, and that in the future it would be financed by high receipts from indirect taxation and budget reallocations. All these factors serve to keep poverty rates low in Finland (Figure 3.3).

Compared to other EU economies, Finland recovered from the 2008 global financial crisis and the eurozone crisis at a slower pace, taking until 2018 to match its pre-crisis productivity levels (Honkapohja & Vihriälä 2019: 24). Finland's capacity to recover was hindered in part by its earlier dependence on Nokia, whose success was short-lived and was overtaken by the Apple iPhone released in 2007 (Honkapohja & Vihriälä 2019: 26). Contraction in the electricity and electronics industry led to a 4 per cent fall in GDP between 2008 and 2015.

The overall fall in GDP also explains why public spending as a proportion of GDP rose so rapidly in Finland between 2008 and 2015. This was because public spending levels were not cut when GDP fell while industries outside of the ICT sector, including forestry and chemical industries, contracted with declining global demand.

In 2015 Reuters reported that Finland had "suffered three years of economic contraction and is currently performing worse than any other country in the euro zone" (Rosendahl 2015). *The Telegraph* newspaper and the BBC announced that the country had become the new "sick man of Europe", with unemployment rising to 9.5 per cent (Walker 2016). This is when Finland tumbled from twelfth on the international HDI league table to twenty-fourth by 2014; before returning to twelfth again in 2019 (see Table 3.1 above).

By reducing unemployment benefits, income tax and early childhood education funding, and by implementing a competitiveness pact that helped the export industry, Sipilä's cabinet (2015–19) increased the employment rate to 72 per cent and the number of employed individuals rose by over 100,000 by 2018 (Orjasniemi 2019). Note that the employment rate is not simply the opposite of the unemployment rate as many adults not in work are not seeking work. It is also worth noting that at this time the debt-to-GDP ratio was improved via spending cuts, rather than tax increases.

Conclusion

The Bank of Finland announced in December 2016 that the recession that began in 2008 would soon come to an end, as the economy had begun to grow again (Kiviranta 2016). However, Finland's economic boom ended in 2019, with economic forecasts predicting more moderate GDP growth. At the time of writing, the trade wars proliferating around the world were especially concerning for Finland, as the export of goods and services accounts for 39 per cent of the country's GDP (World Bank 2018a; also see Carrington 2019). Following EU sanctions against Russia instituted in 2014 due to the annexation of Crimea by the Russian Federation, Finnish exports to and imports from Russia fell by over 30 per cent (Jonker-Hoffrén 2019: 198). The future of the Finnish economy remains highly dependent on global economic trends because of its reliance on export earnings and it has been clearly affected by the Covid-19 pandemic. Strong economic recovery elsewhere is very much in Finland's interest. Whether Finland proves to be more (or less) resilient than other countries is not yet clear in early 2021 – but its social solidarity and excellent health service should prove to be key assets.

The employment rate in mid-2019 was at its highest in almost 30 years, standing at 73.5 per cent (Honkapohja & Vihriälä 2019: 30) although it had fallen to 71.17 per cent by November of that year (Findikaattori 2019). The unemployment rate dropped to below 7 per cent in mid-2019 and was at 5.9 per cent by November of that year (Findikaattori 2020). As an ageing population threatens to slow growth and increase demands on the public sector (Honkapohja & Vihriälä 2019: 31), Finland must institute policies that will enable it to attract and integrate immigrants who will sustain the economy (Vartiainen 2011: 82).

Finland has been able to build a globally competitive economy on the basis of equality and investment in its people. As Finland continues to depend on exports, investment in sustainable technology is crucial for Finland to gain a competitive edge as its global demand grows. The start-up culture in Finland is helping spread Finnish innovation globally (Medium 2019). In November 2019, the winner of the MIT Inclusive Innovation Challenge was Finnish company Reaktor for its free online course "Elements of AI", which was developed in partnership with the University of Helsinki (Reaktor 2019).

Finland's economy is constantly changing in terms of the work people are doing and so no neat conclusion here is possible. In November 2019 a two-week long strike by Posti, the state-owned postal service, took place after 700 packaging and e-commerce workers protested against a plan to move them to another collective agreement that would lower wages (Yle Uutiset 2019c). Conflicting reports about whether or not Prime Minister Antti Rinne and Minister for Ownership Steering Sirpa Paatero knew of this state-owned company's plan before the strike led first to Paatero resigning, and (in a shocking sequence of events) to Rinne resigning when the Centre Party coalition partner withdrew support from the prime minister (Kaarenoja 2019).

While there was criticism in late 2019 of Rinne overstepping his mandate in the negotiations as prime minister, there was likewise criticism from the left of the recent involvement of the former (as they termed it "bourgeois") government in labour markets. The most recent Competitiveness Pact had been passed by the centre-right government led by Sipilä, under the threat of "system-weakening legislation" (Jonker-Hoffrén 2019: 202). The main aim was to improve the competitiveness of Finnish companies, which is important for the export-led Finnish economy and in particular for the manufacturing sector (Jonker-Hoffrén 2019: 199). The Finnish economy did grow, employment reached 72 per cent and debt-to-GDP ratio growth stalled, but the terms of the Competitiveness Pact, especially regarding additional unpaid working hours and cuts to holiday pay, were under revision in the negotiation rounds of late 2019 and early 2020 (Simula 2019).

The resignations of late 2019 led, famously, to five women working in coalition at the top of Finnish politics and with the power to steer its economics in a new direction by December 2019 (see Chapter 7). With an ambitious left-wing government led by Sanna Marin, it remains to be seen how Finland will attempt to reconcile participation in the global economy with its welfare state, and if it can reverse policy decisions by the previous government which, while restoring growth, also withdrew key investment in its people – namely, in education (to which we turn next).

As this chapter has shown, Finland has weathered numerous economic crises, both in recent years and recent decades. This is not well understood outside of Finland. It is now clear that the ways in which its people have handled these crises have, ultimately, been successful. However, for a country that is now very reliant on export earnings the current pandemic crisis is yet another great risk. Demand for buying both goods and services from around the world is expected to drop severely during 2020 and possibly in subsequent years also. It is far too early to say how Finland will fare. But what matters most is how it manages in comparison to other affluent states. One conclusion that could be drawn from its recent economic history, is that it is likely to fare better than most. Finland – as a collective economy – is now more resilient, flexible, imaginative and caring than others.

PART II

Social policy

In this section there are three chapters that cover the human lifespan, discussing issues that most affect people in their youth, mid-life – which we define as ages 21 to 61 – and old age. We discuss childhood and education in the first chapter, general equality in the second, and health in the final chapter of this section.

We begin by demonstrating how Finland's very high levels of income equality for older people are related to high levels of social mobility for the young; and how schools in Finland further accelerate social mobility. Social mobility is easier when the gap between top and bottom is so much narrower than it is in other countries. We show that Finland is second only to Norway in how little money is spent on private schooling and look at how Finland manages to be a world leader in education without spending more overall than many other countries. We also show how Finland has the lowest variation in school outcomes of any OECD country – which partly explains why its educational results are so good. We end by discussing Finland's work opportunities for the young, youth unemployment and higher education.

In Chapter 5, on the middle years of life, we begin by discussing data that confirm that income inequality in Finland has been low for some time and show how this contributes to high levels of social mobility. Of all the countries in the world, only in Denmark does it matter less who your parents are for your prospects in later life. We show that in the workplace Finnish employees of all grades have much greater flexibility over the hours they work than in all of the 35 other OECD countries for which there is data. This is as true for Finns without formal qualifications as for those with university degrees – employees in Finland are the most trusted to determine their own hours of work. We then discuss the paradox of Finland having one of the lowest proportions of women working in jobs that require science, technology, engineering and mathematics qualifications – despite Finland ranking joint highest on the global index of gender equality, which includes how well girls and women do at school and university in general in Finland. We end the chapter by looking at the taxation that keeps inequality low.

In Chapter 6, on old age and health, we demonstrate how Finland – along with Japan, Norway, Sweden and the Netherlands – has the lowest rates of health and social problems in the world today; how Finland, along with France, funds its well-financed public services via conventional taxation; how the numbers of foreign citizens coming to Finland, often to work in public services, have recently increased; and we end by considering how and why life expectancy in Finland is continuing to rise so quickly.

Kouluaamiainen helsinkiläisessä kansakoulussa – School breakfast in
an elementary school, under the former Finnish educational system.

Photograph taken by Hugo Sundström in 1949 or 1950. Used with
permission of Helsinki City Museum; photo licensed with CC BY 4.0 licence.

4

Childhood and education

"In Finland, where children don't start primary school before they are 7 years old, the government requires that all children must be given opportunities to play, have a voice in what and how they will learn, and must have at least 1 hour for physical activity every day, mostly outside, in addition to physical educational classes."

Pasi Sahlberg and William Doyle (2019)

Introduction: improving upon the best

According to the economist and Nobel laureate James Heckman, investment in children produces a high return, benefiting not only the immediate family and child, but society as a whole (Center for High Impact Philanthropy 2015). In 1951 the future of Finland was predicted to be "grey and dreary", but the Finns were tenacious (Sletholt 1951: 126). More importantly than that, they eventually chose the right route to trudge determinedly along.

Finland's postwar recovery and its capacity to establish itself as a serious country depended on the transformation of its (now world-renowned) education system. Alongside providing sufficient support for parents, good housing and high-quality healthcare, education is one of the most important investments in society that a government can make to ensure both the productivity and the well-being of future generations. Politicians such as former Prime Minister Jyrki Katainen of the National Coalition Party have emphasized the role of a highly educated society in promoting global competitiveness (Nygård 2015: 153–4). However, such aspirations may fall short if they are not accompanied by policies that also invest well in public services and education funding.

The frequency with which Finland is acclaimed as the best in the world for education does not mean that it cannot improve further, nor that some of its politicians won't squander that success in the future. Educational mobility is a measure of the degree to which the education system of a country increases or decreases the importance of parental finances and parental power in determining a child's future. Figure 4.1 shows the performance of countries in terms of the social mobility they have achieved and their levels of income inequality, with both factors shown to be influenced by levels of educational mobility within each country. Ten years ago, Denmark achieved slightly greater social mobility than Finland, but as Figure 4.1 shows, that was not the fault of Finland's educational system. Finland has high educational mobility due to its equitable schools, which in turn leads to an increase in social mobility, but not by quite as much as in Denmark. In contrast, Norway's schools' system, while of high quality, appears to operate to slightly reduce social mobility. What Figure 4.1 illustrates is data which suggest that its more equitable schools are the reason why Finland does better than Norway, overall, in terms of social mobility.

In Norway, overall social mobility is almost as high as in Finland, and so the extent to which people are likely to earn more (or less) than their parents during their working lives is high, despite the fact that the education system in Norway serves to reduce social mobility slightly. In both Finland and Norway income inequalities are low, so if you earn more than your parents it is not greatly more, and if you earn less it is not usually much less. This, above all else, helps parents in both countries not to try to determine their children's future as much as elsewhere. Nevertheless, Norway should look to Finland to improve its schools. Of course, all three of these Scandinavian countries look like educational and social Utopias in comparison to states such as the UK, US and Brazil, where in 2009 children's outcomes in life depended, and still depend today, so much on who their parents are (see also Figure 5.1). Figure 4.1 reveals that schools in the US and UK play a greater role in increasing social mobility than in most countries because educational mobility is high, since few American or British children are tested around age 11 and assigned a secondary school on that basis. Nevertheless, schools alone can do little in such unequal countries to alter social mobility overall, which is primarily determined by overall income inequality.

Figure 4.1: Social and educational mobility versus income inequality, 2009

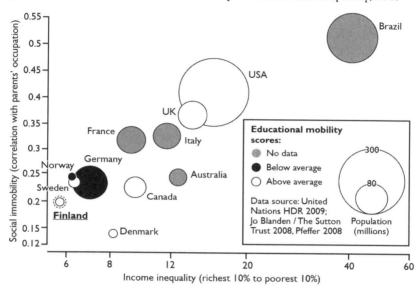

Source: Dorling & Hennig (2010).

If a country aims to build a more equal society, policies on education and families should play a key role, among many other factors, in working towards mitigating the influence of family circumstances on a child's future prospects. In Finland, where the gap between rich and poor is smaller than almost anywhere else, social mobility is understood to be about the freedom to choose what you want to do irrespective of your origins, rather than becoming "better" by climbing above the people around you on a social ladder with widely spaced rungs. When measured conventionally, social mobility is higher in Finland than in almost any other country in the world, but even the Finnish education and welfare system still does not provide for anything near complete equality of opportunity.

According to a recent OECD report on social mobility (OECD 2018a), it would take a child from a low-income (bottom 20 per cent) family in Finland an average of three generations to earn the national average income, assuming his or her children's and grandchildren's position advanced with the usual variance for Finland today (Inman 2018). Sweden and Norway had the same results, whereas for a Danish child in the same situation it would take only two generations. For the UK and US that figure now stands at five generations, for Chile six, India seven, Brazil nine, and Colombia eleven.

There is a wealth of research evidence pointing to a strong correlation, in both economically equal and unequal countries, between a child's educational level and that of their own parent(s), which is then further correlated with other markers of well-being such as parents' income, their overall employability, and their health (Salovuori 2016). A study published in 2016 assessed the educational attainment of all adults born in 1987 in Finland – approximately 60,000 people. It measured the level of education they had attained by the age of 25 and sought to account for the variation. This age group had lived through two deep recessions, and their parents had been subject to welfare cuts affecting daycare, maternity and child health clinics, and school healthcare. The study found that among the Finnish children whose parents were most highly educated, almost 75 per cent had an upper secondary qualification or university degree, while for those whose parents did not have high school or university degrees, only slightly more than 20 per cent had been educated to an upper secondary or university degree level. This study underscored the fact that despite Finland doing so well in international rankings, spending cuts in the 1990s hampered social mobility.

There is great public concern in Finland over any possible reductions in social mobility and increasing wealth and income inequality. Spending cuts that may (possibly) have improved GDP growth have certainly exacerbated the risk of Finland not moving forward in these areas in future. For example, in 2016, 10.2 per cent of Finland's children lived in low-income households. This was despite Finland being one of the EU and OECD nations that most often reports one of the lowest child poverty rates in the world (Karvonen & Salmi 2016). Allowances paid during state-subsidized parental leave have decreased by up to 30 per cent since 1994, when the official child poverty rate was only 4.5 per cent. By 2014, the child poverty rate had more than doubled over two decades to reach 11.7 per cent – although as a comparison, almost a third of children in the UK live in poverty and an even higher proportion suffer very damaging high relative poverty in the US. The small increase in child poverty in Finland has been attributed to the increasing gap between incomes within the country, coupled with adverse political decision-making (Yle Uutiset 2018c). Spending cuts, and poverty, have particularly affected families with children. Childhood poverty can have significant negative impacts on development and later life, and a country willing to tolerate even Finland's (still) relatively low levels of child poverty risks hampering attempts to build a more equal and even better educated society.

In part because of constant vigilance, it is clear that Finland has developed a remarkably equitable education system alongside progressive childhood and family policies that are increasingly lauded worldwide. Progressive politicians in so many other countries can only dream of reducing their child poverty rates to one in ten children. Alongside Sweden, Finland is one of very few countries in the world to provide free school meals to all students from early childhood education to upper secondary education. School meals are not termed "free" in Finland; they are just called "lunch". The legislation to provide them was introduced in 1943 and fully implemented by 1948, a time when Finland was far poorer than the countries debating universal free lunch programmes are today. Thus, just as pupils expect to be provided with a chair and a table to work at, so they (and their parents) expect there to be food as well. It is almost always more efficient to provide food communally. Furthermore, during the summer holidays, play-schemes in Helsinki provide free noontime meals for all children under the age of 16 (Palvelukeskus Helsinki 2019). Playground meals date back to 1942 when wartime food shortages affected the majority of inhabitants of the nation's capital.

Other countries began to provide free meals for some children earlier than 1942; but they still often fail to do so universally today. Free school meals in the UK are provided to roughly 15 per cent of pupils, but only to those from the lowest-income families, although universal free school meals have been available for five to seven-year-olds since 2014 (IFS 2019). The US has means-tested free school lunches. The take-up in the US is larger than in the UK, at 30 per cent of 5–17 year-olds who all come from families living at or below 130 per cent of the poverty line (the poverty line is set so low in the US that many children above it would still go hungry if they were not fed at school). In addition, 20 per cent of poor children in the US also receive free breakfast (Ruffini 2018: 2). However, this seems insufficient in the light of findings reported by the *Washington Post* in 2018 that children in the Washington DC area had collectively built up a debt of over $500,000 because of their parents' inability to pay for lunch at school (Lukacovic 2018). In the US state policies vary, however, and New York City public schools have provided free lunch since 2017 for all children, 75 per cent of whom would in any case have qualified, so high are US rates of child poverty in most of the country (Piccoli & Harris 2017).

Healthcare is also provided at Finnish comprehensive schools (peruskoulu), and in some circumstances the costs of travel to and from school are also covered. In Finland, schools with tuition fees are very rare, often partly state-subsidized, and not necessarily educationally superior: the highest-performing schools are all free. Regional differences in the quality of schools are very small (Info Finland 2019a). In 2013 a report issued by the OECD's Programme for International Student Assessment (PISA) indicated that differences among schools in Finland accounted for only 7.7 per cent of variation in student performance, against an OECD average of 42 per cent.

In some countries, such as the UK, despite its state schools not dividing most children at age 11, the school that children attend still has the greatest influence on how they later perform when tested at age 18 (Morris *et al*. 2016). A child that shows very little ability at age eight, but who has rich parents who can pay for private education, can nevertheless be coached to appear to do well at later "A level" examinations and end up at a prestigious UK university, despite having little personal interest in study. This has the result of much university teaching in elite universities in the UK having to be banal to ensure that the largely uninterested students do not find it too difficult (Dorling 2019b). Such a situation would be unimaginable today in Finland.

Finland is the most literate nation in the world according to a measure that combines test scores with educational inputs, newspaper readership rates, library use and computer access (Central Connecticut State University 2019). Finland is second only to Iceland in having the highest number of library users per inhabitant, and Finns purchase the most books per person per year. It is worth noting that the Finnish writing system is phonemic: "Finnish children only need to learn 23 letter-phoneme pairs, whereas in

English, the possible grapheme-to-phoneme mappings are about 2,000, and whatever rules and mnemonics there are [in English], are quite complex and often require seeing (and considering) the pattern of the entire word before one can assume much about its pronunciation" (Aho 2016).

Finland scored relatively well in some of the earlier international assessments of educational performance, such as TIMSS (Third International Mathematics and Science Study) in which Finland performed above average, and beat the US in both mathematics and geography in 1999. However, it was the later PISA rankings, launched in 2000, which served to attract so much international attention to this small Nordic country's education system (Ukkola 2011; Dickinson 2019). There has been a great deal of criticism of the PISA comparisons, but not in how they describe Finland (Dorling 2015: figure 2).

On the darker side, however, Finland has experienced deadly incidents in schools, most recently a machete attack in Kuopio in October 2019 (BBC 2019b; Happonen 2019). This latest event has called into question the effectiveness of the prevention work done since the school shootings in Jokela (2007) and Kauhajoki (2008), which saw multiple casualties.

A short history of education in Finland

Finland's current educational system, for which it eventually became internationally acclaimed, was the result of a drastic transformation that took place more than half a century ago with the passage of the Basic School Act into law in 1968 (Kupiainen *et al.* 2009). However, the ground was prepared for these changes some years before that.

In around 1900 only a third of Finland's rural children attended school. However, by 1911, 50 per cent of Finnish children went to school and in 1921 six years of education from the age of seven became compulsory (Pekkarinen & Uusitalo 2012). At the age of 11, children could transfer to one of the 338 grammar schools that provided the only possible route to higher education.

In 1950, only 27 per cent of Finland's 11-year-olds entered grammar schools (Sahlberg 2015: 34). Even by the late 1950s, access to grammar school education was dominated by city dwellers. Some 20 per cent of children from the rural areas, where the majority of the Finnish population then lived, entered grammar schools; as compared to 47 per cent from towns. Entry was competitive, and skewed to the better-off, because it depended not only on having sufficiently high grades, but also on a pupil's family having adequate finance. Two-thirds of grammar schools were privately owned, and most required parents to pay tuition fees. Students unable to get into grammar school by impressing a teacher, or by buying their way in, could instead attend civil schools that would lead to further vocational, but not further academic education (OECD 2010).

Beginning in the 1950s, Finnish government funding and control of grammar schools was increased, and the pedagogical approach gradually changed from formal teacher-centred education focused on moral development (behaviour and conformity) to a focus on cognitive development based on new evidence emerging from educational research (Sahlberg 2015: 35).

Legislation introduced in 1957 and 1958 extended the period of mandatory education to eight years. The 1968 Basic Education Act mandated nine years of comprehensive schooling (six years of primary and three years of secondary education). Grammar schools were gradually phased out during the 1970s (Palonen 2019). At the same time, teacher education was upgraded to master's degree level (for primary as well as secondary teaching) in expanding faculties of education. Teachers and their union actively supported these changes, but the primary advocates were Finland's left-wing political parties (the Social Democratic Party and the predecessor to the present-day Left Alliance, the Finnish People's Democratic League) on the grounds that it built greater social and regional equality. Support was also forthcoming from the Agrarian League (now the Centre Party), which advocated for greater regional equality (Parliament of Finland 2019b).

Agreement on reforms was a long time coming, however, as teachers, universities and politicians questioned whether it would ever be possible to guarantee an equal-opportunity education to all children. Some argued that educational levels would suffer from putting all children in the same classroom, and that the children of Finland as a whole would be better off under conditions of competition and selectivity (Palonen 2019). Some of the compromises made between the opposing parties included having different levels of teaching being offered within the same class, but such compromises were soon abandoned when it became clear that instead of being beneficial, they discouraged the educational attainment of boys in particular, who tended to choose or gravitate towards easier levels.

Winning the arguments for reform depended on the desire for greater equality and a national sense of unity; equally importantly, the national consensus that greater economic growth was necessary made it harder to argue against reforming a system that perpetuated inequality and hence inefficiency. With such a small population, the country could not afford to let large numbers of Finns fall behind if it wanted to achieve higher productivity levels, and the conclusion that inequality would stall economic growth seemed (and in hindsight was) logical.

In 1955–56, grammar schools in Finland enrolled about 34,000 pupils; in 1960 there were 215,000; in 1965, 270,000; and in 1970, 324,000 (Sahlberg 2015: 42). Parents were clearly keen to improve their children's economic and social opportunities; the new educational system that was introduced by the 1968 reforms aimed to show that equal educational opportunity could promote social cohesion and strengthen individual development. Importantly, the reforms had been influenced by evidence from abroad, such as the 1966 US Coleman report on Equality of Educational Opportunity. Based on a survey of 650,000 students and teachers in more than 3,000 American schools, it had been mandated by the US Civil Rights Act of 1964 (Sahlberg 2015: 43).

Finland's 1968 educational reform was passed in parliament with 123 votes for and 68 against, with most of the dissenting votes belonging to right-wing parties: the National Coalition Party and members of the party now known as the Centre Party. The vote is likely to have been influenced by events outside of Finland, from the 1967 summer of love in the US through to the student demonstrations in the spring of 1968 in France and around the world, including in Helsinki. There was a sense of change in the air internationally. What is most interesting is that in Finland, the reaction to that zeitgeist took the form of progressive thinking that would be to the great benefit of future generations.

While reformist educators and policy-makers were drawing on international evidence, including that from America, they were also learning from local experience and adapting as they went along. The high quality of teacher training resulted in teachers becoming greatly respected by parents, the public and the authorities, and this made it easier to allow them greater autonomy.

Initially, comprehensive education was highly centralized, but decentralisation in the 1980s gave municipalities more freedom over their schools whilst still following the same common core curriculum and classroom scheduling guidelines (Kupiainen *et al.* 2009). All post-16 education in Finland is selective in that there are varying exam point thresholds that determine which route a pupil may take at that point. However, for those who do not manage to get into a more academic upper-secondary school at age 16, there is a voluntary additional basic education year that will allow them to resit their age-16 year school assessments and apply again (Studyinfo 2020).

Nowadays, only a small minority of schools in Finland levy tuition fees. Most schools with tuition fees specialize in foreign language-medium instruction, such as the German school in Helsinki, whose fees for the academic year 2018–19 were €336.50 (Deutsche Schule Helsinki 2019), or slightly less than one euro per day! Some international schools, such as the International School of Helsinki, charge much higher fees at €12,000–16,000 a year (International School of Helsinki 2019). But if you want to take the International Baccalaureate (IB) education typically offered by fee-paying international schools, you can opt instead to attend a public (known in the UK as "state") school for free as long as you pass an entrance exam. Some of those state schools have better average scores than the very few private international schools, which, as a result, are not seen as more prestigious than others.

Today private education has all but disappeared from Finland, despite not being outlawed. Luck and chance will have also played a part in the development of a system that works so very well in a country that a century ago was considered an educational backwater – a place to leave if you wanted to get on. It may have been a matter of luck that no effective opponents to the 1968 educational reforms emerged. However, there were political debates for almost two decades before these changes ushered in comprehensive education in Finland, so the tenacity of those who had been calling for change was hugely important.

Figure 4.2 shows that countries with higher levels of enrolment in private education do not spend less on education overall. When four to six times as much is spent per head on children in the private sector, educational spending is very inefficient. In the more unequal countries of the affluent world, most money is invested in just a few children drawn from the richest of families.

Figure 4.2: State and private school spending, OECD countries, 2016

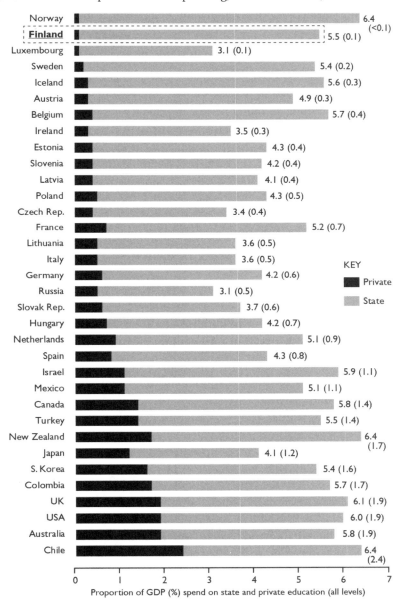

Source: OECD (2019c).

Note: Data for Denmark, Greece and Switzerland is missing from the OECD table released in September 2019; countries are sorted by percentage private of the total amount.

In recent years, Chile, Australia, the US and UK are among those countries, many of which have been involved in conflict and war, that tend to fare quite badly in many international rankings of education and related achievements. Their people now often suffer the symptoms of societal breakdown and a lack of social cohesion, and income inequality levels are extremely high in all four states. It is hard to believe that it is mere coincidence that these are also the countries in which so many people in power were educated separately, away from the rest of the population – not just separated at birth due to affluence, but throughout their childhoods due to private schooling. A truly comprehensive education system, that treats all children as equally deserving, appears to have far wider social implications than just being beneficial in terms of educational results.

Early years' education

Finland has a long history of intervening to help mothers and their babies. The Maternity Grants Act came into law in 1937 in response to the high infant mortality rates (69 per 1,000 births). This was one of the first major public social and health interventions made by the first coalition government of the SDP and the Agrarian League, which is now the Centre Party (Laurent 2017: 92–3). Mothers from low-income backgrounds were among the first to receive the maternity package in 1938, and all mothers began to receive it in 1949 (Kela 2019a). Kela, the comprehensive Finnish Social Insurance Institution, still provides new mothers with a generous and justly renowned maternity package today.

In 2018 the Finnish package comprised 64 items including bedding, baby clothes, nappies, bottles and toys, and packed in a box that can double as a baby's first bed. It is very unlike the commercial advertising-heavy "Bounty Pack" that mothers in England receive, and much more like the package now being introduced in Scotland (Kela 2019b). In order to apply for the maternity package, the mother has to provide proof of an antenatal (prenatal) medical examination before the fifth month of pregnancy, thereby ensuring that the health of both the foetus and the mother is assessed and monitored much more rigorously than in other affluent nations. Such measures, provided by Finland's maternity clinics, helped reduce infant mortality rates. Early childhood development is further supported by Finland's maternity and paternity legislation, which will be discussed in the next chapter.

Today, once a child in Finland turns three years old, he or she is entitled to subsidized or free-to-access early education at daycare, which can be full-time if both parents are working (Infopankki 2019a). At this point in a child's life, parents are no longer entitled to parental or home leave from work, unless they have younger children. The maximum fee for municipal daycare is €290 a month, although this cost may be waived for low-income families depending on their circumstances. From three to four years old, each child is entitled to 15 hours of free daycare per week, which can be increased to 30 hours for certain parents (via means-testing). Children can also enter private daycare, for which Kela pays an allowance directly to the daycare provider, with costs for private provision similar to the cost of municipal day-care (Kela 2017). Preschool education (about four hours a day) which almost all children attend, begins one year before compulsory education officially begins at the age of seven (Infopankki 2019b).

Early childhood education attendance in Finland has increased in recent years, but in 2019 it was still below the OECD average, with one out of five children not attending (Ministry of Education and Culture 2019a). The OECD average is 87 per cent, and other Nordic countries tend to achieve an average ranging from 94 to 98 per cent. Finland's investment of 1.2 per cent of its GDP in early childhood education is, however, still much higher than the OECD average of 0.8 per cent.

Most Finnish children attend early childhood education for at least 20 hours a week, although it can be extended if the parents are working or study-ing. Early years education involves developing skills useful for school and lots of playtime and outdoor activities to promote learning ability. Later, sports classes are introduced, including outdoor activities such as orienteering and ice skating. In Finland the forest is often close by, and it is not surprising that educational innovations such as "forest school" began in Scandinavia. Language support is also provided if the child's mother tongue is not Finnish or Swedish.

Early childhood education, which in other countries is often called nursery school or kindergarten, is very different in Finland from the norm elsewhere in the affluent world. Adults providing the care must hold at least a university degree in educational sciences (OAJ 2019). The job of providing such care is respected, and bears little resemblance to the warehousing of children so that their parents can work longer hours. Sending a child to formal school at an early age has never been shown to be beneficial in any international comparisons of educational outcomes; but helping children to play with other children, rather than being trapped at home most of the day, is one of the reasons why Finland is seen as an educational model today – Finns let their children play with other children. But to enable children to play and learn at the same time, you have to be a well-trained teacher.

Teachers' salaries are competitive within Finland, but average across OECD countries; the highest are found in Luxembourg starting at €74,400 a year in pre-primary education (OECD.Stat 2018a). The median monthly wage of all Finnish earners in 2018 was €3,079, and the median wage of public sector workers was €2,834 (OSF 2019a). Compared to the OECD averages, starting salaries are higher in all Nordic countries, but the maximum salaries are lower (OECD 2019b: 396). In 2018, the median monthly wage for early childhood and primary school teachers in Finland (including those teaching school years 1–6 of comprehensive school) was €3,363 for men and €2,918 for women; those teaching the last three years of comprehensive school or upper secondary school had median wages of €4,079 (men) and €3,974 (women); median wages for vocational teachers were €3,918 (men) and €3,964 (women); and finally the highest median wages were found amongst university teachers at €4,743 (men) and €4,505 (women) (Hiilamo & Ala-Risku 2019). Teaching remains a popular profession, and only just above 10 per cent of applicants are accepted into the degree programmes (Kumpulainen 2017: 209). We discuss the gap between women's and men's pay in Finland later, in Chapter 5, in relation to Figure 5.3. For now, if the discrepancies above surprise you, it is worth knowing that they are probably wider where you live.

Comprehensive school and upper-secondary education

Comprehensive primary (followed then by lower-secondary) schooling begins at the age of seven in Finland, but it is strongly encouraged that children attend at least one year of preschool education or other similar activities before starting school. Like early childhood education, and formal preschool with qualified teachers, comprehensive primary education in Finland further prepares a child for later school life, and can continue to provide language support if needed, but it still comes with significant amounts of playtime and outdoor activities.

Comprehensive schooling lasts for nine years: primary (ages 7–13) covering grades 1–6, and lower secondary (ages 14–16), covering grades 7–9. Spending per student in the final three years of comprehensive school in Finland was recently found to be the third highest of the OECD countries measured (Ministry of Education and Culture 2019a). The most recent 2019 OECD "Education at a Glance" report showed that in Finland there is one teacher for every nine students, against an OECD average of thirteen. Fewer than 2 per cent of students in Finland attend private schools and the few private schools that still exist are often largely state subsidized, with parents having to pay very little (Ministry of Education and Culture 2019b).

Recently, playtime has become a prominent pedagogical area of study, with Finnish academic Pasi Sahlberg and his colleague William Doyle writing a well-received book on this subject (see the quotation at the start of this chapter). For every 45 minutes of class time in Finland, students are given a 15-minute recess, and they are encouraged to spend it outside. Frequent recesses have been shown to increase attention during class. Such breaks do not necessarily have to be spent outside, but in Finland they often are. After school ends, sometime between noon and 2.00pm for lower age groups, schools provide free afternoon activities in public playgrounds for one to two hours (City of Helsinki 2019).

In Helsinki, children learn foreign languages such as English, Spanish, French, Swedish and Russian from the age of ten for two hours a week, and a second language can be chosen the following year (City of Helsinki 2019). Swedish is introduced in grades 6 to 9 (ages 13–16) if it is not chosen earlier. Not only do Finnish children emerge from school with the practical skill of fluency in one or more foreign languages, but the lessons are an aid to imagination and foster an understanding of other cultures. Education is also provided in minority languages. Some 5 per cent of students attend a school where lessons are taught in Swedish (Ministry of Education and Culture 2018), and authorities in Sámi-speaking areas of Lapland are required to organize Sámi-language education. Educational institutions must also provide opportunities for students to learn, or extend their knowledge of, their native language. Additional funding is available to help schools provide these opportunities for minorities such as Sámi and Roma people, and pupils who use sign-language.

There are no national tests in basic education in Finland. The matriculation examination at the end of upper secondary education is the only national examination. Entry to further education, including Finland's universities, usually depends on the results of the matriculation examination alongside any entry tests. Entry to upper-secondary education (ages 16–18) does depend on grades received at the end of basic education, but these grades are provided by teachers and not by a national examination (Ministry of Education and Culture 2018).

Owing to concerns that national examinations at lower secondary level (especially age 11) in other countries have led to an unhelpful fixation on exam results and competition between schools rather than on well-rounded learning, the Trade Union of Education in Finland remains opposed to them (Salo 2018). Instead, for some years clarified assessment criteria have been recommended, and the Finnish National Agency for Education (OPH 2019) published the most recent draft criteria in 2019.

Finland has not had school and textbook inspections since the 1990s, when the system was decentralized (Yue 2014). In addition to evaluations by public authorities and the independent Finnish Education Evaluation Centre, teachers are provided with skills to systematically evaluate their own work as part of their on-going training (OAJ 2011). The Trade Union of Education in Finland (OAJ 2011) further highlights that for teaching to remain as a respected, ethical profession, teachers must be provided with the freedom and responsibility to teach and aid students in their all-round development, rather than purely to train them to perform well in tests.

Following the completion of comprehensive primary and lower-secondary school, Finns can choose between upper secondary academic education, called *lukio*, or vocational education and training. Acceptance into either type is dependent on the choice of children themselves, along with their parents, then on school grades, and, in some circumstances, on entrance exams, so there is selectivity after age 16. While these upper-secondary education opportunities remain free of tuition fees and free school meals are still provided, until 1 August 2021 students and their parents had to pay for upper secondary textbooks and school materials.

Nationals of EU countries have the right to pursue university education in any member state, and their typically high level of foreign-language skills makes it easier for young Finnish adults to do so. As those heading out of the country usually opt for continental mainland European universities, the cost is generally minimal, or even free. However, most choose to remain in Finland for university study, and the variation in quality between Finnish universities is negligible. Degrees from all Finnish universities are well respected, in contrast to those in other countries with a far more rigid hierarchy of status, resourcing and quality, real or perceived.

Diversity in education

Amongst Finnish students, significant differences in outcomes have been found between boys and girls, and for children of immigrants.

When, in 1982, Elina Lahelma found that girls received better grades than boys in school, but then competed for work in care services, whereas boys applied with worse grades for science, technology, engineering and mathematical (STEM) subjects, she was surprised at the extent to which the media focused on the idea that schools were apparently not doing their best for boys (Lahelma 2019). When not held back by educational systems that put them at a disadvantage, girls tend to perform better than boys, especially at age 15.

According to the 2015 PISA results, girls in Finland are on average about half a year ahead of boys (Björksten 2016). Finnish girls were most recently placed second among OECD countries in natural science tests for 15-year-olds, while boys were tenth. Four years earlier, in the 2011 PISA exams, there had been no difference between girls and boys in science performance (Pöysä & Kupiainen 2018). Finnish girls, however, displayed the least interest among OECD countries in pursuing science or technology careers (Björksten 2016). Finland is not untypical in having a media that expresses more concern over the fact that boys lag behind in grades than that girls receive less encouragement to pursue STEM subjects and careers. As in many other countries, boys in Finland become men more likely to be in higher paying jobs than their female peers. Even so, there is a growing and very real concern about boys and young men who become excluded from society.

In PISA examinations in recent years, Finland's second-generation and first-generation immigrant children performed well when compared with similar children in other countries (Arkko 2018). Compared with Finnish-origin children, however, their results were much lower on average. In the most recent PISA examinations published in 2018, Finnish children scored an average of 531 in reading, while second-generation and first-generation immigrants scored averages of 484 and 419 respectively (Arkko 2018). Jouni Välijärvi, emeritus professor of educational research at the University of Jyväskylä, has remarked that while this difference is not as pronounced as it is in countries such as Canada or Australia, it is also important to remember that the language skill requirements are stricter for residency permits in these countries than in Finland. Leena Nissilä from the Finnish National Agency for Education has argued that mother-tongue language teaching should increase, referencing an OECD study that found that this enhances other learning. Participation in early childhood education should also be increased as children of immigrants are less likely to attend daycare with their peers, where they have the opportunity to improve their Finnish or Swedish.

One obstacle noted by the OECD was the substantial home care support provided to parents, which sometimes discouraged women in Finland who were not Finnish from working or pursuing language education when their children were young. It should also be noted that there are regional differences in terms of how many hours of mother-tongue education children can receive. Helsinki provides additional funds to prevent discrimination in schools with low performance, high levels of poverty, or a significant number of foreign-born students for whom Finnish is a third, fourth or fifth language, and research by Mikko Silliman has found that in recent years (and mostly in Helsinki) the number of children of immigrants attending the more academic streams of upper secondary education has increased (Silliman 2017).

Investment in children and education in Finland did suffer significantly in the 1990s and then again after the global financial crisis of 2008. Education expenditure in 2017 decreased by 2.3 per cent, in real terms, compared with 2016 (OSF 2019b). However, this does not apply to preschool or comprehensive education, for which expenditure in real terms has grown since 2010.

Figure 4.3: Between and within school variation, OECD countries, 2009

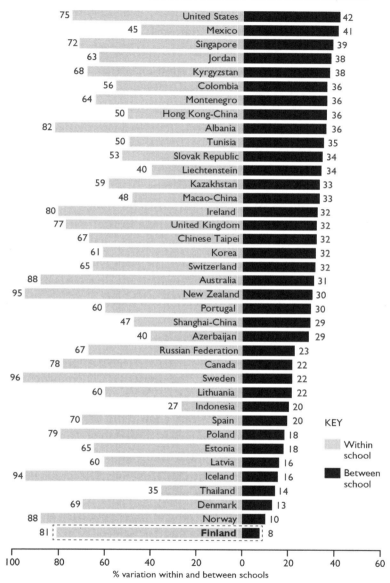

	Within school	Between school
United States	75	42
Mexico	45	41
Singapore	72	39
Jordan	63	38
Kyrgyzstan	68	38
Colombia	56	36
Montenegro	64	36
Hong Kong-China	50	36
Albania	82	36
Tunisia	50	35
Slovak Republic	53	34
Liechtenstein	40	34
Kazakhstan	59	33
Macao-China	48	33
Ireland	80	32
United Kingdom	77	32
Chinese Taipei	67	32
Korea	61	32
Switzerland	65	32
Australia	88	31
New Zealand	95	30
Portugal	60	30
Shanghai-China	47	29
Azerbaijan	40	29
Russian Federation	67	23
Canada	78	22
Sweden	96	22
Lithuania	60	22
Indonesia	27	20
Spain	70	20
Poland	79	18
Estonia	65	18
Latvia	60	16
Iceland	94	16
Thailand	35	14
Denmark	69	13
Norway	88	10
Finland	81	8

KEY

■ (light) Within school
■ (dark) Between school

% variation within and between schools

Source: OECD PISA 2009 database, Table II.5.1; OECD 2013.

Note: Countries are ranked in descending order of the between-school variation; and only those with under OECD average between school variation are shown here.

Vocational education suffered the most in the wake of cuts made after 2008. In national as well as individual terms, such austerity measures are surely false economies, as research indicates. A recent working paper by Silliman and Virtanen for the Research Institute of the Finnish Economy underscores the value of vocational education, in particular for those unlikely to succeed in higher secondary education. The researchers also found that even after the transformation of the labour market following the financial crash, the labour market in Finland still provides a great range of opportunities for those with the skills developed in vocational schools (Silliman & Virtanen 2019) and as Figure 4.3 shows, students in any school prior to age 16 do not have significantly lower exam scores than found in other schools, and so there is a great deal of variation within each school.

Figure 4.3 demonstrates that having a low level of variation between school outcomes tends to place a country near the top of the education league table: Finland, Norway and Denmark have the least variation in outcomes between their schools. In contrast, very economically unequal countries such as the US, Mexico and Singapore tend to have a much greater range of outcomes between schools.

Outcomes *within* schools, rather than *between* them, are most variable in Finland, Norway, Iceland and Sweden; but children are not "held back" by mixing with their peers. Note that the poorer OECD countries tend to be those not included in the table, and they are the nations that have variations above the OECD average. However, a few more affluent OECD states – Germany, Israel, Austria, Luxembourg, the Netherlands, Japan and several wealthy Middle East states – are excluded from Figure 4.3 because the variation between their schools is above the OECD average. Often this is because entrance exams are used in these countries to divide children between different types of school at around age 11. None of these countries achieve what Denmark, Finland, Iceland, Norway or Sweden achieve in terms of overall educational outcomes for their children; but they almost all achieve more than the US and the UK, where the negative consequences of social and economic inequalities outweigh schools' best efforts to give children a more equal start in life.

Conclusion: a model for the rest of the world?

Investment in children's education and the transformation from an elitist system to one based on equal access and opportunity have thankfully survived the debates that followed Finland's dramatic reforms of the 1960s. Finnish children all receive the same education until their late teens, all of them eat lunch for free, and all may continue to higher education without having to worry about tuition fees. Many welfare reforms have also reduced the overall financial burden of children on their families. Contrary to Marin's predecessor, her cabinet declared in its manifesto that it would break with austerity and chose education as a funding priority. In early 2021, with the aim of improving employment and the rate of students gaining upper-secondary qualifications, parliament approved legislation to extend compulsory education to the age of 18, meaning textbooks and other expenditures for older students will now be provided for free.

The means-testing of benefits appears, at first glance, to be the best way to achieve an efficient allocation of resources, but it has its own pitfalls, especially the social stigma it can foster, which is exacerbated in societies that emphasize individual responsibility and self-sufficiency (Gugushvili & Hirsch 2014: 2). In addition, the administrative and cost burden it incurs is significant; and the stress of claiming and proving eligibility inevitably means that those most in need often go without.

Universal programmes, on the other hand, can create a sense of national pride across classes, and they are more difficult to roll back, as their eligibility criteria cannot be changed without undermining the system itself (Wilkinson 2017; Corbyn 2019). Walter Korpi and Joakim Palme (1998: 663) came to the same conclusion in looking at Finland, finding that targeted support meant that classes were split into different coalitions, which contributed to a backlash against taxes and the welfare state. The alternative, universalism, produced an intra-class coalition that provided lasting support for the welfare state. Universal benefits in Finland, like the maternity package, have become seen as a right in the eyes of Finns, and no longer a source of stigma, as policies for the poor used to be interpreted (Harjula 2019).

When Finland's PISA scores started dropping after 2006, even though the country remained one of the top performers, Pasi Sahlberg feared the education system might suffer from the same hubris that led to Nokia's downfall – not innovating at its peak (*The Economist* 2016). However, just as PISA results were received with scepticism when they were first published at the dawn of the millennium, the criticisms of crude rankings remain relevant, and they reflect only one aspect of educational quality.

International assessments of education can be narrow in terms of the subjects and skills assessed, and too test focused. What is remarkable is that a school system that places so little emphasis on testing can perform so well in international tests. However, it is important not to assume that Finland's successful school system can be transferred to other countries without further analysis or consideration of the underlying factors that helped develop these systems. Nevertheless, it is worth noting that neighbouring Estonia has copied the Finnish system with considerable success (Sahlberg 2011).

What Finland has achieved is also by no means the end of what can be achieved. The system certainly needs further reform, in particular in terms of better integrating the children of immigrants, encouraging boys to learn more and to be happier learning, and encouraging girls to pursue STEM subjects. The fundamental goals that drove the reforms of the 1960s, however, should remain: to prioritize investment in the education system; to use education as a means to promote social mobility and the well-being of children and families; and, in turn, to promote the well-being of the economy and the nation as a whole.

The Wealth Parade drawn by Ella Furness in 2016 and reproduced here with kind permission. Ella is currently working as a research associate in the Sustainable Places Research Institute (Sefydliad Ymchwil Mannau Cynaliadwy) at the University of Cardiff, in Wales (Prifysgol Caerdydd). This is one of many illustrations she drew for *A Better Politics* (Dorling 2016).

5

Mid-life and equality

Onnelllisuus on se paikka puuttuvaisuuden ja yltäkylläisyyden välillä
[Happiness is a place between too little and too much]

Finnish proverb

Traditionally, mid-life is hard to define. When does it begin and end? In Finland currently, average life expectancy for men is 79 and for women 84, with both still increasing and the gap between them narrowing. Because of this we have decided here to define mid-life as being aged 21 to 61, the 40 years after the first 21 years of life and before what, for most people, is typically the last 21 years of their lives.

For most of us mid-life begins after the completion of studies and at the start of employment and possible career, after having left the family who brought you up, but before settling down with a family of your own. This stereotype has undergone various changes, but these key points still remain milestones in the average person's life in one way or another. A growing number of people have no children, but for the majority of Finns, mid-life ends when all your children have left home and you are on your own again. It draws to an end as the career or varied set of jobs you have been doing wind down. It ends as retirement approaches or starts and as your life begins to have more and more in common with everyone else in your age group. Equality is greatest in childhood and young adulthood, and again in old age – especially in Finland. Mid-life is a period of specialization and also the time when people tend to be most unequal.

In Finland children are born remarkably equal. As detailed above, a Finnish child's arrival is marked with a very comprehensive maternity package containing things that the baby and its parents actually need. In Finland the government, and the town or village you live in, ensures that your start in life is one of the most equitable on the planet. As explained in the previous chapter, all children in Finland have access to good schools. The influence of your parents' income on your outcome in mid-life is minimal (when compared to their influence if you grow up anywhere else). See Figure 4.1 in the previous chapter and Figure 5.1 here, which help put into context the Finnish experience of how much your mid-life is determined by your parents' lives.

Figure 5.1: Social mobility and income inequality, 2009

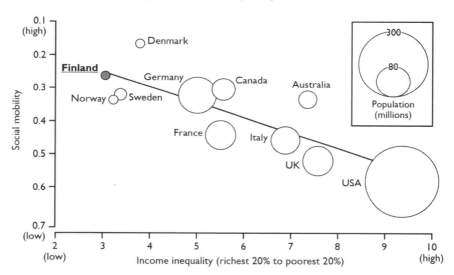

Source: Redrawn from data provided in Wilkinson & Pickett (2009), based in turn on intergenerational mobility data in Blanden (2009).

Note: in this version the area of each circle is made proportional to the population of each country. The horizontal axis is the ratio of the income of the richest fifth of households to the poorest (Wilkinson & Pickett 2009: 17), and the vertical axis is the measure of elasticity as reported in Blanden (2009: table 1).

Greater equality at the beginning of life in Finland does not create a Utopia in and of itself. If you have ever worked at a university that selects students with similarly very high exam results, it quickly becomes evident to any university teacher that starting them off equitably also has the effect of making many people fear that they will "not be good enough". Many of the young students in elite universities such as Harvard and Princeton, Oxford and Cambridge found school easy and did well there. They can then find being among so many equals – all their undergraduate peers who appear to be as capable as they are – a shock. In contrast, in Finland, the children of better-off parents are aware, from a much earlier age, that they will have to compete with all of their cohort for jobs. However, they also know they live in a society that values cooperation. If they are fortunate enough to live in another less equitable country for a year or so, they see just how unusual valuing cooperation is and realize how lucky they are.

Despite the remarkably level social playing field that Finland has built and collectively maintained, its young people can easily be daunted by adulthood. This is even the case for those who have greater social and economic advantages than peers from groups that have traditionally been discriminated against, such as women, LGBTQ and ethnic minorities. Although any debts they might have accrued tend to be very small by international standards, many young Finns do now enter this stage of their lives with some private debt and uncertain career prospects, all within a broader global political climate that is frequently referred to as being "in crisis". These are fairly universal problems, but is it any better for older adults in Finland? What does the state do to help mitigate circumstances of birth and timing and help adults realize their dreams for a home, a career, a family and security?

Quality of life still varies greatly among different demographic groups in Finland. Men earn significantly more than women in almost half of the career fields for which wage measurements are made (Hiilamo & Ala-Risku 2019). Students from working-class backgrounds are eight times *less* likely to continue education into university (Tram 2018). Foreign-born Finns are also less likely to enter or complete tertiary education than their Finnish-born peers. In fact, foreign-born Finns are less likely to do so than foreign-born residents of several other EU member states (Eurostat 2019a). Educational opportunities for children who are either immigrants or the children of recent immigrants is an area in the Finnish system in clear need of improvement.

Higher education, adult inequality and debt

Mid-life begins as higher education ends, but we start by considering higher education in this chapter as it is what most divides the lives of Finns in mid-life. As previously discussed, good education is available for everyone. The numbers of students in Finland studying at university rose from 14,000 in 1950 to over 153,300 in 2017 (OSF 2018b).

The student population of universities in Finland is increasingly diverse, but even though tuition is free – whether you are Finnish, a Finnish resident or an EU citizen – class background still influences educational attainment in higher education (Mikkonen & Korhonen 2018). Students from working-class backgrounds are less likely to go to university than those from the middle classes who have highly educated parents. They are also more likely to work during their studies, more likely to take out a student loan; and – according to the EUROSTUDENT VI survey conducted in 2016 – more likely to see them-selves as less suited for university. Often the first in their families to attend university, young working-class Finns are less likely to receive support at home in making decisions about courses of study. Their middle-class peers, in contrast, still have much higher chances of growing up in environments that value academic forms of learning, where spending time studying at home is seen in a positive light, and where parents feel confident in engaging in their children's education.

It is worth noting that young parents in today's Finland appear not to be quite as accepting of greater and growing equality as were their own parents. Despite Finland having the lowest variation between its schools of any coun-try in the OECD (see Figure 4.3 in the previous chapter), recent studies have found that school choices by parents have now slightly increased segregation between schools. Moreover, of late there has been some evidence of increased variations in performance between schools in the most recent PISA results, compared with earlier years (Bernelius & Vaattovaara 2016).

Although children are enrolled in the schools that are closest to them, laws introduced in the 1990s enabled parents to choose another school for their child, and it is this policy that has played a key role in increased levels of school segregation (Bernelius & Vaattovaara 2016: 3162). Those who choose not to enrol their children in their nearest neighbourhood schools tend to opt instead for schools associated with higher income and education levels. In contrast, the schools that are less often specifically chosen by parents for their children tend to have a higher proportion of immigrants and the children of more poorly educated adults. This trend is less significant for secondary schools than for the primary level.

The decisions of middle-class families to move their children out of what they deem to be less suitable school environments was highlighted in 2015 as a possible new driver of segregation in Finland. Parents naturally want to do the best for their children, but some have sharper elbows than others. When their individual choices cumulatively alter the make-up of schools, it creates a hierarchy of little or no long-term benefit to the top-ranked pupils. However this hierarchy is very much to the detriment of the bottom-ranked, which then exacerbates inequality. Segregation between families along income lines in mid-life can be reinforced by new apartment block building patterns. For decades in each new housing area in big cities, at least 25 per cent is affordable social housing (called ARA Housing). This reduces social class segregation, but individual apartment blocks tend to contain either all homeowners or all renters (Puttonen 2019). Underperforming children benefit from mixed-ability classes, but this is harder to achieve if social classes become more geographically segregated in society.

Statistically, young Finnish adults from highly educated families are eight times more likely to become a university student, regardless of the school they attended. According to researcher Mari Käyhkö, herself from a working-class background, the difference is due to the variation in the demands and expectations at home. Some families may never consider an alternative to university for their children; they would not countenance technical education or apprenticeships (Tram 2018). Conversely, young adults from working-class backgrounds often cannot imagine themselves ever attending university. It does not help that in Finland most university degrees have entrance exams, and affluent parents can pay for their children to take private preparation courses outside of the state education system. Reforms introduced in 2020, however, have increased the threshold of students accepted on the basis of their matriculation exams alone, even for law and medicine.

Instead of pursuing an academic route, some students pursue post-16 education at a vocational school, following on from lower secondary comprehensive school. However, in Finland there are no dead ends. Vocational education is not an inferior choice, unlike, say, England's extremely poorly funded further education system, but the class divide between those who attend Finland's universities and vocational schools remains a concern. Additionally, recent spending cuts in Finland have disproportionally affected the vocational school sector. However, as Figure 4.1 in the previous chapter demonstrated, when the effects are averaged over recent decades, Finnish and Swedish schools have played positive roles in further lowering social inequalities in their respective countries. This contrasts with Norway and Germany, which are countries of relatively high income equality, but where the school systems tend to slightly increase social inequalities. In those two countries, the majority of children are divided into different educational streams at age 11; in Finland, in contrast, the division takes place at age 16, with the majority remaining together in their teenage years.

Table 5.1 shows that Finnish people are the happiest in Europe, Of particular note is how the least educated are happier than anywhere else in Europe, presumably partly due to less financial inequality. The country's educational researchers also keep a close and careful watch on the system, as we have demonstrated through the many references presented in this book. Contrast this with how little concern is shown in the UK at the fact that a child in the lower half (second quartile) of the measured ability range at age eight is, if sent to a private school, 6.17 times more likely to gain AAA grades at A level and 3.03 times as likely to do so as a state school-educated child of above average ability at age eight (Morris *et al.* 2016). The implications for top-ranked UK universities that require AAA grades or above are obvious. This discrepancy is not because the UK's private schools provide a good education, but because the majority are paid to ensure children learn how to perform well in tests (Dorling 2019). Scottish universities at least now account for this and offer contextual admissions, with entrance grades based on social educational background. Finland, however, offers an example of how such problems can be avoided entirely. Unfortunately, data on happiness in Table 5.1 are not disaggregated for the UK's individual nations, or even reported for the UK as a whole, but they are included for the UK as a whole later in Figure 9.3 (where the UK, predictably, ranks low – although the UK is at least not as unhappy a place as is the US).

Table 5.1: People who said they were happy all or most of the time in Europe, 2018

% OF ALL PEOPLE AGED 16 AND OVER	RANKED	HIGHEST EDUCATION LEVEL ATTAINED		
	All People	Lower (0–2)	Medium (3–4)	Higher (5–8)
Finland	75.9	73.0	76.1	79.0
Austria	75.9	66.8	77.7	79.0
Netherlands	76.2	72.3	77.2	78.1
Switzerland	75.4	66.9	75.8	78.4
Belgium	76.3	68.8	75.7	82.8
Luxembourg	73.9	68.3	75.0	79.7
Germany	64.5	59.8	65.2	66.3
Malta	61.8	54.7	68.3	72.1
Denmark	69.7	68.5	70.9	69.0
Norway	65.6	64.0	55.0	64.1
France	67.7	60.3	68.8	73.2
Poland	68.5	56.4	68.1	77.3
Sweden	64.6	64.6	66.9	61.6
Slovenia	57.8	46.1	56.4	66.3
Av. European Union	**58.9**	**53.9**	**63.4**	**70.3**
Hungary	57.8	43.7	58.5	70.1
Cyprus	54.7	46.7	54.5	61.7
Czechia (Czech Republic)	51.6	44.1	48.1	61.9
Estonia	51.4	39.9	49.7	58.7
Spain	71.5	64.7	75.2	79.2
Romania	46.1	36.0	48.1	61.1
Portugal	56.0	48.0	67.6	71.4
Serbia	56.0	40.9	52.6	65.1
Lithuania	45.4	31.4	41.0	57.8
Greece	46.4	40.3	47.6	53.6
Croatia	41.8	29.7	45.0	50.0
Italy	49.1	41.1	65.6	57.8
Bulgaria	34.9	23.0	34.6	49.3
Latvia	30.7	24.5	27.0	40.9

Source: Eurostat (2019c). *Note*: data missing for Iceland, Ireland, Slovenia, and the UK. Lower (0–2) is pre-primary, primary and lower-secondary education; higher (5–8) is tertiary education, usually degree level.

One of the most under-represented groups at universities in Finland is immigrants and the children of immigrants. This is despite the thousands of highly motivated people who now come to Finland every year, often having achieved considerable academic qualifications before they arrive. Refugees are frequently the best educated of their homelands. However, the arrival of refugees in significant numbers is a very recent experience for Finland. In 1990 only 0.6 per cent of the Finnish population had a mother tongue that was not Finnish or Swedish. By 2017, that level had risen dramatically to 5.7 per cent.

In the spring of 2018, the University of Helsinki joined five other Finnish universities in providing specific assistance through a programme titled Supporting Immigrants in Higher Education (SIMHE) (Peltonen 2018). One of the biggest obstacles to learning is a lack of language skills, especially when it comes to entrance exams. Refugees can face further obstacles, such as the difficulty of providing secondary education certificates from their home countries. Thankfully, SIMHE now has processes for refugees to overcome some of these challenges.

Although tuition in both academic and vocational higher education remains free for Finnish and EU students, and despite comparatively generous government aid, many students now graduate with fairly significant levels of private debt which they carry into (and often now throughout) their midlife. Finns are increasingly concerned about debt accumulated while studying, including the cost of accommodation (Mäntylä 2019). From 2010 to March 2019, total student debts increased from less than €1.5 billion to more than €3.6 billion (Bank of Finland 2019b).

Juha Sipilä's government, which held power between 2015 and 2019, cut student support grants and increased student loans. Another factor in the rise in student loans is their low interest rate: a tiny number of borrowers even take out these loans in order to invest the money (Mäntylä 2019). Today, two thirds of students who receive student support also take out a loan, while in 2010 just one third did. Student support is around €250 a month and housing support can be up to €300 a month. A government-backed student loan, arranged via a bank of your choice, can be up to €650 a month if you study in Finland, and up to €800 a month if you study abroad (Kela 2019c). Up to a third of the debt is written off for students who successfully complete their studies within a set period of time (Kela 2021).

It is not just students who are concerned about private debt. Although Finns were traditionally very wary of debt, and banks did not hand out loans as easily as they do now, Finns have become accustomed to living in a low-interest rate environment in which loans are encouraged (Salmi 2019). The European Systemic Risk Board (ESRB) has issued recommendations to Finland since 2016 concerning increasing household indebtedness and lending standards (ESRB 2019: 3). This represents a significant shift from the years before the credit markets were freed, when spending borrowed money was a new and unfamiliar concept. We are living in odd times. For instance, in Denmark some mortgages carry negative interest rates (Collinson 2019a).

Household indebtedness in Finland was 113 per cent of GDP in the second quarter of 2016 (ESRB 2019: 10) and 115 per cent in the third quarter of 2018. It is even higher in Sweden at 174 per cent (ESRB 2019: 11) and Denmark's stands at a whopping 230 per cent (ESRB 2019: 9). As fears grow that global financial insecurity will intensify, lending practices are in urgent need of reform.

Working life

In August 2019, the employment rate in Finland, which represents the percentage of all 15–64 year-olds in paying work, was 73.5 per cent. For men it was 74.2 per cent and 72.8 per cent for women, and that small gap is narrowing (Findikaattori 2019). In 1988 the employment rate had been almost 80 per cent. It fell dramatically to below 60 per cent in 1994, but has remained above 65 per cent since 2000, even through the global and eurozone financial crises. The World Economic Forum ranked Helsinki as the world's best city for work–life balance in 2019, with a 40-hour working week and an average commute of just 26 minutes (Wood 2019). In 2018, the median hourly wage for men in Finland was €19.20, and €16.50 for women.

In addition to administering the PISA tests, the OECD also assesses the information-processing skills of young people and adults between the ages of 16 and 65. Of the 24 countries examined in 2012, Finland ranked second in literacy and numeracy, only beaten by Japan (Brink & Nissinen 2018). Additionally, Finland ranked first among OECD countries for the flexibility that workers had over choosing when they worked, which days they worked and where during each day. Over half of all workers who had a degree said they had some such flexibility in Finland, as did 40 per cent of those with the lowest educational qualification. These figures were higher for every group of workers in Finland than in any other OECD country for which such figures are available (Figure 5.2). As Figure 5.2 makes clear, there are many interesting variations, such as less skilled workers in Turkey, who are often farmers or day labourers, having relatively high flexibility; however, nowhere else in the affluent world comes even close to what Finland has achieved when it comes to work hours flexibility and hence work–life balance and happiness.

Despite Finland ranking first worldwide in terms of in-job flexibility, there is still much that could improve, and a few things that have worsened in recent years. The gender divide in outcomes in working life has barely changed in Finland since the 1980s and follows on from the gender divide in education. As briefly mentioned in Chapter 4, even though girls perform better in PISA results, they are less likely than boys to undertake further study in STEM subjects and then subsequently to be employed in these areas. There are even fewer women in Finland who work in, or who have previously studied, information and communication technology (ICT) subjects. In the 1980s, over one third of women in Finland studied these subjects, but the figure has now dropped to around 15 per cent. Other Nordic countries, all highly ranked for gender equality in education, suffer from the same segregation in employment owing to choices made and norms that prevailed in earlier years (see Figure 5.3).

Despite fewer women now working in STEM jobs, the proportion of women working is high in Nordic countries, with relatively few choosing to be stay-at-home mothers. Women in Finland, however, still do a disproportionate amount of unpaid care work compared with men. According to the OECD, on average women in Finland spend nearly four hours a day on unpaid work, while men spend only 2 hours 37 minutes (OECD.Stat 2019a).

In 46 per cent of job categories in Finland, men earn significantly more than women (Hiilamo & Ala-Risku 2019). Furthermore, in those fields where Finnish women earn more, they do not tend to earn much more. Where women earn more than men, which is only 6 per cent of all jobs by career group, the largest differences are found among vets in the municipal sector (where for every euro a man makes, a woman makes €1.14), property

Figure 5.2: Job flexibility by educational attainment 2012–15, OECD countries

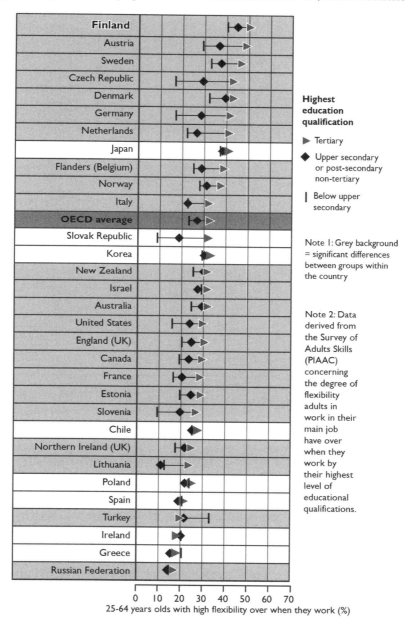

25-64 years olds with high flexibility over when they work (%)

Source: OECD (2019c: 120, table A6.4).

Figure 5.3: The paradox of high gender equality and low STEM uptake by women

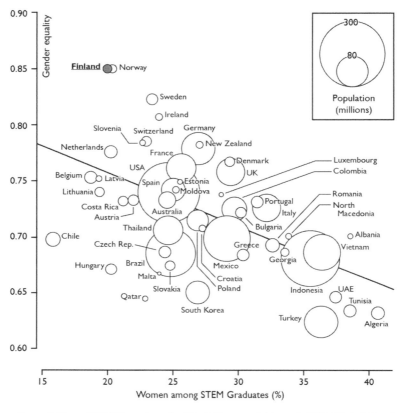

Source: Stoet & Geary (2018) based on the World Economic Forum's 2015 Global Gender Gap Report.

Note: the vertical axis measures the Global Gender Gap Index GGGI. Data on STEM ratios for Iceland were missing, so it does not appear on the graph.

maintenance and cleaning service managers in the public sector (€1.23 for women) and teaching experts in the public sector (€1.81 for women for every euro earned by a man).

In contrast to the few areas where women in Finland earn more than men, the most pronounced differences in the other direction are found among professional services managers, along with financial and insurance services branch managers in the private sector (€0.63 earned by women for every euro earned by a man) and in the public sector (€0.66), and legislators, senior officials, and managers in the private sector (€0.71) (OSF 2019a). Of course, all these statistics look quite equitable when measured against the rest of the OECD countries and they are significantly more equitable than the social divides found in most poorer countries that are not members of the OECD. Greater equality is much more prevalent in more affluent countries. But the highest levels of equality can only be maintained through constant vigilance.

One remarkable aspect of the world of work of Finland, and similarly that of Norway, is that these two countries, alongside Iceland, rank highest – being least divisive – in the Global Gender Gap Index (GGGI). The GGGI is a measure of the degree to which women fall behind men on 14 key indicators that include earnings from work, tertiary education, life expectancy, seats in parliament and so on. A measure of 1.0 would represent complete parity or even men falling behind (which is not yet the case anywhere in the world). For the countries for which there are also PISA educational statistics, the GGGI in 2015 ranged from a low of 0.59 for the United Arab Emirates to a high of 0.88 for Iceland. These statistics were used to produce Figure 5.3.

Family life

Finland takes its social statistics very seriously, for good reason, and Statistics Finland is among the very best statistical agencies in the world. (Statistical agencies rank many things, including each other; Canada's agency also often does well in this particularly geeky list.) Without good statistics you cannot begin to know what is happening to families, or how your country is dealing with challenges such as equality in mid-life. Far more than statistics is needed, but they are the first essential in monitoring and assessing the impact and effectiveness of policies. In the year 2018 there were 1,468,681 families recorded as living in Finland, including unmarried couples without children, with an overall average family size of 2.8. There were 404,142 couples with children, with an average family size of 4.0. There were 152,888 single mothers, and 33,292 single fathers (OSF 2019c). In 2018 the fertility rate was 1.41 children per woman in her lifetime, representing a new low (OSF 2019d).

The decreasing fertility rate in Finland makes headlines every year, partly because of what it portends about the tax base that funds the welfare state and the social contract that binds Finland together. This continued drop in fertility further exacerbates the implications of an ageing society (United Nations Population Division 2001). Even so, research into why fertility in early mid-life has fallen so low in Finland is still scarce (Hiilamo 2019a).

In later chapters in this book we discuss the extent to which immigration to Finland can compensate for the country's very low fertility rate, although the number of people who move to Finland is as yet too low to do so. For centuries, Finland was a net exporter of people. In this it was very much like its neighbour Sweden: "Between about 1860 and World War I roughly one-third of all the natural increase in Sweden [births] was lost through emigration, principally to the United States" (Wilson *et al*. 2013). Only recently has Finland become a net immigration state (the implications of which we also touch on later in this book). Research published in 2013 found that for European countries: "The amount of migration required to maintain the working-age population – a proxy for the labour force – was higher, but nevertheless still within the scope of recent migration levels for many countries" (Craveiro *et al*. 2019).

In Finland, having children in mid-life (although not as an older teenager) is encouraged by the state. Allowances are provided for the entirety of parental leave, although it is always less than a person's normal income – typically around 70 per cent of it (Kela 2018a), but never below €24.64 a day (Kela 2018b). If you continue to be paid by your employer, your allowance is paid to your employer by Kela, Finland's Social Insurance Institute. Maternity leave is granted for 105 working days, or about four months. Paternity leave, introduced in 1978, is provided for 54 working days (nine weeks), but only 18 working days of paternity leave can be taken while the mother is also on maternity leave (Kela 2019d). Parental leave, which begins when maternity leave ends, is 158 working days. Furthermore, paternity leave can be continued after parental leave if the 18 working days are not used up prior to parental leave, as long as the child is under the age of two. These parental leave policies are dictated by the state, rather than left to individual companies to decide. Based on a league table developed by UNICEF, Finland has the twelfth most family-friendly policies in the world – Sweden was top, the UK ranked only 28th (Chzhen *et al*. 2019).

In Finland, nearly all mothers take maternity leave as well as shared parental leave. In 2014, 78 per cent of all fathers in Finland took paternity leave, but on average they take only four weeks of the maximum nine weeks of paternity leave (Aulasmaa 2017). The highest proportions of parental leave taken up by men are found in the Nordic countries and Portugal (OSF 2018c). Finland still lags behind other Nordic countries in this respect. In Iceland 30 per cent, Sweden 27 per cent, and Norway 21 per cent of parental leave allowances are taken by men, but in Finland this figure is only 10 per cent (OSF 2017a). This may be low, but it has increased significantly from 1997, when it was 4 per cent, and from when it was 6 per cent in 2007.

Persuading more men to take their paternity leave and shared parental leave is still a challenge in Finland, even though it has been almost two decades since Paavo Lipponen – who was the Finnish prime minister from 1995 to 2003 – became the world's first head of government to do so. He took six working days of paternity leave in 2000, and said that "in this way, a new masculinity is arising, a culture of fatherhood that is very positive for children" (quoted in Chincilla & León 2005: 33).

According to research by Eerola *et al.* (2019), men's greatest motivator for taking paternity leave is the wish to have a break from work and help the child's mother return to work or study; while among the obstacles they cite, the greatest is the family's economic situation. That research concluded that international comparisons suggest that fathers are more likely to use their leave when their exclusive leave is extended, and the loss of earnings are effectively compensated. For Finland to increase fathers' take-up of parental leave, these researchers also recommended that the maternity, paternity, parental, and home care leave schemes should be simplified and made more flexible for diverse family arrangements (Infopankki 2019a).

It should also be noted that family life is still far easier for heterosexual couples to organize, as legislation has yet to continue to progress beyond heterosexual couples and binary genders. The law makes it even more difficult for same-sex male couples. The spouse or registered partner of a mother has access to parental allowance regardless of their gender, but the male spouse or registered partner of a father does not have access to parental allowance, and their eligibility for paternity allowance is limited (Kela 2019e). Nor is there a category that addresses the needs of non-binary or intersexual people; in matters of parental leave, as in other matters, the Population Information System assumes that you are either a man or a woman (Saure 2019).

Sipilä's government (2015–19) tried and failed to reform parental leave, which is still generally seen as extended maternity leave (Eerola & Lammi-Taskula 2019). In February 2020, the new government agreed on a parental leave reform, to come into force in 2022 after further planning and parliamentary approval (Parliament of Finland 2020). The reform would increase parental leave allowance to 160 days (six allowance days per week) allocated for each parent, with the option of transferring up to 63 days from one to the other. This is in addition to a pregnancy allowance of 40 days. With gendered language removed from the legislation, both parents would have equal access regardless of their gender. A single parent will also have access to the same amount of allowance as is intended for two parents. This reform intends to accommodate more diverse families, increase the father's share of parental leave, and help reduce the gender pay gap – although the home care allowance will remain untouched.

Earnings and tax

Finland's welfare state is not cheap. It is logical, however, that if people themselves benefit from the services their taxes fund, not just individually but through the benefits that the system brings to the broader society, then they will accept it. And indeed, the majority of people we interviewed in Finland while researching this book actively welcomed the higher rates of taxation that they paid. If you pay taxes but are offered only poor public education, and if you cannot rely on public healthcare or other services that some people opt out of, you may well consider taxes to be an unfair burden. But if the services provided through taxation are of a high quality, then you should be happy to contribute financially. However, you must at least be aware that such a comparison is possible, even if you have never experienced living in a low tax, highly unequal affluent country.

While it is not strictly true that taxation funds public spending, it is a useful approximation. In practice a country can choose to increase its borrowing instead of raising more through taxes, as the US does when it borrows ever more from abroad. Alternatively, the people of a country can choose to have relatively low taxes, as Japan does, but also have very equitable earnings and leave families to be their own safety nets. However, that approach does not work when family members become estranged, or for people who have small or no families; and it is particularly unsuited to people with severe disabilities for whom families cannot provide enough support. In Finland disability benefits are generous, including for carers, and: "If you are blind or immobile without assistance, you are entitled to a disability pension even if you work" (Info Finland 2018). Progressive taxation that is effective and hard to avoid also serves the purpose of curbing extravagant spending by the rich, because the rich have less to extravagantly spend; not least because that money is being used for people with severe disabilities to ensure their quality of life is high.

If income tax was lower in Finland, more people who received a high salary could own an apartment in central Helsinki for use during the week, a large house in an outlying town for the family, and two or three holiday homes. Such a scenario is common in the US, and less common but increasing in the UK and a part of the causes of the British housing crisis (Dorling 2014). In contrast, this situation is extremely rare in Finland. Ownership of multiple residences has led to greater homelessness in both the UK and US, as more and more dwellings are no longer used most of the time as main homes. Figure 5.4 shows the main sources of tax in Finland and how those sources differ slightly from the usual OECD distribution of tax-bearing assets. Figure 5.4, perhaps surprisingly, shows that in Finland the share of tax raised from corporate profits is just over half that in the OECD as a whole (5 per cent instead of 9 per cent), while taxes on property are also half the OECD average, and both combined are equal to the amount that personal income tax is higher for Finns as a share of all taxes.

In 2020, the highest marginal tax rate applies to annual incomes of €88,000–93,000 at 60.6 per cent owing to lower tax deductions, and then decreases to 57.8 per cent on annual incomes at €130,000 and above (TAF 2019). Following the Nordic dual income tax model, investment income is taxed separately, at 30–34 per cent. Figure 5.4 compares only the distribution of taxes. Overall taxes in Finland are around 27 per cent higher than in the OECD as a whole, so all the bars for Finland in the graph are drawn 27 per cent wider than the OECD average bars. The totals still equal 100 per cent. The graph represents a snapshot in time of a slowly changing distribution of what is taxed, and how much, in a more equitable affluent country, compared

Figure 5.4: The tax structure of Finland as compared to the OECD average

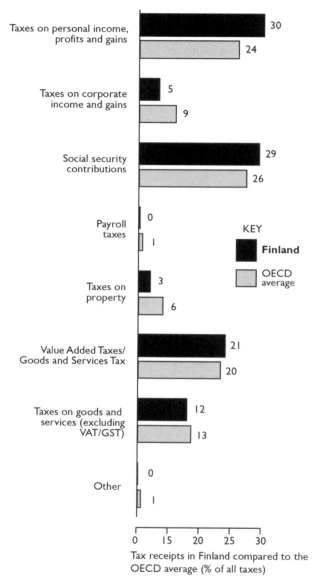

Source: OECD (2018b).

Note: tax revenues in Finland were 26.9 per cent higher than in the OECD as a whole in the year 2018 (43.3 per cent of GDP rather than 34.2 per cent) and so the bars for Finland are drawn that much wider.

with the OECD average. The reason that this distribution is slowly changing is that Finland is adapting its taxation system to a changing world and
changing priorities over who needs the most and can afford the most (rights
and responsibilities).

In Finland, capital income tax – the taxing of income from the receipt of
interest and sources such as rents – became progressive in 2012, but remains
lower than the taxation of earned income and is a significant source of
income for high earners. Prior to this, it was levied at a flat rate (Riihelä 2009:
48). Finland abolished a small net wealth tax of 0.8 per cent in 2006. In 2017,
Finland's tax-to-GDP ratio was 43.3 per cent, against an OECD average of
34.2 per cent (OECD 2018b). In this, Finland was ranked fifth out of the
36 OECD countries, coming after France, Denmark, Belgium and Sweden in
terms of countries that tax and spend the most. Low taxation does not save
people money. People have to spend more on private provision for what
would otherwise be public good, such as a university education, and they
tend to go into debt more often. Furthermore, in countries where overall taxation is lower, and spending is more often personal rather than public, more is
spent by the more affluent who have the spare money. In such countries, that
spending tends to be more frivolous and less wise (Frank 2016).

The UK's tax-to-GDP ratio in 2017 was about a percentage point below
the OECD average, at 33.3 per cent. The US had the sixth lowest tax ratio,
at 27.1 per cent. The richest 1 per cent in the US take over 22 per cent of all
income per year, compared with around 15 per cent in the UK, less than 9 per
cent in Sweden, and nearer 5 per cent in Finland. See Figure 9.4 later in this
book, which shows how these statistics for the richest 1 per cent are derived
and how they have changed both in recent years and over the course of the
past century.

Finland has long practised the redistribution of income, and to an extent
wealth, so what do the wealthy say? In an interesting interview, Anders
Wiklöf, the richest man in Åland, which is a Swedish-speaking archipelago
in the Baltic Sea and an autonomous region in Finland with its own MP (see
Table 7.1 in Chapter 7), said that he considered high taxes for the wealthy
to be just (Pallaste 2019). He further added that when politicians privatize
too much, the power and the tax money in effect goes to businessmen, when
taxes should go to those most in need. Wiklöf went on to say that Juha Sipilä

of the Centre Party, Finland's prime minister from 2015 to 2019, had treated Finland more like a business than a state (he had previously been a business-man). The one tax that Wiklöf disagreed with was inheritance tax – claiming that this amounted to being taxed twice over. Wiklöf also estimated that he has paid over €300,000 in fines, including speeding fines, which are levied on a sliding scale based on income.

Inheritance tax raises such a small amount of money in Finland that it does not appear in Figure 5.4. For close relatives of the deceased, the tax rate begins at 7 per cent for inheritance valued above €20,000 and rises progres-sively to 19 per cent on inheritance exceeding €1,000,000. For other relatives and non-relatives, the respective range is 19 per cent to 33 per cent. The top rates would affect Wiklof's heirs, but he is one of very few Finns likely to bequeath more than €1 million to a number of individuals, and the highest inheritance tax for close relatives is less than a fifth of the sum bequeathed.

Anders Wiklöf is not wholly representative of Finland's super-rich. A contrasting view can be seen in some of the 28 interviews with anonymous male entrepreneurs conducted by Anu Kantola and Hanna Kuusela (2019). Entrepreneurs are often seen as exemplars of capitalism who promote indi-vidualism and whose outlook is the result of their rags to riches background (although few successful entrepreneurs were ever in rags). In Finland over 80 per cent of entrepreneurs are male, and all who are very successful belong to the top 1 per cent of Finnish earners. Kantola and Kuusela's interviewees reit-erated familiar criticisms of the welfare state, including the accusation that some people are living off benefits that are higher than certain salaries (they do not mention that this is mainly people with severe mental or physical disabilities) and that recipients see benefits as a right; Kantola and Kuusela (2019: 378) also highlight one interviewee who characterized politicians and public sector workers as "unproductive people who exploit the productive".

Wage earners' demands and strikes were also frequently cited as unwel-come events by those whose income is already in the top 1 per cent in Finland. Nevertheless, among this group there were some entrepreneurs who supported high taxes, because of the services such taxes funded and from which the rich also benefit, and because they contributed to maintaining a functioning society. It is not hard to prove this. Nurses, teachers and vari-ous other professions work tirelessly, alongside an army of low-paid private sector workers whose low pay is set by people such as entrepreneurs, and who are essential for a functioning society regardless of their total supposed contribution to the country's GDP. That Finland's severely disabled people have their complex needs met by receiving benefits greater than the wages of the lowest paid able-bodied workers should surely be a matter of pride, not derision (Info Finland 2018).

Because Finland taxes very wealthy people more, it is possible for it to provide better services to those who most need them than are often found in European countries with lower tax rates. For instance, although Finnish winters pose difficulties for wheelchair users and, according to a post for disabled expats, finding accessible flats can be difficult (Venesperä 2018), the Finnish state and municipal services work together to provide for disabled individuals' needs. In Finland, it is a matter of course that, for example, deaf children have the right to receive education in sign language (Katsui *et al*. 2018: 2). Some efforts have been made to increase employment rates among disabled people, but further initiatives are still needed. That, too, requires public funding, as something not to be offered purely on a whim or by charity, but by right.

Noting how closely some of the remarks of Finland's very highest-paid entrepreneurs resembled conservative American views, the researchers highlighted how it is possible to give too much political weight to the top earners in the private sector. This occurs frequently in a country like the US, which is plainly not serving the large majority of its citizens, its children, its newborns (so many more of whom die in their first year of life than newborns in many other wealthy countries) and most of its elderly (who do not live as long as the elderly do in any other affluent country). Giving too much weight to the few who are very well off could undermine what Kantola and Kuusela (2019) see as the source of Finland's success, namely, compromise, recognition of others' value, and the effort to understand other people's position in society, rather than creating boundaries and conflict.

Figure 5.5 shows that the take-home pay of people in Anders Wiklöf's position (the lowest line in the figure) has fallen slightly since the mid-1990s, which might be part of the reason for a little discomfort among the very-best off in Finland. You can study the figure to see the very small changes that have occurred over time for each of the four groups shown. But the noteworthy thing is that these are all small changes. In contrast the same graph as shown in Figure 5.5 for the UK and USA would show the top 1 per cent taking more and more almost every year from 1980 onwards; and the next 9 per cent scrabbling to keep up with them, leaving less and less for the next 40 per cent and a dwindling and so much smaller amount for the worst-off 50 per cent of the population.

Figure 5.5: The income share of the different groups in Finland 1980–2016

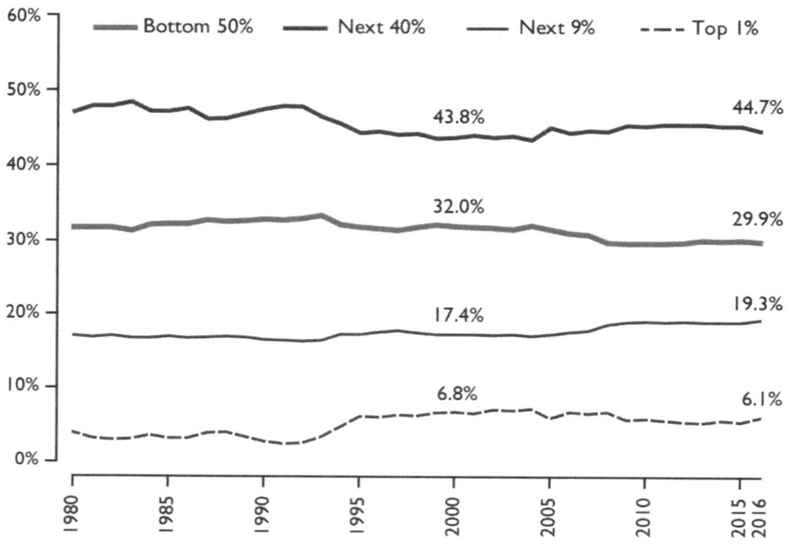

Source: World Inequality Database

Note: Shown here is the total post-tax income share of each group from all sources including employment, rents, capital and profits. If this was not unequal, any 1 per cent would get 1 per cent.

The most recent income inequality data for Finland (shown in Figure 5.5) illustrates (if you look carefully) the growing divide between the top 10 per cent and bottom 50 per cent, which widened in 2016. When a divide grows in Finland it tends not to grow very much. It also shows that the share of the top 1 per cent has been falling since 2000. It also fell remarkably over the century – from a high of 15.3 per cent in 1920, to 7.5 per cent in 2009 (see Figure 9.4 for further details).

These changes in income distribution have created a great deal of discussion about rising inequality within Finland. This is part of the constant social surveillance by the Finnish press, academia and parliament of whether progress is being achieved. It is worth noting the dominance of the Finnish press in the reference list at the end of this book. All this surveillance helps prevent great rises in inequality occurring unrecorded and uncriticized, and helps more radical political parties to win power every so often and set Finland back on course towards greater equality once again. Figure 5.5 demonstrates the equitable and stable distributions of income in Finland. But those inequalities tend to grow if they are not monitored. Even small income inequalities leave the best-off with spare money with which they can purchase assets that rise in value and enable them to accumulate wealth and from some of which they can then also supplement their income.

While progressive taxation is meant to redistribute wealth across the population, the wealth gap increased in Finland in the 1990s nevertheless. It is no coincidence that the 1990s also featured a tax reform which differentiated between the taxation of earned income and capital income. This disproportionately benefited the wealthy and has undermined progressive taxation (Riihelä 2009: 167). The top 10 per cent of Finnish households received about 25 per cent of all income in 2016 (as Figure 5.5 illustrates), but they owned approximately 47 per cent of net wealth by that same year; a significant increase of two percentage points from 2013 when that top decile owned 45 per cent (Yle Uutiset 2018d). At the same time, housing debt increased by 3.5 per cent, making it harder to narrow the wealth inequality gap in future. For those in the bottom half of society in Finland, that 2 per cent increase would be an enormous amount of money to receive, doubling (or more) the scant savings of the majority of people. That same Statistics Finland report showed a fall in the wealth held by the median Finnish citizen in recent years. However, the share of the top 10 per cent in Finland was a very significant five percentage points below the share held by that group in the UK at the same time (51.9 per cent), which was itself a social world away from the share of all wealth in the US that the wealthiest 10 per cent there now own (73 per cent), leaving little for everyone else (World Inequality Database 2019).

Finns are vocal about rising inequality. Scarred by the financial crisis of the 1990s, Finns saw the rise in inequality that it precipitated as a rupture from the norm. Attitudes towards the provisions made by the welfare state in Finland have varied over time. In interviews conducted by Kantola and Kuusela (2019) it was found that the most controversial use of tax-payers' money was the payment of unemployment benefits, which were often viewed as supporting many indolent people who preferred benefits to working. Sipilä's 2015–19 government introduced a welfare-to-work policy, the "activation model", to try to remedy this. This cut unemployment benefits by 4.65 per cent, if the applicant failed to meet criteria such as receiving entrepreneurial income (finding self-employment) of at least €241, undertaking training, or working for at least 18 hours within a three-month period (SAK 2019b). Employment during Sipilä's government did rise to slightly higher than it was back in 2008, but the actual contribution of government policy to having achieved this is uncertain. The Economic Policy Council (2019: 11) attributed the greatest impact on employment as being a result of the tripartite Competitiveness Pact, not the welfare-to-work policy.

The various hoops that the unemployed were being asked to jump through varied – being enforced differently in different regions – and was considered by many politicians, the unemployed themselves and others to be "humiliating" and "a time-consuming exercise in bureaucracy" (SAK 2019b). Furthermore, the reduction of unemployment benefits by a third (if recipients were members of a trade union unemployment fund), and by 40 per cent (for those receiving benefits from Kela), increased families' dependency on basic security such as income support and housing benefits (Kela 2019f). Such hoop-jumping then hinders finding full-time work (Honkanen 2018). Hardening attitudes towards welfare spurred a political response that worsened the situation for many people and cost the government more in other benefits and in bureaucracy.

The activation model, which has only recently been disbanded, was a false economy. As the problem largely stems from a mismatch between the skills of the unemployed and prerequisites for available jobs, more structural reforms are needed. Despite its criticism of the activation model, Marin's left-leaning government may be forced to make similarly unpopular decisions as, like most governments do, it relies on increasing productivity and tax revenue to support its ambitious programme. Meeting its employment rate target is seen as crucial for achieving its social benefit aims (Luukka 2019a).

Housing

Housing in Finland is primarily divided into private housing and housing provided by ARA (Asumisen rahoitus- ja kehittämiskeskus), the Housing Finance and Development Centre of Finland (Ara 2013). ARA was set up in 1949 to provide subsidized housing when the private sector was unable to provide sufficient funds for the building of new housing (Tulla 1999). The state gives ARA long-term (40 year) loans. Until then the state's role in housing had been limited to intervention in crises (Ruonavaara 2003: 54).

Approximately half of all rental apartments in Finland have been built with financing through the open market and the other half have received funding from national ARA loans or interest-subsidized loans (Environmental Administration 2018). Priority is given to people in housing need – the homeless, the evicted, those currently living in inadequate conditions, and those with limited assets (Juntto 1992). State housing loans to institutions also apply to student housing associations and old-age housing associations (Tulla 1999).

Government housing support almost doubled following the 1990s depression, so that by the year 2000 some 15 per cent of the Finnish population received housing support (reducing the rent they paid) from Kela (Ruonavaara 2003: 56). However, the availability of this housing support has contributed to increasing rent prices in the privately rented sector. Rents for ARA-apartments have also risen by 15 per cent on average between 2011 and 2016, while those of privately financed apartments have risen by 18 per cent (Alho *et al.* 2018: 8).

In all ten of Finland's largest cities, rents for tenants living in privately owned properties have recently risen faster than incomes. Due to continued urbanization and the increased popularity of the city as Finland rises up the global ranks, in Helsinki the demand for state funded ARA housing now far exceeds supply, with four times as many households applying in 2017 to be placed in ARA housing than had succeeded in doing so in 2016. Nevertheless, and especially outside of the capital, the home-ownership dream of the US and UK is a reality in Finland: in 2017, two thirds of Finnish households lived in a home they owned (OSF 2018d).

Only just over half of Finns live in houses (53 per cent), with almost all of the remainder living in apartments (OSF 2017b). In 2017, 317,000 house-holds, just over a fifth of all households, lived in what is generally very high-quality social housing. However, some 31 per cent of Finns aged 20–24 are now living with their parents, a rise from 27 per cent in 2017. By way of comparison and to illustrate how much better housing is organized in Fin-land than elsewhere, 58 per cent of the same aged young adults in the UK live with their parents. Only 6.6 per cent of 25–29 year-olds in Finland were still living with their parents in 2017, compared to 20.1 per cent of that age group in the UK (Eurostat 2018a). Few young adults in the UK want to live with their parents, and very few had to do so in the 1970s and early 1980s. Home ownership is increasingly an impossibility for the great majority of young people in the UK, and increasingly it is becoming impossible for middle-aged people too (Fransham & Dorling 2017).

Although home ownership has traditionally been relatively high in Fin-land, in recent years it has become more popular to rent. Housing benefits have increased, making renting more affordable for those who are poor. Meanwhile, the state has also gained revenue, as rental incomes are taxed and that tax is now progressive (Soininvaara 2016). Until a landlord receives a total of €30,000 a year in rent across all his or her rental properties, the tax is 30 per cent, and after €30,000 it is 34 per cent (Verohallinto 2017).

Some changes are arguably less progressive. Rent control was abolished in 1992 in Finland (Lyytikäinen 2006) and the criteria for eviction were also relaxed. Only rent for state-subsidized housing continues to be regulated (Ministry of the Environment 2013a). Because of this rents have risen signif-icantly faster than inflation (Alho *et al.* 2018). In the first quartile of 2018 rents increased by 2.4 per cent (OSF 2019e). Additionally, a larger propor-tion of disposable income is now being used on living costs. Increased living support payments and applications for social (ARA) rental apartments have increased rents above many tenants' ability to pay, as demand to live in some areas rises. While regional differences in apartment prices have widened, considerable new building has mitigated some pressures on price increases in areas of high growth (Bank of Finland 2019c). However, rental prices within Helsinki outstrip the rest of Finland and remain out of reach of many Finns.

Immigration, emigration and equality in mid-life

While only 6 per cent of the total Finnish population were born abroad, 8 per cent of 15–29 year-olds were (Helminen 2017). A study in 2014 by Statistics Finland found that over half (123,000) of foreign-born people had moved to Finland to be with family or to pursue relationships (Sutela & Larja 2015). Only 18 per cent (41,000) of those people came for employment reasons, and men were twice as likely as women to migrate for work. Some 10 per cent came to study and a further 10 per cent of immigrants were refugees.

Like many developed Western states, Finnish society is greying, with falling birth rates threatening the ability to raise sufficient tax income to pay for Finland's welfare system in future. In the view of many policy researchers focusing on this issue, greater immigration is a solution. Research on Finland has now determined that immigration would not have to be on a massive scale to solve the demographic problem, but more people are needed, and perhaps there needs to be a little less emigration (Craveiro *et al.* 2019).

Life for an adult in Finland who was born elsewhere can be very different than for those born in Finland, and foreign-born people may not benefit as much from all the things that Finland is ranked so highly for. Among western European countries, Finland has one of the lowest numbers of foreign-born residents, and yet an EU study of 12 countries found the highest rates of racially motivated violence and harassment against people of African descent were to be found in Finland. In recent reports, the European Commission against Racism and Intolerance has underscored the efforts that are required to help people, in particular those of Somali descent, better integrate into Finnish education, housing and employment and to be better protected from racist attacks. At some 20,000 people, Somalis are the fourth largest diaspora in Finland (after Russian, Estonian and those grouped together as Arabic speakers), and half of all Somalis live in the Helsinki area. Most came in the early 1990s, partly in the wake of a failed $1.7 billion intervention by the US (Lee Hogg 2008) into the civil war in Somalia, and many have since had children born in Finland.

The Somalis were some of the first immigrants. Most of Finland's immigrants, and especially most of the refugees who were not white, came in the past decade. Considering how recently many of these foreign groups arrived in Finland, it is not surprising that it is more difficult for immigrants to have achieved the "Finnish dream". It will be an important challenge for Finland in the near future to narrow the current divides that the statistical agencies measure in both opportunities and outcomes, without making authoritarian demands for extreme assimilation.

Immigrants in Finland are covered by the Finnish social security system if they intend and register their intent to reside permanently in the country. According to Osten Wahlbeck, "the extensive welfare system based on universalism has been argued to be one of the most important inclusion mechanisms, as the basic accessibility to benefits and services reinforces wide participation in other areas of society" (Wahlbeck 2018). Integration into the labour market has been more difficult, even though resettlement programmes include language and labour market training. The unemployment rate for immigrants is up to three times higher than for the general population.

Refugees or immigrants with little education are especially vulnerable. Unemployment rates are much higher, income much lower and health problems more frequent (THL 2018a). Differences have also been observed in long-term illnesses and reproductive health. Additionally, immigrants experience discrimination in finding work, in work relations and in renting apartments. Research has shown that merely having an Arabic name is a problem in Finland. Researchers at Åbo Akademi University sent out 1,459 rental enquiry emails across the country. They found that if the email was signed with a male Arabic name, the response rate was 16 per cent, while a Finnish woman's name received a response rate of 42 per cent (*Turun Sanomat* 2017). Ethnic segregation in the Helsinki metropolitan area has also increased in recent years (Vilkama 2012: 8).

Remarkably, less well-educated immigrants from conflict countries use health services less than the general population, despite being much more likely to have health service needs as a result of the trauma most have experienced – many find access difficult and are often scared of appearing needy.

Conclusion

Life is generally better in your mid-life years in Finland than in almost any other European country. It is also improving. As Nobel laureate Paul Krugman

(2018) explains, people in the lower deciles of the income distribution are better off in Finland than in the US, and while counterparts in the top deciles may have a smaller income, the benefits of living in a country like Finland can more than make up for it.

The greatest challenge facing Finland is the effective integration of increasing numbers of migrants, coupled with overcoming the racism and discrimination that they experience. Over the centuries, millions of Finns have left the country. The majority of people in the world with Finnish ancestors do not live in Finland. Finns have been accepted around the world as migrants. Today this most successful of all countries needs to prepare for the inevitable outcome of that success. More people will want to come to Finland, and Finland needs them to come (Londen *et al.* 2008).

The world's first female Members of Parliament, Finland, 1907. Pictured seating from left to right are: Hilja Pärssinen, Alli Nissinen, Lucina Hagman, Alexandra Gripenberg, Evelina Ala-Kulju and Liisa Kivioja. Standing, from left to right, are: Dagmar Neovius, Hedvig Gebhard, Iida Vemmelpuu, Hilda Käkikoski, Miina Sillanpää, Hilma Räsänen and Maria Laine. In 1906 Finland was still an autonomous Grand Duchy of the Russian empire, but its national assembly granted universal suffrage to all adult men and women, including not only the right to vote, but also to stand for election. In 1907, 19 women, most of whom are shown in this photograph taken that year, were elected to Finland's single-chamber parliament. Among them was Miina Sillanpää, who in 1927 became the first female minister and was a Member of Parliament for 38 years. In 2016 the government made 1 October a flag day to honour her (Korpela 2006).

Source: Helsinki City Museum (2019) (photographer unknown).

6

Old age and health

"Only the Nordic countries are known for their pared-down simpli-
city . . . *The Nordic Guide to Living 10 Years Longer* applies this ethos to
health – and it is important for me to express that to live a healthy life,
you do not have to go to extremes. It's the small and simple changes that
amount to a happier, healthier life."

Bertil Marklund, author of
The Nordic Guide to Living 10 Years Longer

The secret word

There has been a recent boom in books about how, if you live the Nordic way,
you too could live longer. Hundreds of little tips essentially all boil down to
an instruction to be more Swedish, more Danish, more Finnish. Each country has its own special word that signifies the secret to success. In Swedish,
according to Bertil Marklund, the word is *lagom*, meaning "just the right
amount". However, in each case we are told that there is no exact translation,
and hence an entire book on "the word" is needed for the reader to glean the
secrets it holds.

In Denmark the magic word is *hygge*, meaning an atmosphere of cosiness,
closeness and comfortable conviviality, which in turn generates feelings of
greater well-being and contentment (Norway has *koselig*, meaning nearly the
same thing, with some subtle differences.) Candles, cushions and closing the
door on unwanted intrusions feature heavily in *hygge*, and wrapping yourself

in chunky hand-knitted blankets and indulging in pastries is how the concept was presented to the outside world (*Country Life* 2017). Inevitably, there is no exact English translation or short definition that quite summarizes the concept correctly.

It is not just the Nordic countries that have received this treatment. In Japan the equivalent concept is *ikigai*. According to *The Times* "Forget hygge. It's all about ikigai (that's Japanese for a happy life)" (*Country Life* 2017; Mogi 2017). Unsurprisingly, the Japanese term also defies translation and requires an entire book to explain it. What none of these books point out are the many similarities between these countries. For instance, the Finnish land reforms of 1918 and 1919 (that we documented in Chapter 2) helped establish a way of living, behaving and treating each other that is very similar in some of its outcomes to the reforms for the better sharing out of land that took place in Japan between 1947 and 1949.

Apart from these untranslatable words for the secret to a good life, what do Norway, Sweden, Denmark, Japan and Finland have in common? The answer is not these societies' international bestseller-spawning cultural concepts, but that they are all amongst the most remarkably equitable countries in the world. These are the five countries clustered to the left in Figure 6.1. It has become an accepted fact that economic inequality is the driving force behind most societal problems. It has nothing to do with soft furnishings, cosiness and lighting, but everything to do with genuine equality of opportunity and outcome.

So what is Finland's untranslatable secret concept? The word is *sisu*.

Sisu and other mystical words

Various origins are claimed for *sisu*. It was a brand name of a liquorice sweet that has been around in Finland since the late 1920s, but that is just one of many theories for the origins of its use to mean more than sweets. The best translation – and of course there is the obligatory caveat that the true deep meaning cannot be translated into English – is that it's about not giving up, especially when things get tough. Apparently, *sisu* is behind The Moomins, the children's stories created by Tove Jansson, who was born in 1914. As one writer suggests: "... those original Moomin stories carry doses of *sisu*, too.

Figure 6.1: How health and social problems are related to inequality in rich countries

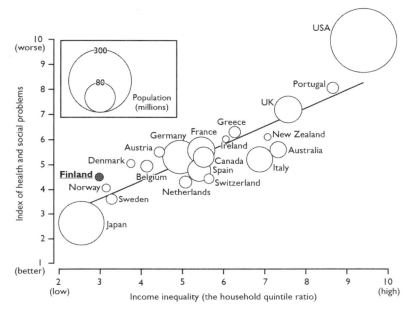

Source: Wilkinson & Pickett (2009: 20, figure 2.2).

Note: no numbers were included on the scale of this original diagram when it was first published.

Little My, the fiercely independent, brave and mischievous little girl who is adopted by the Moomins, always manages to get herself out of a tight spot – no matter what happens" (Pantzar 2018). But have you ever read a children's story where that did not happen?

Finland and the other equitable countries in the world are not special because they each have their own special way of being (and a special word to go with it). Instead, they each have a special way of being as a consequence of having become more equal. But what it feels like to live in a more equal society is something that the rest of us find very hard to imagine.

Today, people in Japan are among the longest lived in the world, but in the 1930s when Japan was one of the most unequal affluent countries in the world, this was far from the case. The aristocracy were becoming richer, the old were often not well cared for, and there were too few resources to do so.

131

Although *Ubasute*, the practice of abandoning old women to die, may well be a myth, it was the case that childless old people were removed to the outskirts of the village in remote rural parts of Japan to live together – where the soil was not as fertile and the harvest likely to be inadequate.

Similar stories can be found all around the world. They may be myths, but they provide an echo of how in past times, an old age without children to support you meant destitution and despair. In the Nordic countries, *ättestupa* (in Swedish) is the name of a mythical cliff that elderly people were thrown off, or leapt from, when they were no longer wanted. The most equitable countries of the world today were, a century ago, much like everywhere else, but typically also places with thinner soils, shorter growing seasons and an especially treacherous path into old age. It is no coincidence that Finland was one of the first countries in the world to see the need to systematically address the problem of old-age destitution.

Security in old age

Kela (Kansaneläkelaitos), the Social Insurance Institute of Finland, was founded on 16 December 1937. A contributions-based old age pension scheme began in 1939, but paid out only from 1949. In 1956 it was changed to a means-tested pension, and Kela broadened its services to include wider social security. Today Kela even sends monies abroad to Finnish students studying in other countries. It was established as, and remains, an independent body, but one that works under the supervision of the Finnish parliament. It relies on that parliament to raise the taxes it requires to function (Kela 2018c).

State pensions in Finland are subject to a residency test: all those with a right to be resident in the country are eligible to receive a pension. There is no contributory element. Everyone is entitled, regardless of whether they have paid taxes or not, although length of residency matters. Once you have been resident in Finland for 40 years you are entitled to a full state pension.

If you had moved to Finland 20 years ago from another country at the age of 45, you would be eligible for half the state pension. In 2010 the pensionable age was allowed to increase to take account of increases in life expectancy, but by no more than two months a year, regardless of how quickly life expectancy rises in Finland (see Figure 6.4 at the end of this chapter). The full basic benefit for a single pensioner in 2019 was €634.30 per month, but the Finnish authorities will top up that amount as they guarantee that no pensioner without other sources of income should have to live on less than €784.52 a month, and that top-up rate rises in line with prices (Kela 2019f).

On top of the state pension there are also employer based earnings-related pensions, which are carefully controlled in Finland to ensure they are fairly administered and reliable. Here reliable means ensuring that the provider does not go bust. This is achieved both through government oversight and the way the schemes are devised. The higher your earnings-related pension is, the more is (in effect) deducted from it in the form of a reduction in your basic state pension. This not only ensures that Finland's richer pensioners are not hugely better off than poorer pensioners, but also helps to fund the state pension system itself.

In contrast, in the UK, receipt of the basic state pension requires at least ten years of contributions to National Insurance before any state pension at all can be received. Someone who has paid national insurance contributions by working in the UK for 20 years can expect to receive £418.91 a month, but a full state pension of £730.60 per month requires a minimum of 35 years of payments (UK government 2019). There are minimum income guarantees in place in the UK to ensure no elderly person is utterly destitute, but the entire system is far more complex than in Finland, less generous, and based on a completely different model (see Table 6.1).

In Finland, state pension age is 63 for those born in 1954 or earlier, rising progressively to 65 years for those born in or between 1955 and 1964, with retirement age for those born in or after 1965 linked to future rises in overall national life expectancy (Finnish Centre for Pensions 2018). Finland is doing very well in a context where pensions systems across many countries are now under pressure to reform, in order to address the changing nature of work and the increase in temporary and part-time employment, as well as higher levels of inequality amongst people of working age (OECD 2017a: 16).

In the UK, the state pension age is 65–68, depending on your date of birth (Department for Work and Pensions UK 2017). However, the rate of growth in life expectancy has fallen more in the UK compared to other developed countries (Siddique 2018). This fall, which began for frail elderly women in

Table 6.1: Social statistics concerning old age and poverty in Finland, the UK and the US

		Finland	United Kingdom	United States
Social expenditure % GDP, old age (OECD.Stat 2018b)	**1980**	5.4%	5.3%	6.0%
	2015	11.4%	6.2%	7.1%
Income poverty levels of the elderly (2015), all aged 65+ (OECD 2017a: 135) (Percentage with incomes less than 50% of median household disposable income)		5.2%	13.8%	20.9%
Income poverty levels of the elderly (2015), aged 76+ (Percentage with incomes less than 50% of median household disposable income)		8.5%	18.5%	27.7%
Income poverty levels of the elderly (2015) aged 65+ (Percentage with incomes less than 50% of median household disposable income)	**Men**	3.2%	11.1%	17.2%
	Women	6.8%	16.0%	23.9%

Source: OECD (2017a: 135) and OECD.Stat (2018b).

Note: Around 45 million people in the US are retired and receiving social security payments, less than 14 per cent of the total population. Roughly 12 million people in the UK are aged 65 or over, 18 per cent of the population, and a further quarter of a million UK pensioners live in other EU countries. In comparison, 1.6 million people in Finland receive a pension, 28 per cent of the Finnish population, of whom 58,000 live abroad (Finnish Centre for Pensions 2019).

2014, and then the population as a whole in early 2015, means that by 2018 life expectancy was still below the levels it had reached in 2014 for both men and women (Hiam *et al.* 2020). The past president of the European Public

Health Association, directors of public health, NHS doctors and academics in the UK have "demanded an urgent inquiry into whether austerity policies could be behind a stagnation in life expectancy" (Asthana 2018). No inquiry has happened yet, although one was promised in 2018. Furthermore, income poverty levels for the elderly are higher in the UK than in Finland. According to the OECD, the high levels of poverty among the elderly in the UK can be attributed to the low level of state pensions, which are the lowest among OECD countries despite the "triple lock" that ensures they rise by at least 2.5 per cent a year (OECD 2017b).

In the US the model is even more complex, key decisions are left almost entirely up to individuals to make, and they are expected to finance their own pension arrangements. One report (Dinkin 2018) has stated that the complicated means-testing of state benefits for people in old age ensured that in 2016 in the US, a single pensioner was assured only 17 per cent of the national average wage, or just 25 per cent for a couple (an eighth of average pay each). Another report, using earlier data from 2013, revealed that 85 per cent of older Americans rely on social security benefits, which average $15,132 (at that time £9,852) annually, or 33.7 per cent of the national average US wage (O'Hara 2015).

Most working-class Americans will spend their retirement in destitution. Even some 40 per cent of their middle-class peers face poverty under the current US system "... causing 74 percent of Americans planning to work past traditional retirement age. Additionally, both private and public pension plans have been allowed to become seriously underfunded" (Dinkin 2018).

Life in old age in Finland and England/UK

Finland and the UK appear to be at opposite ends of the spectrum in Europe – and when you compare Finland to the US, it is as if you are comparing life on different planets. Finland is increasingly presented as the most socially progressive of all European states. In August 2018, the UK's Office for National Statistics released a report showing that of the 20 countries it had compared, Finland had seen the greatest improvement in the health of men in the most recent six years (ONS 2018). In great contrast, the UK has seen the worst health decline of any European country in the same period. In Finland by 2017, women's life expectancy had reached 85.6 years and total life expectancy was 81.7 years and rising (Eurostat 2019b).

In the year after 2014, across the UK as a whole life expectancy for both men and women fell, dropping from an average of 81.4 years (for both sexes combined) to 81.0 years in 2015. By 2018, women in the UK had a life expectancy of 82.93 years, and men 79.24 years; but below their 2014 levels (Hiam *et al*. 2020). It is worse still in the US, where average life expectancy has declined fairly continuously since 2014 to reach 78.6 years in 2017 (Bernstein 2018). With comparators such as these in mind, Finland is often presented as the greatest of success stories, and the UK is increasingly seen across Europe as a state that represents failure. But what would it take for the UK to become more like Finland?

In 2012 Ed Miliband, who was then leader of the UK's opposition Labour Party, observed: "If you want the American dream, go to Finland" (Fleetwood 2013). That dream – of opportunity, of a happy life, of the chance to live free and equal, and the ability to enjoy a long and comfortable old age – is, of course, about far more than simply receiving an adequate pension to live on when you can no longer work. It is about the entire environment around you and everyone else that matters, especially in old age. If you live in a country where you have to drive or go online to access the social security system, then what happens once you are too old to drive, or if you have never used the internet, or – like so many people in advanced old age – you have multiple disabilities? What happens if you are afraid and lonely? What happens to you if you are living in a society where people have been brought up not to care, and just to look out for themselves?

Ed Miliband mentioned Finland because he was calling for slight increases in public spending in the UK, at a time when such spending was being cut so severely that it would converge, by 2022, with the incredibly low state spending of the US (Figure 6.2). All countries in the affluent world saw what on the surface appeared to be a dramatic rise in public spending after 2008; but that was because states had to bail out their banks and often GDP at that time fell, so public spending as a proportion of GDP appeared to quickly rise in most countries in 2008 and 2009 due to bank bailout spending. After that different states took differing paths.

When Miliband explained that if you wanted to achieve the American dream then you had to move to Finland, public spending in Finland was rapidly rising toward 58 per cent of its GDP. That rise was Finland's response to the global economic recession that began in 2008. All affluent countries increased their public spending then for the reasons given above, but Finland increased taxation significantly to ensure that public services and state pensions and benefits did not have to fall, or fell only slightly. Since 2014, public expenditure as a proportion of GDP in Finland has reduced to the level of France, hovering slightly over the 50 per cent mark.

Two other countries, Sweden and Germany, are included in Figure 6.2 for comparison. They represent the OECD norm for the more affluent of its member states. In November 2019, Britain's Labour Party presented a manifesto for the December election that included promises to increase public spending in the UK to just below German levels by 2024. This was characterized

Figure 6.2: Public expenditure as percentage of GDP, six countries, 2001–22 (projected)

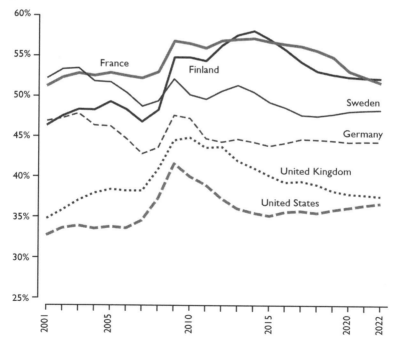

Source: International Monetary Fund (2018).

in almost all of the British media as an incomprehensibly reckless proposal, and Labour lost the 2019 general election, shedding almost one third of their seats in Parliament, albeit with only a small (7.9 per cent) drop in overall support. The winning party, the Conservatives, increased their share of the vote by only 1.3 per cent on 2017, and are likely (pandemic aside) to continue on the low public spending course they were on before (while simultaneously making promises to spend more). As Figure 6.2 makes clear, Finland (and France) are as far above Germany in terms of how much they spend on public services as the UK and US are below Germany. Sweden is almost exactly half-way between Germany and Finland in what it taxes and spends. Before 2008, it was Sweden that taxed and spent more than Finland.

Finntopia is about being better than that German norm, and Finland usually achieves that in a very different way than France does. Nevertheless, and similar to France, there is also a place for traditional labour disputes in Finland. In 2018, there were 128 cases of industrial action and 28 threats of industrial action. A total of 282,096 workers participated, and 214,428 working days were lost. This figure is still lower than the number of working days lost in the years 2000 (253,838), 2005 (672,904), and 2010 (314,667) (OSF 2019f). During this time, as in other European countries such as France, far-right populism has seen electoral success. Back in 2011, when the Finns Party had their first significant gains in electoral support, the most common party from which they took voters was the Social Democratic Party, although they attracted voters from almost all parties apart from the Swedish People's Party (Isotalo *et al.* 2019: 15). A significant proportion of their votes that year, however, also came from people who had not voted the year before.

In Finland, people complained about the small public service cuts that had been made since 2014; in response, in 2019 they elected a government that by June (after convoluted negotiations) was formed of a coalition of the Social Democrats, the Centre Party, the Green League, the Left Alliance and the Swedish People's Party. In contrast, in France with no election scheduled in 2019, people had to take to the streets in violent protest to oppose President Emmanuel Macron's plans to cut state spending.

Although one third of Finns live in the greater metropolitan area in and around Helsinki, the elderly are less likely to do so. Rents are cheaper outside of Helsinki, where the average monthly rent in 2016 was €11.50 per m², compared to €13.65 per m² (or €18.08 in non-subsidized housing) in Greater Helsinki (OSF 2017c). In the same period in central London, average monthly rents were £33 (€39) per m² for a privately rented 2-bed flat (Wainwright 2017). Across Europe as a whole, only Monaco is more expensive than central London, at £45 (€53) per m² (Global Property Guide 2019a). In the most expensive of locations in the US, such as New York City, monthly rents peak at $143 (€129) per m² (Global Property Guide 2019b).

Partly because of affordable property prices, but also because of the leave parents can take from work, Helsinki was ranked the best city in the world for families in 2020: "The Finnish capital was handed the accolade after researchers analysed 150 cities and 16 factors including paid parental leave, high-quality education, healthcare, employment rates and general affordability. And parents living in each location were polled on what they think about where they live. Quebec in Canada comes second in the ranking, Oslo third, and London a lowly 55th, while Los Angeles ranks top for kids' activities." (Thornhill & Kjellsson 2020). However, for children, Helsinki is also a great and incredibly safe city, as is all of Finland; but there is increasing criticism, however, that rent prices in Helsinki are increasingly out of reach for lower-income individuals.

Grandparents in Finland spend a great deal of time with their grandchildren, but much more at weekends or after formal daycare – not as a substitute for daycare. In contrast to Finland, in the UK childcare is often too expensive for many families to use, especially if a parent has two children aged under five. Out of necessity, grandparents often have to undertake regular childcare. Children are often happier playing with other children than only with their grandparents, and grandparents may well find that a playgroup where there are other parents and grandparents is less isolating for them. But in the UK, where social classes find it hard to mix, and in the US, where racial divisions are even more marked, children are very often brought up in isolation from other children and also often live far away from their grandparents.

Long-term cohort studies of the health of children in different countries are beginning to show evidence of the negative impacts of these factors. Equally significantly, the take-up of paternity leave is lower in the UK and US than in Finland. Nevertheless, in Finland men not undertaking paternity leave is seen as more of a problem than it is in the UK. Surveys in the UK indicate that many people are not even aware of parents' right to 18 weeks of shared parental leave per child. This is not surprising, as it is unpaid leave – unlike the five months of paid leave offered in Finland – and so it is unlikely to be a realistic option for many British parents.

In 2019 in Finland the healthcare giant Attendo and nursing home provider Esperi Care made headlines when it became clear that the quality of their services was seriously suffering, in particular because of understaffing (Yle Uutiset 2019d). Legislative chief Vappu Okkeri of the Union of Health and Social Care Professionals noted that issues of negligence were far more common in the private sector than in public services, owing to competitive pressures (Yle Uutiset 2019e). Validia, a private provider of housing to disabled people, has also faced similar allegations (Malin 2019).

Finns, unlike people in the US and the UK, are still surprised by cases of neglect of the elderly in institutions, and neglect of children is incredibly rare. In contrast, in the UK, the number of cases of neglect rose between 2010 and 2019 under the Conservative/Liberal Democrat coalition government and the Conservative government that followed it, as cuts in public spending increased. Cases of neglect deemed worthy of headlines almost always involved deaths, and the reporting of them had no noticeable effect on policy or funding, even when it was revealed that over 1,000 unexplained deaths under the care of just one care provider, Southern Health, had not been investigated (Sambrook & Ryan 2017). Care provision for people with disabilities, including funding, is far more comprehensive in Finland (Info Finland 2018).

Homes and homelessness in Finland

Due to the changing demography, Finland's national housing policy now includes measures to renovate and develop housing for the elderly in order to provide more accessible housing and to allow them to live safely in their own homes for as long as possible (Ministry of the Environment 2013b). In Finland, the generations have much greater choice over whether to live together or separately because the latter is financially feasible and need not require living far away from friends and relatives. As in the rest of Scandinavia, the proportion of Finns who are able to afford to live alone, if they so choose, is very high. In fact, it is amongst the highest in the world, other than in Japan.

Life for the elderly in Finland is very different from that in other affluent nations in many ways – not only in the provision of affordable, convenient housing. For instance, crime rates in Finland are much lower than in other countries. The elderly tend to worry about crime more than other people, but in Finland they have less cause to do so. Nor do Finns encounter homeless people living on the streets, as is now common in UK cities and as has been the case for decades in the US. It was recently pointed out that many homeless people on the streets in the UK are slowly, or more quickly, dying (Kerry 2019). The almost complete absence of street homelessness in Finland has not come about by chance or because of the winter cold; but because people worked hard to combat it.

Thousands of people used to live on the streets in Finland. The depression of the 1990s left a large section of Finnish society unemployed and excluded from working life (THL 2019a). Income inequality and poverty grew as distributive policies were weakened. Despite this, however, Finland has managed to reduce homelessness at the same time as it has increased in almost all other European countries, including, most notably, the UK which has the highest rates in Europe. Only Germany comes close, with the high rates of homelessness among the 1.5 million Syrian refugees now living in the country being considered a special case (OECD 2017c). A tiny proportion of those 1.5 million people are living in tents, like so many homeless people in the UK. Finland leads the way in Europe on homelessness policy with its Housing First approach, which is being copied across the continent and is now being trialled in England, in Liverpool, Manchester and the West Midlands.

Finland's Housing First initiative was introduced in 2008, and is based on the principle that housing is a basic human right. It is a national strategy, with a tripartite approach that has integrated efforts by the state, municipalities, and NGOs (Pleace *et al.* 2015: 17). As a result of these policies, in recent years "... some 12,000 people have found a home" (Y-säätiö 2018). In the 1980s, the homeless were only given social housing and allowed to keep it after they proved that they were rehabilitated, either by stopping drug or alcohol abuse, or ceasing to display violent behaviour. NGOs, like Y-Foundation (Y-Säätiö 2018) bought apartments specifically for homeless people and the state supported the development of new affordable housing units for that purpose.

The Housing First policy deliberately reverses the order in which homeless people's needs are addressed: first giving them somewhere to live, and then providing support services to help with their often complex needs (including mental health, addiction and disabilities) that resulted in them ending up on the street in the first place. The programme has shown that providing housing for the long-term homeless can save as much as €15,000 a year per person. Resources that would otherwise be used to provide a place to sleep overnight can better be utilized for rehabilitation and support. Housing First's aim is to develop societal integration and a long-term way out of homelessness and poverty. Tenants must pay for their housing, and it is their responsibility to arrange their own affairs. Importantly, however, they receive not only financial support, but other practical support and advice, to allow them to do so.

In 2017 there were 6,620 homeless people in Finland, most of whom were concentrated in Helsinki; this was 331 fewer people than in 2016 (Asunto Ensin 2018). By 2018 there were only 5,482 homeless people in Finland, of whom 4,882 lived alone; there were 105 couples and 159 families with children. Fifty-five per cent of all homeless people lived in the Helsinki Metropolitan area. Almost no one sleeps on Finnish streets: partly because of the cold, partly because public toilets are heated, but mainly because of Housing First. In March 2018 it was reported that there were 70 fewer homeless people in Finland, and 150 fewer in long-term homelessness. The number of homeless families decreased from 325 to 214.

In Finland today, 25 per cent of those who are homeless are foreign-born. Youth homelessness has recently increased by 190 people, and long-term homelessness (more than a few days without a home) amongst young people increased by 30 people. Some 84 per cent of homeless people are living temporarily with friends or family (Ara 2018), 10 per cent live in lodging or other facilities, and the remaining 6 per cent live outdoors, in staircases, or in shelters. Unlike Finland, the UK has no reliable figures for homelessness because adults without accommodation who don't have children or a specific disability or vulnerability are not considered in need of state support. In an international review, it was noted that "more recent data (beyond 2003/4) on homelessness service activity in England are incomplete, as government funding for data collection has been withdrawn, and now represent only a large sample of homelessness services" (Pleace *et al.* 2015: 54).

The UK charity Shelter estimated in 2018 that at least 320,000 people were living in (usually unsatisfactory) temporary accommodation or emergency hostels, or sleeping on the streets (Richardson 2018). In 2019 there were 84,740 households (up 77 per cent from 2010) living in government funded temporary accommodation in England. These households included 126,020 children and were mostly housed in exorbitantly expensive and extraordinarily unsatisfactory bed and breakfast style accommodation (Wilson & Barton 2019). Rough sleepers are visible in considerable numbers in all large UK cities. During 2019, the situation worsened further across the country (Brimblecombe *et al.* 2019). The Housing First project and Finland's decisive drive to tackle rough sleeping and homelessness have proved to be so effective that Finland is now the sole EU country where homelessness is both very low and falling.

Old age, immigration, emigration and minority groups

Finland's population last shrank in 1969 and 1970 due to emigration. For decades and centuries before that, large-scale emigration prevented significant population growth and any immigration was largely the return of former ex-pats. The emigration rate eventually slowed down, and from the 1980s onwards there has generally been a net gain in migration to Finland.

Because of its past high fertility rate, Finland did not need immigrants to sustain its workforce, including those who care for the elderly and provide health services. But following the dramatic fall in the fertility rate that occurred in all affluent countries, and which began in Finland in the 1960s, the rising number of foreigners coming to Finland since the 1990s has compensated for the demographic deficit (Figure 6.3). Although this was not the outcome of policy, greater in-migration almost always happens in times and places where there is a growing demand for people.

For some of the older generation, adapting to a more diverse Finland has been difficult. This is a common experience across Europe, where older people tend to be more conservative and more anti-immigrant, even as services provided for the elderly are increasingly reliant on the labour of immigrants; as is evident across the health services, social work, and care home provision. Racism can be just as easily found in Finland as elsewhere in Europe.

Because of its migration history, Finland today is less culturally diverse than many other European countries. In 2016, there were 364,787 foreign citizens in Finland, or just under 7 per cent of the population. As in almost any country, it is possible to be classified as foreign even if you were born in Finland, but that is rare. Nearly all of the 7 per cent were born outside of Finland. Finland also has its own significant ethnic minority populations born within the country, including more than 10,000 Roma in the south and west and 9,350 Sámi, who live mainly in the far north. Like immigrants in general, and refugees in particular, significant minorities in Finland also currently experience social integration difficulties.

Figure 6.3: Foreign citizens in Finland, 1870–2015

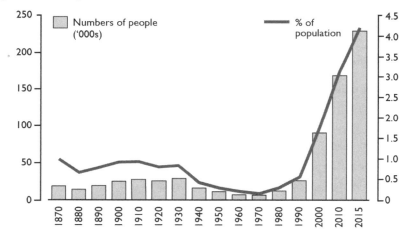

Source: Anttosen (2015).

Roma people in Finland are native Finns, but are sometimes treated as if they are foreigners. They have been in Finland since the latter half of the sixteenth century. Roma are spread mostly around the south of the country, and now live mainly in the larger cities. They are a recognized, protected ethnic minority, but experience measurable socio-economic inequality in relation to education, employment, housing and health – including using health and maternity services less than the general population (THL 2018a).

The Sámi are Finland's indigenous people (THL 2019b). Their linguistic and cultural rights are protected in constitutional law; including Sámi district and language law, the Non-Discrimination Act, and in various international human rights agreements. However, Finland has yet to ratify the International Labour Organisation (ILO) Indigenous and Tribal Peoples Convention No. 169 from 1989, owing largely to its implications for land management (Government Communications Department 2017). Their traditional way of life, including reindeer herding, fishing and handicrafts, their diet, exercise, and strong cultural identity has been noted to protect them against certain diseases such as cancer and cardiovascular disease. However, their rapid transition to a western lifestyle has brought negative consequences for the overall health of the Sámi population.

The limited research that has been carried out to date suggests that mental health problems and other physical diseases have increased in recent decades among Sámi people, including higher suicide rates among younger reindeer-herding Sámi. The National Institute for Health and Welfare attributes this to the lack of psychosocial services and the tendency among Sámi people to not seek professional help. The almost total destruction of a traditional way of life has been identified as the fundamental underlying cause. Although the Sámi receive social and health services in their own languages, these are currently judged to be insufficient compared to what is provided for the rest of the Finnish population. The structure of the Finnish welfare system has recently been reviewed by the National Institute for Health and Welfare and found to be inappropriate for the needs of the Sámi people.

Threats: suicide, speeding cars, alcohol and other addictions

Car accidents and suicide pose an increased threat to people as they age. In the UK and the US, the most common cause of death of those aged 15–24 is being hit by a car. From 30 onwards, suicide becomes the most common cause, and after 45 it is a heart attack. Suicide is the second most common cause of death of children in the age groups 11–16, and young adults aged 17–19 and 20–24 in Britain (Dorling 2011).

The popular perception is that Finland has a high suicide rate; but that description was significantly more accurate in the bleaker past. Its suicide rate shrunk rapidly from the 1990s to 2015, but increased slightly in 2016–17.

Finns monitor the numbers carefully. There were 14 fewer suicides in 2018 than in 2017. As we write in February 2020 the figure for 2019 has yet to be released. Suicide in Finland is less disguised than in countries such as the UK where many suicides are recorded as "accidental deaths"; and it is well below that of the country with the worst rate in Europe, France. It is the old and the young who are most at risk from speeding cars because both groups find it harder to judge the speed of a car moving towards them and both tend to be frailer and smaller in size and weight than mid-life adults. In 2016 in Finland, road fatalities were 5.0 per 100,000 motor vehicles. The equivalent figure for the UK was 5.7, while in the US it was 14.2. In Sweden, whose policies are built around reaching zero road deaths in the very near future, the rate is now 4.6. Switzerland currently has the lowest road death rate in the world per vehicle (3.7), and Norway has the lowest rate in the world per vehicle kilometre travelled (Wikipedia 2019a). Norway, Sweden and Switzerland protect lives by levying very high speeding fines, with fines proportional to drivers' income and the extent to which the speed limit is broken.

This policy has made international headlines. In 2002 Nokia executive Anssi Vanjoki was fined €116,000 for driving his Harley Davidson motorbike at 75km/h (47mph) in a 50km/h zone. Reima Kuisla, a Finnish millionaire, was handed a speeding ticket of €54,024 for driving at 103km/hr (64mph) in an 80km/h area. His fine was calculated based on his income in 2013 of €6,555,742. Following an appeal, however, Kuisla paid only €5,346 but through posts on Facebook, he continued to call it a punishment for his success, suggesting that: "Finland is now an impossible country to live in for people with a large income and wealth". Kuisla warned that taxpayers would leave if Finland continued taxing the wealthy and that tax revenue would decrease in the long-term (BBC News 2015). Kuisla still lives in Finland.

Of course, Finland has plenty of vices. It is well known for high rates of alcohol abuse and gambling, although, as we mentioned in Chapter 3, gambling is now under better control (see also Gillin 2018; *The Economist* 2019). In the wake of a steep increase between 1968 and 2008, alcohol consumption has fallen by nearly a fifth since 2007 (Suomenash 2019). Some 13 per cent of Finnish drinkers, however, consume so much that it is deemed detrimental to their long-term health, and 78 per cent of total alcohol consumption is identified as being at the hazardous level (THL 2018b).

Spirits can be purchased only at state-owned Alko stores. Although national policy remains focused on reducing the negative social and health impacts of alcohol, legislation that came into force in 2018 allows retail stores to sell alcoholic beverages with up to 5.5 per cent alcohol by volume (a rise from 4.7 per cent by volume limits) and permits bars and restaurants to advertise "happy hour" discounts (Ministry of Social Affairs and Health 2018). Serious crime in Finland is generally very rare; although minor crimes, many of them alcohol-related, are not, and the Finns are as assiduous as the South Koreans at recording minor crimes (Dorling 2017: figure 4.12).

In 2017 in Finland, the average daily prison population was just 2,884 people, including 203 women and just 95 prisoners aged under 21 (Criminal Sanctions Agency 2018). In England and Wales, that figure was 84,399, or 29 times higher (Ministry of Justice *et al*. 2017). This included about 4,200 women and 4,900 people under 21 (Sturge 2019). The population of England and Wales is only ten times greater than Finland's, so Finns are three times less likely than English or Welsh people to have a child or other relative in prison, almost never a daughter, and virtually never a relative under 21.

Even including those detained pre-trial or on remand, only 213 women were in prison in Finland in 2018, and only three people aged under 18. In contrast, 2.1 million people were in prison in 2016 in the US, rising to 2.3 million in 2018, including more than 200,000 women in prison at any one time and 63,000 people aged under 18. The total population of the United States is only 60 times that of Finland, which is similar in population to many US states. The statistics for Finland are exact, whereas for the US they are only rough estimates and often out of date (World Prison Brief 2019).

Murder is rare in the UK, because there are so few guns. Murder is equally uncommon in Finland, where there are far more guns. UK data show that young men are the most common victims of homicides, and children and people in their later mid-life the least likely to be murdered. Murders of elderly people are somewhat more common, with murder rates for male victims in their nineties being higher than in their eighties or seventies. For women, the chance of being murdered is very low, but it is higher in their seventies than at any point other than in their twenties (Dorling 2006). In Britain, alcohol is involved in half of all murders, and it is even more frequently involved in murders in Finland.

147

In Finland, male, socially excluded alcoholics are the most likely victims and perpetrators of homicides. As Finnish policies addressing alcohol abuse have become increasingly effective, a higher proportion of such victims are elderly, especially men, according to the Ministry of the Interior (2019a). In both Finland and the UK, the homicide rate is 1.2 per 100,000 people per year, while it is 5.3 in the US (UNODC 2017). The Ministry of the Interior identifies alcoholism as the primary reason for Finland's higher homicide rate than those of other Nordic countries (the comparable figures are 1.1 in Sweden and 0.5 in Norway, although Denmark matches Finland at 1.2).

Homicide rates, suicide rates and accidental deaths involving firearms are much higher in Finland than in most other affluent countries. Although they are still far below the US (where 12.21 people per 100,000 die from these causes per year), among high-income countries Finland (at 3.25 per 100,000) ranks above Sweden (1.6), Norway (1.75), Denmark (1.47), and the UK (0.23) (World Population Review 2019). One reason these rates are higher in Finland is that there are far more guns in Finland.

Due in part to the legacy of Finland's wartime and rural past there are far more guns and gun-owners in Finland than in other European countries: 1.5 million licensed firearms, and over 600,000 licence holders (Ministry of the Interior 2019b). Many gun-owners are elderly and most are men, with the vast majority of weapons used for hunting. However, some 200,000 of those firearms are handguns (Sandell & Tebest 2016). With licences becoming more expensive and regulations tightening, fewer are now being issued. In order to obtain a gun licence, Finns must first undergo extensive background checks, interviews and aptitude tests. The police registry is checked daily to see if anyone arrested for acts of violence or acts involving substance abuse holds a gun licence; if so, the gun is confiscated. Per gun, the murder rate in Finland is extremely low.

Healthcare

The publicly run health system in Finland is decentralized across its municipalities, of which there were 310 in 2020. Half of the municipalities have fewer than 6,000 residents (so those areas often cooperate) and only 107 are towns or cities. The country has some of the best health outcomes in the world, including the lowest infant mortality rate ever recorded for a nation state: "In 2015, the infant mortality rate was 1.7 deaths per 1,000 live births: only 97 children died during their first year of life. This was the lowest figure ever recorded in Finland [and for any nation state to date]" (THL 2017).

The national health service in Finland works alongside a heavily state-subsidized, semi-private system of physicians and hospitals (Saltman & Teperi 2016). The main channel of funding is public. Service vouchers for private care are provided by Kela when the waiting lists are too long in the public sector (Pantsu 2017). By agreement all patients have to be able to access care within three months of having their needs evaluated, with the starting date for that limit being within three days of first calling the doctor. Some employers offer private healthcare insurance (Kallio 2008: 478).

The average waiting time for non-urgent care across health services in Helsinki was 16 days, as recorded on 4 June 2018. Waiting times ranged nationally from 2 days in the neighbourhood of Laajasalo (an island to the east of Helsinki) to 35 days in Kontula which is a suburb to its north east (City of Helsinki 2018). People who are unemployed are more likely to experience (slightly) longer waiting times, because employed people have access to occupational healthcare or can afford semi-private healthcare (OECD/European Observatory on Health Systems and Policies 2017). Despite the complexity of the system (Miettinen 2018), health outcomes in Finland are excellent and are still rapidly improving (see Figure 6.4). This can be attributed to the speed with which patients are seen, diagnosed and treated, which has been shown to lead to better health outcomes in any setting.

Figure 6.4 shows the changes in life expectancy in four European countries since 1993 through to 2017. Finland rose from being 26th highest in the world in 2016 to 24th highest in 2017 (Country Economy 2019; Eurostat 2019b). People now live longer in Finland than in New Zealand (which is now 25th highest), Belgium (26th), Greece (27th) and the UK. The UK has now fallen to 28th place in the world life expectancy ranking and is expected to fall further down the ranks in the near future. It now has the worst postwar record of any western European country (Hiam *et al.* 2020).

Life expectancy is falling in the UK mainly because mortality rates for the elderly are rising, but a very small part of the reason is the absolute rise in infant mortality in the UK since 2015. In contrast, by 2015 Finland had

Figure 6.4: Life expectancy in Ireland, the UK, Norway and Finland, 1993–2017

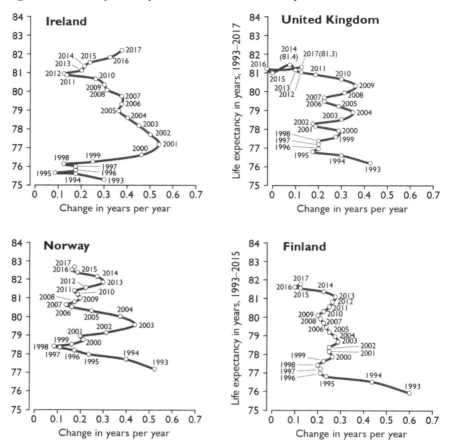

Source: updated version of a figure originally published in Dorling & Rigby (2019).

Note: life expectancy is shown on the vertical axis and the rate of improvement is shown on the horizontal axis. In Finland it has risen by almost a fifth of a year every year since 1995.

already achieved the highest survival rates for newborn babies of any large country in Europe, and in the world, with a neonatal (first four weeks of life) mortality rate of only 1.3 per 1,000 births. In 1990 Finland ranked fourth in Europe just behind Germany, Sweden and France. It is now a safer place to give birth than any of those countries. In 1990 the UK ranked seventh best, just below Denmark and above the Netherlands. By 2015, 18 EU countries had a better neonatal mortality rate than the UK (ONS 2017). After that point, neonatal mortality rates actually began to rise in the UK.

The US, where men and women combined lived to 78.6 years on average in 2017 (Bernstein 2018) now ranks 37th in the world for life expectancy, and its rank is dropping as the health of its people fails. It is now below Slovenia (29th), Costa Rica (32nd), Cuba (33rd), Lebanon (34th) and Chile (35th). The US has an almost identical life expectancy to one of the poorest European countries of all – Albania (38th) and will soon be overtaken by it, and by Turkey (39th) Estonia (40th), Qatar (41st) and Panama (42nd), if current trends for US life expectancy continue; all before the 2020 pandemic struck.

In Norway today, life expectancy is 82.7 years, 4.1 years higher than the US and exactly one year more than in Finland. In 1993, Norway was furthest ahead of all the four countries shown in Figure 6.4 with men and women (combined) expecting, on average, to live to 77.2 years at that time. Norway's life expectancy was also rising at a remarkable six months per year at that point, but it was rising even faster in Finland where, at that time, it was below all the other countries shown in the figure except for Ireland. Indeed, Ireland has seen the greatest increase in life expectancy between 1993 and 2017 – a total rise of almost seven years, or 15 weeks a year. The second highest increase was for Finland, at almost six years. The third was Norway, at 5.5 years. Fourth was the UK with only 5.1 years, averaging 11 more weeks a year – until the year 2015.

Finland does not spend that much on healthcare – just 9.5 per cent of GDP in 2017 – a proportion as low as the UK, which spends less than most affluent European countries (OECD.Stat 2018b); and almost half of what is spent in the US. Finland does not need to spend too much because its population is healthier (less obese, with better mental health, and happier) than in other countries, thanks to the positive public policies that start with decent maternity care and later include good food at school and outdoor play as routine; and because it does not have a large private healthcare market whose costs must be considered in international comparisons. Despite not spending more than the UK does on health, in Finland there are eight doctors for every seven doctors in England: 3.2 per 1,000 people as compared to 2.8 (OECD. Stat 2018c).

Doctors are not paid as much in Finland as they are in England or the US (or as in much of the rest of Europe). The lower cost of living in Finland does not require salaries in the public sector to reach the same levels as elsewhere. Fewer elderly people – the most significant group in need of healthcare – live in poverty in Finland, and poverty exacerbates ill-health. Interestingly, in the 1970s, the UK used to pay NHS doctors half as much as it does today in real terms, but back then the UK was a far more equitable set of nations by income inequality and the doctors were among the top 1 per cent of earners. High and rising economic inequality makes providing healthcare far more expensive.

Despite not spending more than the UK on health, Finland still has 50 per cent more hospital beds available for its population: 397 for every 100,000 people as compared to 258 in the UK (Eurostat 2018b). This greater number of beds also means that there is less need to hurry patients out of beds before they are better, or before support services can be properly organized. The average length of stay in a hospital in Finland is 8.3 days per patient as compared to 6.8 days in the UK (Eurostat 2018c). In the US, hospital treatment for the uninsured is simply not available unless it is a life-threatening emergency, and even then people try to avoid going, so great is the fear of medical bills which can often lead to bankruptcy.

Although the general health of the Finnish population has improved according to the National Institute for Social Services and Welfare, inequalities in health based on socio-economic status have widened in recent years (Rotko *et al*. 2011). Finland has been criticized by some groups within the country for failing to invest as much in health as it does in education. The 1990s depression led to a weakened decentralized healthcare system, because decreased funding failed to keep pace with need. The Global Financial Crisis of 2008 also contributed to a decline in public spending on health, despite the overall rise in public spending shown in Figure 6.2 (OECD/European Observatory on Health Systems and Policies 2017).

There is a concern within Finland that the groups that need health services the most do not use them because they do not trust their organization or officials, or find them inaccessible (Kivimäki 2017). In a 2013 study of 51,400 women and 53,400 men, 44 per cent of unemployed men had not used health services within the past year (Hetemaa *et al*. 2018: 11). Reform has to be considered as inevitable – but of course there are many directions reforms can take (Jokinen 2018).

There are already modest user fees for some services, decided on at municipal level, although taxes largely subsidize service costs and some are means-tested (Social Services and Healthcare Division 2020). Ultimately the goal is to make the Finnish health system fairer, as inequalities in health based on socio-economic status have slightly widened in recent years (Rotko *et al*. 2011), but the issue is more complex than this. An ageing population means that the demand for health services is increasing, but the supply of healthcare professionals and the population that primarily forms the tax base to support the system are both decreasing (Øvretvei 2003). Of course, greater immigration can bring in more younger healthcare workers and a rejuvenation of the economy.

In 2018, the Finnish government reached a consensus on the need for reform of its healthcare system, along with the IMF, the EU, and the OECD (Ministry of Finance and Ministry of Social Affairs and Health 2018). By that point, three successive governments had attempted to implement a regional government, social and healthcare reform, known as Sote, in the face of repeated delays and lengthy debate, and intensified by citizens' concerns over potentially worsening services.

Just before the 2019 elections, Juha Sipilä's cabinet resigned en masse after promising but failing to implement their planned reforms. The issue is sometimes referred to as Finland's Brexit, with widespread "Sote fatigue" brought about by the many policy complications that make it difficult to understand, and the fact that it has not yet been implemented.

The threat of privatization

The possibility of an increased role for the private sector in Finland's healthcare provision is particularly contentious. The Hospital District of Helsinki openly questioned the wisdom of plans for more privatization. The Global Burden of Disease study, financed by the Bill and Melinda Gates Foundation, recently ranked the Finnish healthcare system sixth, the UK's 23rd, and the US system 29th of 88 countries (Kontula 2018). Moreover, the US was found to have the most expensive healthcare system in the world, with a cost-per-person close to €6,900 a year, compared with Finland's €2,800 (Yle Uutiset 2018e). The Hospital District of Helsinki said "the difference in price proves that market-driven, commercial health services are not at the same level as a publicly organized one".

The UK's National Health Service and the recently reformed Swedish model were used as examples of increased freedom of choice in service provision; however, the chair of the Swedish Left Party, Jonas Sjösted, warned that freedom of choice in his country had led to excessive supply in well-off areas. In England (but not Scotland, and less so in Wales and Northern Ireland), private companies have made massive profits from increasing healthcare privatization. Many of the politicians supporting these reforms would appear to have been less than impartial in the outcome. Lists of the members of the House of Commons and the House of Lords with personal financial interests in private healthcare were published at the time of the 2012 Health and Social Care Act, and then again following the election of a Conservative government in 2019, with many of the cohort of new Conservative MPs having close links to the private health sector.

Issues of healthcare reform have dogged recent Finnish prime ministers, being a key reason as to why Juha Sipilä's government resigned in 2019 (Niemelä 2019a). He was succeeded by Antti Rinne who had been leader of the Social Democratic Party since 2014 and served as Prime Minster only from June 2019 to December 2019 after which both men were replaced by women. Sanna Marin of the Social Democratic Party became prime minster (the youngest ever Finnish prime minster and until 7 January 2020 she was the youngest serving state leader). Juha Sipilä was replaced as leader of the Centre Party first by Katri Kulmuni and then by Annika Saarikko.

In Sipilä's government, the National Coalition Party and the Centre Party had reached a compromise between greater freedom of choice (increasing the role of the private sector) and reorganizing the responsibility of providing social and healthcare services from municipalities to new larger, self-governing counties. The Centre Party, unlike the National Coalition Party, is part of the 2020 coalition (Kangas & Kalliomaa 2018; Sutinen 2019). Finland's sparsely populated yet very large geographic area has always made organizing public services difficult.

The burden of successfully bringing about healthcare reform then became the responsibility of the new government, formed in June 2019 (Niemelä 2019b). At the time of writing, no reforms have been passed, but new goals have been introduced, including reducing waiting times to a week, continuing with the division into counties, reducing the role of the private sector from that proposed in the Sipilä government's plan, and bringing doctors back to the public sector from the private sector (Tikkala & Pilke 2019).

The reform currently under consideration also intends to provide better services for issues that require the cooperation of social and healthcare services, such as domestic abuse. The private sector's resources still are needed, but must be better integrated in a way that maintains public authorities (the counties) as decision-makers and prevents profit-making becoming the driver in the decisions of healthcare providers (Merikanto 2019). This latest plan has already been postponed to 2021, and the Green League, Left Alliance, and the Social Democratic Party in the new government are highly critical of market-based approaches to Sote reform. The primary advocate for market-based approaches is the National Coalition Party, which is no longer in the governing coalition. Aino-Kaisa Pekonen of the Left Alliance has been Minster of Social Affairs and Health since December 2019 and is a trained nurse. In the next chapter we turn to the building of consensus politics in Finland which has achieved so much, but does so in such complex ways.

Conclusion: a beacon of hope

Today, Finland has one of Europe's highest levels of health and living standards for the elderly. Finns may not yet be the world's longest-lived people, but they are experiencing one of the greatest sustained improvements in life expectancy anywhere on earth. As Figure 6.4 shows, the greatest change came in the 1990s when the rate of improvement in Finland was even faster than that of Norway, despite the worsening economic situation in Finland at the time.

Life expectancy is affected by what happens to people throughout their lives. Many of the elderly in Finland today grew up in poverty and that will have had life-long negative effects on their health. Today, even among the elderly, poverty is very rare in Finland, much rarer than in other European countries, and this has been achieved without the advantages of huge reserves of oil, such as Norway has. In future we should expect Finland to see even greater gains in health and life expectancy, as the young, who have had a much better start than their grandparents, grow old, and as migration to Finland increases. It was migration that contributed to Ireland's dramatic increase in life expectancy in recent years (as shown in Figure 6.4), as the composition of its population changed. Most migrants who are migrating for work are much healthier than the population they join. Finland can also expect to see future older generations age better and live longer, as they will have had a childhood and mid-life largely free of poverty.

Finland is the best place to be born in the world in terms of neonatal mortality rates and care in the first few years of life, in terms of the schooling that comes after that, and an inclusive university education and inclusive workplaces where all are respected and trusted far more than anywhere else in the world. The young people of Finland do not have to fear homelessness or being unable to find a decent home to live in, and they can expect to grow old in a society in which equality is now inculcated. Grandparents and great-grandparents in Finland today deserve to be very proud of what they, more than anyone else, and for a more sustained length of time than anyone else, have achieved.

PART III

The future

In this final section of *Finntopia*, we begin with politics and populism, looking at how turnout in elections varies among affluent countries and across the states of the United States. Finland, alongside other more equitable countries, has relatively high voter turnout – and it has been rising in recent years. However, voter participation is still lower than in Norway, Sweden, Denmark and the Netherlands. Politics in Finland is complex, with coalition governments made up of many political parties, and voter fatigue is common.

As we write, in early 2020, the country is governed by a very new, politically progressive coalition made up of a diverse group of parties. To explain how this happened, in Chapter 7 we have redrawn a complex political-space map originally disseminated by the Finnish state broadcaster Yleisradio Oy (Yle) in April 2019. That political map helped explain the positions of political parties' candidates on a number of issues. We end by mapping the results of the most recent general election over population-space using a population cartogram.

In Chapter 8, we focus on demography and the environment. We begin by depicting how birth and death rates in Finland have varied from 1749 through to the present day, not only highlighting the impacts of famine and war, but also showing how, since 2014, death rates have consistently exceeded birth rates. Next, we consider the fall in fertility over the past century, and then the fall in migration to Finland in the early 1990s and its rise in the twenty-first century. Today net in-migration is the only reason that the population of Finland is not falling. We show where migrants to Finland have come from, and then link all of this to the major environmental challenges being faced by Finland – and the world – today. In matters of environmental action, Finland punches well above its weight.

Chapter 9, on future challenges and success fatigue, begins with the concerns of young people who are suffering or struggling. Mental health is a problem in Finland, but worldwide only Denmark has a smaller percentage of young people who say they are not thriving mentally. Finland is also ranked as the most politically stable country in the world; has the second most trusted press in the world, after that of the Netherlands; and ranks as one of the happiest countries in the world – the ranking in which Finland excelled in both 2018 and 2019 – and again in 2020.

We end by considering long-term trends in the income of Finland's best-off 1 per cent, showing how its share of income shrank in the 1970s to become one of the lowest in the world in the early 1980s, then rose somewhat to peak around the year 2000, fell with the global financial crash of 2008, and is now falling once again. We close with a discussion of Finland's future.

The leaders of Finland's five coalition parties in power in December 2019. This image was widely circulated in a popular tweet, that "went viral" upon Sanna Marin becoming prime minister on 10 December 2019. People around the world immediately commented on all five being women and four being in their early thirties.

Source: Tuomas Niskakangas (2019), Tweet with the caption: "Finland's government is now led by these five party leaders"; https://twitter.com/hashtag/newgeneration?src=hash (8 December).

7

Politics and populism

"I have lived in a welfare state and am grateful for how society gave me
support in the tough times of my life."

Sanna Marin, just before becoming the world's
youngest serving prime minister at 34 years old
on 8 December 2019, quoted in de Fresnes (2019)

Introduction

In 2019, Finnish politics made international headlines twice. The first time
was when the Social Democratic Party won the most votes in the April 2019
general election (*The Guardian* 2019; Duxbury 2019) and the second was after
the prime minister and the Minister for Local Government and Ownership
Steering resigned over issues involving a postal strike and his successor,
Sanna Marin, became the world's youngest serving prime minister on 10
December 2019 (see Chapter 3). Her appointment meant that the country
was governed by a coalition of five female-led parties.

Finland was flatteringly profiled as a hotbed of progressive politics and
policies by newspapers such as *The Guardian* and *The New York Times*, and
by politicians including Hillary Clinton. The hosts for the podcast for the
newspaper *Helsingin Sanomat*, "Uutisraportti", ended their weekly broadcast
on a gleeful note about the attention Finland was attracting in the wake of
Marin's appointment. It was unbelievable and exciting, they exclaimed, that
William Barr, the US's Donald Trump-appointed attorney general, had asked

the visiting Finnish Justice Minister, Anna-Maija Henriksson, for her views on the new prime minister (Peltomäki 2019). Barr wasn't the only American to want to know more about Henriksson's homeland: when she visited a US prison, the inmates asked her about politics in Finland.

Politics is important to the story of Finland's success because effective social policy and the welfare state were the outcome of choices and policies made by government. Of course, Finland's politicians have not always made the right decisions: as we've discussed in Chapter 6, lawmakers are still grappling with the thorny issue of social and healthcare reform. Nevertheless, Finland's politicians did succeed in setting the country on a successful path to economic development following the Second World War via significant state intervention in the economy, setting a precedent for governments in the decades that followed. Elected representatives persevered through lengthy and complex debates on reforming education throughout the 1950s and 1960s, and since. They would also create a policy for tackling homelessness, Housing First, that has outlasted the government that approved it in 2011 (Y-Foundation 2017: 112). The success of Housing First was confirmed by an international review (Pleace *et al.* 2015: 3) and said to be due to "... decisive moments of commitment and shared will..." by the leading political parties in Matti Vanhanen's cabinet, and their provision of reliable national funding.

Government services are financed through tax, which in turn depends on the Finnish people's trust that their taxes will be spent on services that directly and indirectly benefit them. Trust in political and public institutions is a cornerstone of Nordic societies. It promotes both a greater readiness and willingness to support the state, through paying taxes; and an understanding of the types of public spending that can be most (and least) efficient. Political trust, and general agreement on political issues between the electorate and the elected (responsiveness) further facilitates difficult political decision-making and the acceptance of those decisions during economic and political crises (Kestilä-Kekkonen & Vento 2019: 18).

Political trust can be an ambiguous concept, but this chapter will lean on one provided in governmental research, with numerous academic contributors, which understands it in "terms of [the] support for the political system, accompanied by trust in politicians and confidence in institutions" with natural fluctuations which can lead sceptical citizens to occasionally call for renewal, which is beneficial for democracy (Kestilä-Kekkonen & Vento 2019: 31). The perception that inequality is increasing can lead to a fall in trust and a rise in doubts over state institutions and their effectiveness. A state which has become stronger through its emphasis on equality and inclusivity – concentrating on the right of all individuals to participate and influence the direction of society – can easily flounder if people believe that self-interested groups are gaining undue influence, especially if they are thought to be receiving more than their fair share of funding.

The political system and elections in Finland

As mentioned in the introductory chapter of this book, Finland's parliament is unicameral (having one chamber of government), and the national constitution was amended at the turn of the twenty-first century to restrict presidential powers. However, whoever is president still has a significant role in foreign policy and national security matters. There are four types of national elections held in Finland: parliamentary, presidential, European and local (Parliament of Finland 2019c). Some 200 representatives are elected in parliamentary elections every four years, usually on the third Sunday of April, unless a parliament resigns earlier.

There are 13 electoral districts in Finland and the number of parliamentary seats afforded to each is proportionate to their populations, assessed six months before each election. In addition, one parliamentary seat is allotted to the Åland islands, an autonomous, Swedish-speaking province in the Baltic Sea. Local elections, divided by municipality, are also held every four years. They used to be held on the third Sunday of October, a year and a half after parliamentary elections, but the 2016 elections were moved to the spring of 2017 and henceforth are held during the spring (Solla & Palmén-Väisänen 2017). Presidential elections are held every six years on the fourth Sunday of January and are based on a direct popular vote. If no candidate achieves a simple majority in the first round, a second round is held two weeks later.

The Finnish system requires a high level of trust to operate well, not least because it does not have a second parliamentary chamber, or many of the checks and balances that are commonplace in other western democracies.

In a series of European Social Surveys from 2004 to 2017 that measured political trust across 32 European countries, Finland on average ranked sixth highest for trust. Despite some variation in levels of trust in governments during some years, general levels of trust in government as a whole have been steady.

Figure 7.1 shows that electoral turnout in Finland is not as high as in many other reasonably equitable countries – such as Sweden, Denmark, Norway, the Netherlands, Switzerland and Luxembourg. In general, turnout is closely related to how equitable a country is, or how equitable it was when most voters were growing up. People who have voted once in their lives are much more likely to vote again. In Finland's most recent general election (held in April 2019), voter turnout rose to be more in line with international trends by rates of economic equality.

The outliers in Figure 7.1, countries such as Australia and Singapore, have various mechanisms to compel people to vote. In general people are more easily dissuaded from voting in more economically unequal countries and more unequal states of the US. In the US, a significant minority of people are not allowed to vote, for instance many who have been convicted of a crime or do not have the correct identification papers (often discriminating against poorer black voters).

In the 2019 Finnish general election, 72.8 per cent of the electorate voted. In 1908 the turnout had been 69 per cent for men and 60 per cent for women, but by 1960 this gender gap had disappeared. Between 1954 and 1983, turnout was usually over 80 per cent, falling to just below 70 per cent from 1999 to 2007 (OSF 2007). It is probably no coincidence that 1983 was a year of very low inequality in Finland (see Figure 9.4). Turnout at elections in Finland is currently on the rise as economic inequality falls again. Figure 7.1 uses 1983 as the year in which inequality is measured because that is the year for which estimates for US states are most reliable, but it also gives a useful impression of what the long-term effects of factors such as high economic equality might be on voting turnout later in life.

Political scandals in most democracies have an impact on both levels of trust and electoral turnout. There is now growing support for providing more opportunities for citizens' direct participation in politics, such as via "citizens' initiatives" to debate certain issues, rather than relying solely

Figure 7.1: Inequality and electoral turnout, 2016–19

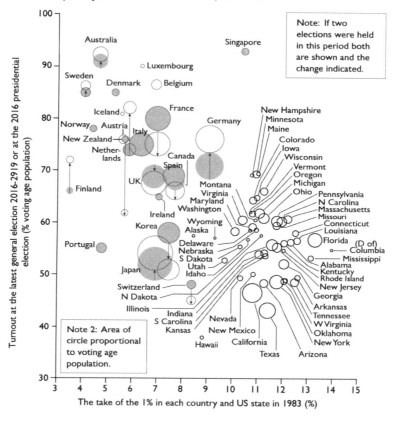

Source: World Wealth and Income database; turnout data from www.electionguide.org and "The United States Election Project, 2016 November General Election results".

Note: inequality data is calculated as the percentage share of income of the top 1 per cent measured in 1983; estimated for Luxembourg from 1985, and in Belgium and Iceland from 1990.

on the traditional model of representative democracy. However, one very recent Finnish government publication about political trust noted that an increasing idealization of participatory and deliberative democracy may be unhelpful and that "more direct citizen involvement [...] is unlikely to solve the long-term dilemmas [such as an ageing population] facing many advanced representative democracies" (von Schoultz 2019: 62, 75). This conclusion stems from the concern that despite popular support for the idea of direct citizen involvement, citizens who were not involved in such bodies would be "sceptical or even resentful" of their fellow citizens and the process itself.

Recent Finnish government research found that the people most inclined to oppose increasing citizen participation tended to hold right-wing views and support increased technocratic decision-making instead. Finns Party supporters typically did not support increased citizen participation (Von Schoultz 2019: 72). Those on the left were more supportive of citizen participation, which is in line with their history of collective mobilization to advance workers' rights.

Although the National Coalition Party and Centre Party are traditional bourgeois parties, and the Social Democratic Party was founded as the workers' party, people also now tend to be suspicious of what they see as the political elite in general: the traditional parties on both the left and right, the National Coalition Party, the Social Democratic Party and Centre Party. Furthermore, one of the contributors (von Schoultz 2019: 74) concluded that individuals' view of the ideal form of political decision-making largely depends on their values and on their opinion of contemporary democratic processes, and so unanimity will never be reached – "the creation of a political system that fulfils all wishes and expectations is complete utopia" (translated). Controversy surrounding the participatory budgeting process in Helsinki in 2019 is one example we were told of more than once while researching this book.

So how will Finnish politics cope with some of the most pressing issues the country faces in the near future? It has long been acknowledged by policy-makers, industry, academics and most lawmakers that Europe needs migrants to address its shrinking working-age population (UN 2000). Finland's overall population has aged more slowly thanks to the influx of younger migrants in recent years. Whether this rise in immigration will precipitate adverse political outcomes has yet to be seen, but in the short term, and given the results of Finland's most recent 2019 election, the critics who suggested that Finland would not be able to adjust have been disproven. However, the issue of immigration in Finland has certainly contributed to political tensions.

Political parties in Finland in context

Political spectrums across countries can be difficult to compare and are heavily affected by national histories. Understanding these spectrums has grown more challenging, as many parties are no longer differentiated by clear and obvious social groups such as class, wealth, religion, or ethnicity. This is seen in the increased popularity of the Green League and the Finns Party, but the left/right divide is still prevalent in debates over collective bargaining and social and healthcare reform. Historically, religion was important to Finland's early national politics and to its writers, such as Zacharias Topelius, who contributed to the formation of the Finnish identity during its time under Russian rule (Poulter & Kallioniemi 2014: 29). The reorganization of municipalities in the nineteenth century led to the church in Finland losing responsibility for poor relief, local administration, and popular education, and it also officially became separate from the state (Markkola 2015: 8).

Religion is not a very significant factor in Finnish politics, although churches have often taken significant responsibility for providing food aid (Ohisalo & Saari 2014: 12), and Protestant societies, combined with low corruption, have been found to enjoy higher political trust among their citizens (Bäck & Kestikä-Kekkonen 2019: 14). In 1900, 98.1 per cent of Finland's population belonged to the Evangelical Lutheran Church of Finland (OSF 2019c). Since 2000, when it was 85.1 per cent, that figure has gradually dropped to 69.8 per cent. Membership of the Eastern Orthodox Christian churches has remained at 1.1 per cent since 2000; the country also has 50,000 baptised members of the Finnish Pentecostal Movement (Mantsinen 2018). Membership of the Lutheran Church is highest among older generations and, briefly, for the many 15-year-olds who attend confirmation camp, so they are able to marry in church or become godparents later in life. In 2015, only every third Finn, when asked, reported having attended church in the preceding 12 months, although attendance has been growing in recent years, and one in four people in the same survey said they prayed every day (Sandell 2016). That survey also found that while participants generally did not mind the construction of an Evangelical Lutheran Church or Orthodox Christian church in their neighbourhoods, one third opposed the building of mosques nearby. Opposition towards mosques was primarily expressed by non-religious participants.

Although Finland has a religious party, the Christian Democrats, it is not very strongly affiliated with the Finnish Evangelical Lutheran Church (Christian Democrats 2019). The party's former chair, Päivi Räsänen, even criticized the church's official affiliation with Finland's Pride Week (Yle Uutiset 2019f). Formed in 1958 as a reaction to secularization, the Christian Democrats won their first parliamentary seats in the 1970s, although they have only once been part of a Finnish government (Simula 2014). In 2019, they won five seats and are currently part of the opposition. There are more important issues that divide the major parties including immigration and the environment.

In a recent publication by the Finnish Ministry of Finance, based on election study data collected between 2011 and 2015, identification with a higher social class correlated with higher political trust (Tiihonen 2019: 171). It is very likely that this particular finding largely reflects the fact that people trust a system more in which they see themselves as doing well – which is why higher paid social classes often have more trust in the government (but see also Berner 2019; Muhonen 2019b).

Nine political parties won seats in the 2019 general election. These nine parties, ranked in order of the votes and seats won most recently, are shown in Table 7.1. That table shows that the proportion of votes each won was almost directly related to the number of seats they were assigned under Finnish proportional representation.

As of 2019, the Finns Party led by Jussi Halla-aho (until his replacement by Riikka Purra in 2021) is the largest opposition party. It holds 39 seats in the 200-seat parliament, one less than the victorious Social Democratic Party (SDP), which formed a majority coalition with 31 Centre Party, 20 Green League, 16 Left Alliance and 9 Swedish People's Party MPs after lengthy negotiations concluded in June, two months after the national election. In opposition are the 39 Finns, 38 National Coalition Party representatives, and 7 other MPs. Such complexity is a common scenario in mainland Europe, but almost unimaginable in a system without proportional representation, like the UK's first-past-the-post system.

In the most recent Finnish election, progressive political parties won sufficient seats to be able to form and lead a coalition government. Women gained an unprecedented number of seats – 93 out of 200 (Konttinen 2019). In 2015, 83 women were elected, and 85 in 2011. A remarkable 87 per cent of the new Members of Parliament for the Green League were women, and over half of the SDP MPs were women. Four out of ten ministers in the government formed in June 2019 were women, and that has now risen to a majority. The current cohort of Finnish MPs constitutes a very young parliament. The average age is 47, with eight MPs below the age of 30, 87 between 30–44, 95 aged between 45 and 64, with just 10 over 65.

Table 7.1: Results of the 2019 general election in Finland

Party	Votes	Seats	abbr.	Finnish name (and note in English)
Social Democratic	17.7%	40	SDP	Suomen sosialidemo-kraattinen puolue
Finns (far-right)	17.5%	39	PS	Perussuomalaiset (formerly 'True Finns')
National Coalition	17.0%	38	Kok	Kansallinen Kokoomus (Conservative)
Centre	13.8%	31	Kesk	Suomen Keskusta (formerly Agrarian Party)
Green League	11.5%	20	Vihr	Vihreä liitto
Left Alliance	8.2%	16	Vas	Vasemmistoliitto
Swedish People's	4.5%	9	RKP	Suomen ruotsalainen kansanpuolue
Christian Democrat	3.9%	5	KD	Kristillisdemokraatit
Movement Now	2.3%	1	liik	Liike Nyt
Blue Reform and others	3.2%	0	Sin	Sininen tulevaisuus
Åland representative	0.4%	1		The MP is Mats Löfström
TOTAL	**100%**	**200**		

Source: Official Statistics Finland (OSF 2019g).

According to political scientist Erkka Railo, the difficulty in achieving reforms when governments are formed of complex coalitions spanning broad parts of the political spectrum has elicited concerns over the stability of future governments (Milne 2017). However, Juha Sipilä's cabinet (2015–19) did pass many reforms aimed at boosting economic performance, to the displeasure of groups including students, the unemployed and trade unions. Unemployment benefits were cut for those who could not show proof that they had been seeking work (the activation model). Trade union negotiating power was restricted by a "competitiveness pact". Sipilä's government resigned in early 2019 over its failures in social and healthcare reform. The challenge of completing these reforms now lies with the government. Compared to previous coalitions, however, the 2019 government is significantly more cohesive along political lines, in this case along the green–left axis, albeit with the addition of the conservative Centre Party.

An oft-cited problem with an electoral system based on proportional representation is that it can lead to smaller parties – including, potentially, fringe or extreme groups – gaining influence quickly. However, this system also forces compromise, a feature that has long been the basis for many of Finland's policy achievements.

The rapid rise of the nationalistic Finns Party has taken many moderate Finns by surprise. Within Finnish politics they are on the far right. They secured 17.5 per cent of the vote in the 2019 election, up from 4.1 per cent in 2011 and 1.6 per cent in 2007. In 2015 they managed to get into the governing coalition and in 2017 the arch-nationalist Jussi Halla-aho became the party's chair. In consequence Timo Soini (the party's previous leader) and 16 other MPs left and formed a new party, Blue Reform, which remained in the coalition government. However, Blue Reform fared far worse than the Finns Party in the 2019 election. As Richard Milne (2017) noted in the *Financial Times*, the party's split and its time in government highlighted "the perils for populist groups seeking to move from protest to power". Under new leadership, and once outside government, the Finns Party message became simpler: anti-immigration and anti-climate action.

A majority of people in Finland, when asked, will say that they are appalled by the nationalism of the Finns Party, which only gained about one in six of all votes (Evon 2019). In 2014, the Finns Party were the source of the lone far-right MEP that Finland sent to the European Parliament in Brussels. In contrast, the UK was responsible for and formed the great majority of the EU's far-right bloc in those elections, when the 52 per cent of Britons who voted in that 2014 election opted to send 40 MEPs who represented parties that lay to the right of the conservative centre-right European People's Party Group – namely the Conservatives and UKIP.

Figure 7.2 shows where the nine major political parties lie in Finnish "political space". The horizontal scale is a traditional left-wing/right-wing division. The vertical scale has internationalist/green attitudes at the top and anti-immigrant, anti-EU, nationalist attitudes – that at times border on

Figure 7.2: Voting in Finland: party candidates in political space, 2019

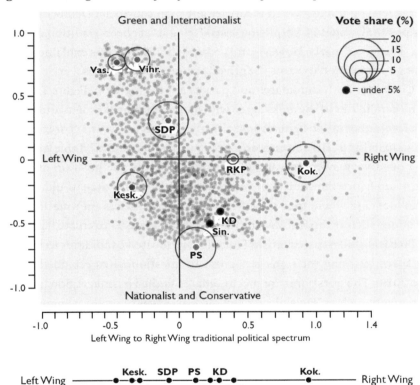

Source: Lång *et al.* (2019).

Note: SDP: Social Democrat; Kesk: Centre; PS: Finns; Sin: Blue Reform (now nearer to "Movement Now"); KD: Christian Democrats; RKP: Swedish People's Party; Kok: National Coalition Party; Vas: Left Alliance; Vihr: Green League. The data used to construct this diagram are derived from answers given by the very large number of candidates standing in the most recent elections in Finland, not from the voters.

a populism of a fascist kind – at the bottom. Each small circle on the graph shows where the attitudes of each party candidate surveyed lie in response to the questionnaire given below. The average positions of the parties are then superimposed on this (these are the larger labelled circles drawn in proportion to the votes won by that party in 2019). The two-dimensional depiction helps to better explain where parties stand. For instance the Centre Party (Kesk), which grew out of the rural Agrarian Party, is more left-wing in the views of its candidates on one axis, but simultaneously more nationalist and conservative than five of the other parties shown in Figure 7.2. Its position on the left–right axis, which is further left than the Social Democratic Party's position, might be surprising considering it has been traditionally seen as a "bourgeois" party. However, this more-left position was explained by its stronger opposition towards the privatization of care services.

Circles for both candidates and parties appear higher in Figure 7.2 when many candidates in the areas agree with statements such as "Finland should be a forerunner in the fight against climate change – even at a cost to private individuals" and "Finland cuts down too much of its forests". Table 7.2 shows how positive answers to various questions affected the position of candidates and hence the choices of voters as to which party they would vote for by influencing where they were in political space. It was information from questions such as those shown in Table 7.2 that was used to create Figure 7.2.

Political analysts working in Finland have located candidates in the voting space by using their answers given to questionnaires provided by Yle (Yle 2019). The questionnaire for candidates in the Helsinki region included statements such as "Helsinki can use nuclear power to produce energy when it shuts down its coal plants"; "The bilingual requirement for official positions should be relaxed to make it easier to hire immigrants"; "The defence forces should give up its garrison in Santahamina to make way for housing"; and "Helsinki should introduce a congestion surcharge during traffic rush hours". An earlier analysis in 2015 gave a more detailed account of the kinds of views that candidates in each quadrant of Figure 7.2 held, with a full description of the two-dimensional political spectrum in 2015 being provided at that time to the general public (Yle Uutiset 2015).

To left-leaning observers in more unequal and more dysfunctional countries, politics in Finland looks close to idyllic. Although Finns with

Table 7.2: Key issues in Finland that helped determine party choice in 2019

Question	Vertical	Horizontal
Finland should be a forerunner in the fight against climate change – even at a cost to private individuals.	0.70	0.04
Finland should not fast track a ban on the sale of diesel- and gasoline-powered cars.	-0.83	-0.04
The state should encourage people to eat less meat using measures such as taxation.	0.88	0.08
Finland cuts down too much of its forests.	0.87	-0.06
The government should cut costs rather than raise taxes to balance the budget.	-0.41	0.50
Universal basic income for all working-age residents should replace some current social benefits.	0.58	-0.18
Finland would be better off outside the eurozone.	-0.01	-0.19
Public authorities should be the main provider of social and healthcare services.	0.00	-0.82
Finland should outsource more senior care to private providers.	-0.02	0.74
A terminally-ill patient should have the right to euthanasia	0.14	-0.10
Under-18s should be allowed to undergo gender reassignment treatment.	0.61	-0.08
Wine and beer should be sold in grocery shops.	-0.21	0.23
Finland should adjust family policies so that childcare leave is equally distributed between parents.	0.35	-0.20
Compulsory education should include vocational and upper secondary school.	0.10	-0.46
Finland should delay the start of school summer holidays by two weeks to mid-June and so that it ends at the end of August.	-0.17	0.01
Finland should downsize its tertiary education network and redirect funds toward top institutions and research.	0.17	0.54
Rising immigration has increased insecurity in Finland.	-0.63	0.06
Faced with an ageing population and declining birth rate, Finland needs more work-based immigration to support the welfare state.	0.29	0.27
NATO membership would enhance Finland's security.	0.05	0.73
Legislators should define hate speech and make it a criminal offence.	0.06	-0.22

Source: Lång *et al.* (2019); questions available in English in Yle (2019).
Note: The numbers in this table relate to the positions in the graph shown in Figure 7.2.

173

traditionally conservative views support polices that largely lie to the left of politicians seen as left-wing in the UK or US, there remains widespread concern at the recent rise of the right in Finland. This alertness to the threat of right-wing populism contrasts with the situation in the UK and the US (especially when Trump was president), countries where racist public statements often go largely unchallenged, as the establishment and mainstream media focus their attention on criticizing the left and liberals. Part of what keeps politics in Finland progressive is fear of the far right and of nationalists. The issue that drives the majority of current support for Finland's nationalist right is immigration, and, sadly, this will likely be the case for years to come.

Immigration and politics

Immigrants to Finland come for many different reasons. It was judged one of the best European countries for retirees, just behind Spain in first place, in a study of 45 countries undertaken by Blacktower Financial Management. "The research was based on crime rates, cost of living, life expectancy, property prices and population age – but not weather, which is one of the main reasons that UK expats flock to Spain, but might overlook Finland" (Jefferies 2019). However, it is not an influx of elderly retirees from more affluent parts of Europe that is up for debate in Finland.

The issue of immigration was introduced into the political sphere by the Finns Party in 2008, and through this initiative they were able to shape the agenda and approaches to the debate. Other parties ranging from right to left on the political spectrum soon caught on, usually framing immigration as a problem and arguing that limits had to be set (Koivulaakso *et al.* 2012: 230–31). In 2009, Arto Savonen, a National Coalition Party MP, argued that if refugee policy, which was based on international agreements and the rule of law, lacked the approval and trust of the Finnish people, it could lead to greater inequality and growth in racism and xenophobia (Koivulaakso *et al.* 2012: 234).

Scholar Miika Tervonen has warned that the far-right, in promoting an image of a culturally homogeneous Finland, has contributed to the rise of racism and nationalism (Petäjä 2017). Finland's labour market needs immigrants to sustain the supply of workers. However, the government in power before June 2019, an alliance of the Centre Party, the National Coalition Party and Blue Reform, imposed new restrictions on refugees, especially following the 2015 European migrant crisis when the new coalition government with the nationalist Finns Party was established.

In 2019 the Finnish Ministry of the Interior said that it practises "controlled immigration", that "takes account of the need to safeguard the legal status of foreign nationals, Finland's international obligations, the capacity of society to take immigrants, and security considerations" (Ministry of the Interior 2019c). It also pointed out that labour migration is set to increase in importance for Finland as those of working age continue to decline in number. The working age population is predicted to fall by 75,000 by 2030 (Ministry of the Interior 2018).

The more right-wing but pro-immigration National Coalition Party has been the most vocal in calls to relax rules on economic migrants, in particular the requirement for proof of labour market needs (referred to as "labour market testing"; Hämäläinen & Rautio 2019). The Greens are also supportive, although other parties remain wary. The "testing" was removed in 2019 for those who already had been employed in Finland for at least a year. Otherwise labour market testing prioritizes the available Finnish and EU/EEA labour force as a whole, before a residence permit is issued for an individual (Migri 2019).

Today the Finnish government's immigration policy has three strands. First, actively attracting highly skilled workers and businesses to Finland, through programmes such as the Talent Boost scheme. The previous government, given the influence then of the National Coalition Party, was keen to streamline and simplify the process of applying for a work-based residence work permit, in order to help attract skilled workers from outside the EU. A new type of residence permit was introduced for start-up or growth entrepreneurs in April 2018, and residence permits for students and researchers were also extended, encouraging them to seek long-term employment in Finland (*Finland Today* 2018a).

Second, the new government has carried on with its predecessor's policy of supporting immigrants and their families in gaining skilled employment. As an example of what is happening on the ground, in the small town of Joensuu a job-seeking club has been set up for immigrants, providing them with information about the Finnish job market and helping those who are not fluent in Finnish to complete application forms, improve their CVs and practise for interviews (Bouzas 2018a). More widely, the rapid integration of migrant children into Finnish schools is being facilitated by expanding the number of schools where the curriculum is taught mostly in English – a language in which the Finnish population is also already very accomplished. New undergraduate programmes have also recently been introduced in Finnish universities in English to ensure that the children of workers who have come from abroad can continue to study in Finland, including children arriving aged 17 or as young adults with their parents. The 2019 "Academic of the Year" in Finland was named as Nafisa Yeasmin who works at the University of Lapland. She moved to Rovaniemi from Bangladesh in 2006. She is the project manager of the Arctic Centre's Aim2Work project, which helps the unemployed and people with immigrant backgrounds find work by motivating small and medium-sized corporations to support them (FUURT 2019).

Third, initiatives aimed at promoting good relations between newcomers and native Finns, in order to reduce discrimination against immigrants in everyday life and at work, have been instituted in recent years. This policy appears to have had some success. In 2014, Finland was ranked fifth (behind Norway, Sweden, Portugal and New Zealand) in the Migrant Integration Policy Index, which assesses the effectiveness of migrant integration policies, based on 167 measures. However, there is still progress to be made: African immigrants and their families are 60 per cent more likely to encounter discrimination in Finland than the EU average for such families, and there is often talk of a risk of spatial segregation increasing, partly because immigrants tend to be accommodated in the cheapest available housing (Bedhall 2018).

The current government's pro-immigration strategy focuses on economic migration, couched in terms of its positive impact on Finland's economy. More controversial as far as some are concerned is its policy with respect to asylum seekers and refugees. Following Europe's migrant crisis of 2015 with many people fleeing war in Syria, Finnish immigration reached record levels in 2016, at 34,905 immigrants (OSF 2016). Of these, nearly all, 32,476 people, were asylum seekers; in the years immediately prior, the annual average had been only about 4,000. The services available to refugees were set up to address the needs of relatively small numbers of incomers, and the bureaucratic nature of the Finnish state has been described as an obstacle to integrating large numbers (Wahlbeck 2018). The majority of asylum seekers in 2015 originated in Iraq (63%), followed by Afghanistan (16%), Somalia (6%), Syria (2.7%), Albania (2.3%) and Iran (1.9%). Note that only a very small proportion were from Syria.

Of course, the more than 32,000 refugees accepted by Finland in 2016 was in reality a very small number, although it was the EU's fourth highest amount per national population. In contrast, the EU country that accepted the most people, Germany, received 890,000 applications for asylum in 2015. By early 2019, Germany had housed (but not necessarily accepted) 1.4 million refugees, the majority Syrians, with another 19 per cent coming from two other countries in the grip of ongoing conflict, Iraq and Afghanistan. However, even the high number of refugees accepted by Germany was lower, both in real terms and measured against the size of the host population, than is the case in many much poorer countries. The vast majority of the world's refugees end up in a poor country near the one from which they have fled. However, it is worth noting that Finland's tally of 32,000 far exceeds the approximately 9,000 refugees a year that the UK took in before 2015, or the 14,000 it accepted for asylum or resettlement schemes in the years that followed.

Within the past decade, about 40 per cent of those who applied for asylum in Finland were accepted. Sweden introduced border controls with Denmark in November 2015, leaving Finland's border with Russia as the only land route for refugees into Finland (Wahlbeck 2018). Following that move, the proportion of positive asylum decisions in Finland fell to 32 per cent. Social integration has been a key goal of government policy, but as some residence permits awarded to refugees are temporary rather than permanent, and reassessed twice a year, the motivation to learn Finnish, attend school and find work is diminished (Järvinen 2015). Finnish is typically seen as a difficult language to learn, especially in a society in which older people tend to be terse and chats with strangers are rare, including with other Finns! Nevertheless, Finnish is relatively easy to learn if you are dyslexic, because it is a logical language with grammatical and orthographic consistency (Aho 2016). However, Finnish is hard for English-speaking people as there is no connection to Latin or the Germanic languages that preceded English.

The inclusion of the far-right Finns Party in the coalition government formed in 2015 marked a low point in recent Finnish political history with respect to immigration. The far right demanded new negotiations on immigration policy, and since 2015, greater restrictions have been put in place, leaving the country conforming to only the minimal requirements of EU legislation. By the end of 2016, Finland had received only 18,401 refugees that year and its officials were dealing with 5,601 pending cases (UNHCR 2017). In 2018, only 4,548 refugees sought asylum in Finland, a mere 1,852 were granted asylum and just 888 received residency permits, while 1,976 applications were rejected (OSF 2019c).

Finland has also taken "quota refugees", which are third-country resettlements of UNHCR registered refugees. It has done this ever since 1973–74, when a group of Chilean refugees was resettled there (O'Shaughnessy 2013). Chile remains the most unequal of the 36 wealthy OECD countries and experienced severe social unrest and mass rioting in late 2019. Finland is the most equal of OECD countries. Nevertheless, under the 2015–19 Finnish government, the annual refugee quota set by the Finnish parliament was just 750 people, raised temporarily to 1,050 for 2014–15.

Municipalities are responsible for carrying out resettlement and integration work. In 2017 the Finnish government, in response to a routine UN investigation, agreed that it would enhance its existing mandate for provision by "developing national monitoring of discrimination, methods for equality planning and assessment, educating key groups and developing a policy of good relations between population groups" (Government of Finland 2017). In 2019, the refugee quota was raised to 850, in addition to accepting 120 additional "emergency" refugees (Ministry of the Interior of Finland 2019d).

During the 2019 parliamentary elections, the Centre Party, the National Coalition Party and the Finns Party said they wished to further restrict refugee policy, the SDP said they would keep it the same, and the Greens, the Left Alliance and the Swedish People's Party said they supported relaxing it (Teittinen 2019).

Racism and Finland

In recent months and years, the Finnish media have documented public concern over crimes committed by immigrants. In December 2018, multiple child sexual abuse offences in Oulu were alleged to have been committed by asylum seekers. By January there were 12 suspects all of whom were reportedly in prison, and the number of alleged victims had risen to nine. By February 2019 there were 29 suspects and yet more alleged victims. The Finnish president, Sauli Niinistö, reflected the public mood when he said, "It's unbearable that some who have sought asylum from us . . . have brought evil to us and created insecurity" (*Finland Today* 2019a).

In response to these child sexual abuse cases, the government promised action to prevent further criminal activity by immigrants – including giving more consideration to criminal records before granting residence permits, and undertaking enhanced surveillance of individuals facing deportation who were thought to pose a threat. In mid-2019, eight men of foreign descent were all convicted of sexual abuse and rape of a 13-year-old girl. One other man is awaiting extradition from Germany to face trial in Finland. The massive media hysteria over these events, including that of the state broadcaster Yle, died down after the parliamentary elections. Subsequently the reporting was described by some commentators as the worst journalism in Finland in 2019. As in other European countries, very little was said about those who commit the vast majority of child sexual abuse, both now and over past decades and centuries – namely the (Finnish-born) members of the victims' own families.

In 2019 the Finns Party released a notorious election campaign video featuring a young woman (dressed in a short skirt) walking alone down a street and then being abducted by asylum seekers: a blatantly racist depiction aimed at provoking hate and discrimination. Crimes against any person in Finland are legitimate security concerns, but they are by no means exclusively committed by immigrants. It should be remembered that Finland's three deadly school shootings in 1989, 2007 and 2008, and a fatal sword attack in Kupio in 2019, were committed by Finns, and that in 2019 five Finnish men were found to be involved in an international paedophile ring (News Now Finland 2019).

The new year messages in January 2019 and 2020 from Finland's President Sauli Niinistö and Prime Minister Sanna Marin focused heavily on immigration, emphasizing that immigrants must be given an opportunity to be part of Finnish society, but must also respect the laws and integrity of the country. However, they also urged people not to incite hatred against refugees or foreigners because of the criminal activity of a small number of recent immigrants. This may well have been a response to the greater visibility of neo-Nazism in Finland.

On Finland's 101st Independence Day, 6 December 2018, up to 300 neo-Nazis with three large swastika flags (which the police later confiscated) marched through the streets of Helsinki. There was subsequently an anti-Nazi counter-protest by approximately 1,800 people, as well as a demonstration by a similar number of people under the "612" (6 December) banner which encompasses most right-wing groups (Öhberg 2018a). The ultra-right vigilantes included members of the Soldiers of Odin, a group so far to the right that they accused the far-right Finns Party leader of being a "traitor of the people" (MacDougal 2018).

The extreme right in Finland is a small minority. The far right is larger. Geographical areas of support for the far-right Finns Party, however, tend to be scattered, and are exaggerated on a normal geographical map that makes lower density areas (where older people tend to live) appear more significant than their number of voters warrants. Figure 7.3 shows the actual distribution of the vote over the electorate. It also has the advantage of not distorting the support for the Centre Party, which tends to be highest in the more rural northern areas of Finland.

Politicians of immigrant origin

In order to increase ethnic diversity at all levels of society and build a more inclusive society, broadening the ethnic diversity among political representatives is crucial. This requires ethnic minorities to have sufficient trust to engage with Finnish politics and become candidates themselves. The most recent and relevant Finnish government study, conducted in 2019, found that political candidates of immigrant origin rely heavily on personal network ties to build a support base, but strong connections between political party networks and those of ethnic minorities are currently lacking in every party in Finland (Bäck & Kestilä-Kekkonen 2019). In order to earn their support, political parties need to engage with ethnic minorities. The report also noted that migrants need to increase their knowledge of voting rights and the Finnish political system. This could be done through "agents of trust", such as candidates of immigrant origin (Sipinen 2019: 196). The Minister of the Interior has also called for greater diversity in the police force, including more Muslims and more Swedish speakers (Saarikoski 2019), with the aim of fostering greater understanding of minorities and build trust.

Immigrants aged 18 and over who live permanently in Finland have the right to vote in municipal elections and to stand for municipal office (Info Finland 2019b). Only Finnish citizens are allowed to vote in parliamentary and presidential elections. Five years of continuous residence in Finland, or a total of seven years since the age of 15, with the last two years being continuous residence, are prerequisites for citizenship, along with a satisfactory level of written and spoken Finnish or Swedish (or relevant sign language). An additional waiting period is required for those found guilty of any punishable offence, or who have had a restraining order issued against them. Candidates for citizenship must inform the Finnish Immigration Service of the source of their means of support, and be able to pay the €420 or €520 application fee (Finnish Migration Service 2019). Conditions for immigrants must be improved, but it is an achievable goal in a country with a history of pioneering social innovation – most famously in women's rights.

The challenge then, is for Finland to be as progressive today as it was 100 years ago when it comes to its most marginalized people – no longer women, but ethnic minorities and recent immigrants. Researchers, activists, journalists, and politicians increasingly emphasize the structural inequality and injustice which withhold the same possibilities in life that native, white Finns can expect to receive. Among the various issues raised in 2020 has been the exploitation reminiscent of human trafficking by cleaning firms, usually of asylum seekers fearful of losing their residence permits.

Immigrants are invaluable in promoting democracy and internationalism in Finland and for reminding Finns of values that can become forgotten or taken for granted in the contemporary political environment. If people lack trust in or knowledge of the political system, however, such benefits fail to be realized, as a candidate of immigrant origin for the 2017 municipal elections noted in an interview in 2019:

Candidate: The country for the Kurdish community from which we are moving to here, we always have problem with the system. I mean

Figure 7.3: The political map of Finland: electoral cartograms of the 2019 election

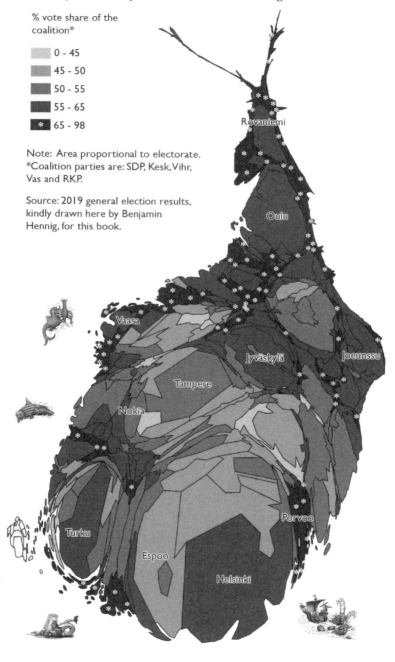

% vote share of the coalition*

- 0 - 45
- 45 - 50
- 50 - 55
- 55 - 65
- 65 - 98

Note: Area proportional to electorate.
*Coalition parties are: SDP, Kesk, Vihr, Vas and RKP.

Source: 2019 general election results, kindly drawn here by Benjamin Hennig, for this book.

Rovaniemi

Oulu

Vaasa

Jyväskylä

Joeunssu

Tampere

Nokia

Porvoo

Turku

Espoo

Helsinki

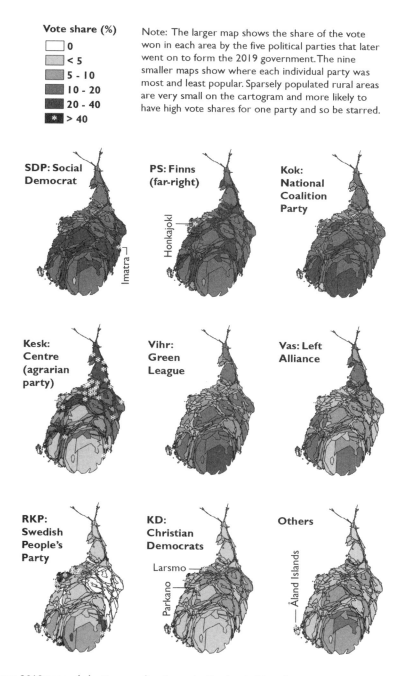

Vote share (%)

- ☐ 0
- ☐ < 5
- ☐ 5 - 10
- ☐ 10 - 20
- ☐ 20 - 40
- ✳ > 40

Note: The larger map shows the share of the vote won in each area by the five political parties that later went on to form the 2019 government. The nine smaller maps show where each individual party was most and least popular. Sparsely populated rural areas are very small on the cartogram and more likely to have high vote shares for one party and so be starred.

SDP: Social Democrat

Imatra

PS: Finns (far-right)

Honkajoki

Kok: National Coalition Party

Kesk: Centre (agrarian party)

Vihr: Green League

Vas: Left Alliance

RKP: Swedish People's Party

KD: Christian Democrats

Larsmo

Parkano

Others

Åland Islands

Source: 2019 general election results, drawn by Benjamin Hennig.

183

you have no rights. Only right you have [is] to exist, as a servant or as a worthless something. But when people move here, they are afraid to be in contact with government. That's scary for them. I mean, the people traumatized that much, it's not easy to explain that hey, you know what, if you have a problem you can go talk with someone. If you are not happy with new plan about your neighbourhood, go and complain to the city planning office.

Interviewer: Are people afraid of doing it?

Candidate: Obviously! And they don't know actually they can complain about it, they don't know that. You know, who says that, I don't remember the name but, "the biggest enemy of freedom [are] the slaves who accept the fact and [are] happy with it." As long as slaves are happy with the fact they are slaves, you cannot free them.

Interviewer: And you wish to change that?

Candidate: I wish to change that. (Sipinen 2019: 190)

Finland's history of electing politicians of immigrant origin is short. By 2015, there had been only four first-generation immigrant politicians: Swedish-born Elisabeth Nauclér (Swedish People's Party Member of Parliament, 2007–15), Estonian-born Hella Wuolijoki (Finnish People's Democratic League, 1946–57), Afghan-born Nasima Razmyar (Deputy Mayor for culture and leisure, SDP), and Turkish-born Ozan Yanar (Member of Parliament for the Green League, 2015–19) (Sarhimaa 2017). A number of people with at least one foreign-born parent made it into office prior to 2019 but we have no count of these.

Right-wing populism

While most politicians are happy to see Finland flatteringly profiled in international media, the Finns Party have little intention of drawing international attention to its advantages. Their 2011 parliamentary campaign advocated reducing "social immigration" by making Finland less appealing (Koivulaakso *et al.* 2012: 240), and in 2019 the party's response to the question "Should Finland attract more foreign labour?" was "Finland is simply not a very attractive destination for skilled workers, reasons including: a hard language, isolated location, cold weather, high taxes, and average wages" (Teittinen 2019).

The Finns Party's economic plan in 2019 was arguably, in one small way, left-wing in wanting to support public services and keeping critical services under public control, but also placed significant emphasis on internal security and defence (The Finns Party 2019: 3). However, the party aimed to do so whilst remaining fiscally responsible and balancing the budget instead of cutting public funding. They proposed achieving this by cutting funds spent on immigrants, the EU, and international development – while failing to consider that international development spending should help reduce the numbers of asylum seekers and refugees. Although the party's aim was to balance the budget for the benefit of future generations, they also argued for a reduction in green policies by cutting wind energy feed-in tariffs. Arguing that Finland should be no more ambitious in its climate policy than the EU as a whole, the Finns Party suggested that as a small country, Finland should play only a small role in such efforts. Their concern for future generations, it would appear, did not extend to addressing the climate emergency to come.

As their 2019 economic plan illustrated, the Finns Party wanted to utilize scarce resources for Finns, pointing to the past success of the country's welfare state and arguing that their party's ability, determination and ruthlessness were necessary to protect it against what they saw as the mistaken moral obligations for accepting immigrants. Indeed, in the 2019 parliamentary elections, their key slogan was "Return to Finland's Future" by "re-establishing the traditional values of Finland and the Finnish society" (Halla-aho 2019). Finnish inadequacies in areas such as healthcare and the environment were blamed on the previous government spending money on supporting immigrants instead. National climate policies are, according to the Finns Party's chair, the costly outcome of "some kind of self-assigned moral position" and they advocate that no further efforts should be taken than what is agreed at the EU level.

In a study by Sitra, the Finnish Innovation Fund, one in three Finns Party supporters said they were afraid of the future because they foresaw threats

– with over twice as many of them foreseeing such threats as supporters of other parties. A lower proportion of Finns Party supporters, just 41 per cent, acknowledged that it is extremely important to adapt to the planet's limits and protect the future of our environment compared to the much larger proportions who believed that in all other parties (Liiten 2019). Emilia Palonen, an expert on populism, suggests that perception of future threats and a sense of powerlessness encourages people to vote for the Finns Party. After the 2019 parliamentary elections, academic Hanna Wass adopted the term "basic bourgeois" (*perusporvari*) to describe Finns Party voters, especially entrepreneurs, who are economically quite well-off, yet increasingly concerned with the future of their status. In another study, Sivonen *et al.* (2018) found that the Finns Party draw their support from the working class, small entrepreneurs, and people in clerical work. They have also attracted some of the poorer voters from the SDP's traditional base, and wealthier voters from the National Coalition Party, although less often the highly educated.

Although the Finns Party's chair may prefer to have his party viewed as the main opposition party rather than an aberrant populist fringe group, the "True Finns" (as they previously called themselves) are widely regarded as the heart of Finnish right-wing populism. Founded in 1995, the True Finns Party replaced the Rural Party, which entered bankruptcy that year. Defending the rural poor is no longer its defining aim, and it now receives variable support throughout Finland (Ylä-Anttila 2017: 345; and Figure 7.3). Since at least 2010, some of its members have been described as thinking along the lines of neo-Nazism (Salminen 2010).

Members of the Finns Party have claimed that "Finnishness" is under threat, pointing as proof to a heated national debate that occurred nearly two decades ago over a song, *Suvivirsi*, that schoolchildren would traditionally sing at the end of the school year (Ylä-Anttila 2017). Being technically a hymn, it has mild religious connotations and the controversy was politicized into an anti-EU debate with arguments that were orientated around particular imaginations of a Finnish cultural heritage. In point of fact, the hymn is of Swedish origin.

In 2002, news outlets such as the high-circulation *Helsingin Sanomat* newspaper claimed that EU and Finnish regulations such as the Religious Freedom Act would result in the banning of the song outright, rather than allowing children and their parents the freedom to opt out of certain religious practices in schools. The debate over the hymn resurfaced in 2010–14, when the Finns Party tried to use it to appeal to the familiar and traditional experiences of Finns and national pride, and to underscore its message that immigration posed an existential threat to Finns. Other parties tried to counter those arguments by emphasizing the acceptance of and respect for a variety of different cultural traditions, including Finnish ones, such as the singing of *Suvivirsi*.

The Finns Party gained its first significant win in the 2011 parliamentary elections (Herkman 2018: 343). It later became part of the centre-right coalition government in 2015, holding four ministerial positions. When the Finns Party split in 2017 the main group became more far-right, and the other parties refused to participate in a coalition with the party's new chairman, Jussi Halla-aho. The chairmen of the National Coalition Party and the Centre Party, Petteri Orpo and former prime minister Juha Sipilä, feared they would risk the cabinet's capacity to work effectively because of their severe disagreement with Halla-aho over immigration policies (Pekkonen 2017). Just three years earlier, Halla-aho had been found guilty by the Finnish Supreme Court of ethnic agitation and breaking religious peace in a blog post that fulminated against Islam.

Different people have different ideas of what Utopia might be. For a small and racist minority, it is a monocultural, mono-ethnic, monolingual, single-religion "pure white state". In Finland, racist views are most common amongst the elderly, not among the young. As we write, the True Finns' voters are ageing. They may still do well in the polls wining a sixth of the vote, but their support is not strong among the younger generation. However, people we talked to when writing this book told us that there is always the risk that young men in particular in small towns could be drawn towards racism, as some were in the depression of the 1990s. More hopefully, if enough Finns have learnt from that experience, then once today's Finnish school children become young adults and discuss politics with their grandparents, it will be interesting to see which group succeeds in changing the views of the other.

Acceptance of the Finns Party into any government coalition, given its new, harder-line leadership, would have compromised the Finnish position on furthering European integration. It also became harder for the Finns Party to aim its criticism at the political elite once it became part of the 2015–19 ruling coalition (Niemi 2015). Those who left the Finns Party following that party's 2017 leadership election and subsequently formed the Blue Reform Party, and stayed in government, failed to win any seats in 2019. Despite being at times out on a political limb, during the Covid-19 crisis their fiscal prudency and stance on taxation has drawn support from less liberal politicians from another opposition party, the National Coalition Party.

Conservative economic positions, however, rarely embrace market absolutist thinking – that is, the idea that everything can be solved by market forces and nothing should ever hinder such forces. Even the country's most fiscally right-wing party, the National Coalition Party, shifted its position in the 1970s towards support for the welfare state and even collective bargaining (Malinen 2008: 6). An exception, however, concerns the continued attempts of the National Coalition Party to increasingly privatize healthcare services. Finland has few far-right lobbyists and none of the far-right think tanks so common in the UK and US today (Sandell 2018; Pirie 2018).

Conclusion

The Finnish cabinet that was in place at the start of 2020 planned to focus government attention on increasing welfare-state funding and action on climate change. In marked contrast, the Finns Party offered no deadline for becoming carbon neutral, or even a target for reducing emissions. Furthermore, Halla-aho, as the de facto leader of the opposition (until his replacement by Riikka Purra in 2021), does not believe that the climate crisis can be curtailed by politics because of the sacrifices it demands of people (Brenner 2019). As they are not a party of climate-change denial, one wonders what hope for the future the Finns Party have (Halla-aho 2006, 2019; Hiilamo 2019b).

The new government had a series of ambitious plans laid out in late 2019, including for new political funding arrangements (Luukka 2019b; Niskakangas & Nalbantoglu 2019). However, once the Covid-19 pandemic forced countries to restrict economic activity and movement, it became clear these would need to be reconsidered.

The 2020 Covid-19 pandemic triggered memories of the 1990s economic depression in Finland, when, at its worst, 22 per cent of the workforce was unemployed. Of course, the nature of the crisis and Finland's global standing are now remarkably different. For one, Finland need not worry as much about its credit rating as its ability to borrow from international markets is far stronger in 2020. Nevertheless, the consequences of prolonged unemployment and spending cuts on the most vulnerable is foremost in the minds of minsters. The income hits in the 1990s left lasting scars on the affected generation who now leads the current government. The 1990s thus serve as a stark warning to hold on to the pillars of Finnish success when reconstruction can begin – meaning investment in education and social security to ensure the most vulnerable, and their purchasing power, are not left behind.

Finntopia is a long way off. Finland's politics remain in some ways fractured and there are constant internal arguments in government. However, with its multiple political parties representing the spread of opinion and proportional representation, coalition government is almost always inevitable. Consequently, politics in Finland is unlikely to become as polarized as it is in the US and UK. Finland can expect to see continued high levels of trust in its political institutions. Coalition governments, and ruling by consensus, help ensure that most policies manage to outlast the government that introduces them.

When politicians know that after an election they will almost certainly end up in coalition and have to work with their opponents, cooperation, compromise and consensus are the order of the day. Across Europe this is the norm, but in Finland it is often taken further still.

What matters for almost all societal groups – no matter how that group may compare in terms of material resources with a similar group living in another country – is not so much how things are at present, but whether the situation is improving and a better future lies ahead. When a significant group feels left behind, there is a risk of rising nationalism, and a growing desire to exclude and marginalize people seen as different and less deserving.

Improvements in well-being, stability and opportunity are always possible and necessary, but should not be cast as being delivered at the expense of others. Once an affluent society recognizes that there is an individual level of wealth above which little greater happiness is achieved, a great deal is possible and there is no need to continue to tolerate poverty. But politicians can still debate how to achieve this, and there are always new problems to argue over.

It is so easy now to forget that Finland was, until very recently, poor, and had been historically a country of extreme poverty for centuries. It is quite remarkable to see what a people and their politicians have quietly achieved in one small (by population) place, essentially by simply caring for each other more and being clever and becoming even more clever (educationally). Finland is still a long way from eradicating poverty, and from becoming fully inclusive and sustainable, but it is much further along that road than almost any other country in the world, and has much to teach others (Petri 2019; Noack & O'Grady 2019). Many of its people, its universities and its private companies are now also at the forefront of the global fight to reduce climate emissions and despite the disbelief of some far-right commentators abroad (Worstall 2019) are looking to produce technological solutions to issues such as future global food shortages (Good News from Finland 2019; Boffey 2019).

By Toivo Fahlenius. Fahlenius studied at the Viipuri Friends of Art Drawing School in the 1930s. During his student years he worked at different advertising agencies and probably painted this in the 1950s. Reproduced with kind permission from the lovely folk at Visit Rovaniemi (www.visitrovaniemi.fi).

8

Demography and environment

"I was with the president of Finland and he said 'we have, much different, we are a forest nation'. He called it a forest nation. And they spend a lot of time on raking and cleaning and doing things, and they don't have any problem. And when it is, it's a very small problem. So I know everybody's looking at that to that end."

> US President Donald Trump in 2018,
> recalling a conversation he never had about
> how Finland avoids forest fires (Kelly 2018)

Decreasing fertility and the effects of climate emergency are phenomena that all western, developed countries face. On the one hand, a shrinking and greying population risks the future tax base needed to fund government policies. On the other hand, a larger population would almost inevitably use up more of the planet's scarce resources and further intensify climate change. Immigration is proposed as the solution. The previous chapter illustrated the difficulties Finnish politics and society have faced in adapting to immigration, and detailed the populist backlash against multiculturalism. This chapter, on demography and the environment, delves further into how the contradictory need for greater fertility and the certain need for climate action has played out in Europe, as this will significantly affect Finland's capacity to sustain its welfare state at current levels.

Population change in historical perspective

Long-term trends in birth and death rates in Finland reflect the country's chequered history. Spikes in the death rate followed major events such as the 1808–09 war between Sweden and Russia, which culminated in Finland being ceded to its eastern neighbour; and in the Finnish famine of 1866–68 some 270,000 people – 9 per cent of the population – died of hunger. The civil war in 1918 that followed Finnish independence from Russia in 1917 led to the deaths of 37,000 people – mostly men in prison camps. There were smaller spikes during the Winter War (1939–40) and the Continuation War (1941–44) against the Soviet Union, when around 96,000 Finns (2.5 per cent of the population) perished. Since 1945, annual death rates have remained low and stable, at 10 per 1,000 population, while in the past few years birth rates have fallen so low that they are now below death rates (see Figure 8.1). However, Finland's population has grown overall between the end of the Second World War and today because births usually exceeded deaths and net emigration was typically not much greater than the difference between these two.

Finland's birth rate has declined steadily, from 40 births per 1,000 people annually in the mid-eighteenth century to just less than ten births per 1,000 people in 2017. More rapid falls in the birth rate occurred during the famine of the 1860s, and the severe economic depression in the 20 years following Finnish independence in 1917. But the sharpest decline occurred in the 25 years after the postwar baby boom, during which the birth rate more than halved, from 27 per 1,000 in 1948 to 12 per 1,000 in 1973.

The postwar decline was due in part to the crippling postwar reparations imposed by the Soviet Union. Settling a bill for $300 million was "achieved only by a complete reorganisation of the country's economy and the combined, almost superhuman effort of every Finn" (Nickels 1977: 94). Birth rates never really recovered, and in recent years have declined further. From 2016 onwards, the birth rate has fallen below the death rate in Finland for the first time since 1940.

From the 1870s onwards Finland, like much of Europe, saw a decline in death rates as sanitation improved, the quality of the food supply increased along with knowledge of nutrition and then of hygiene. The number of deaths in Finland fell to about 1 per cent of the population a year by 1950. At

Figure 8.1: Birth and death rates in Finland, 1749–2017

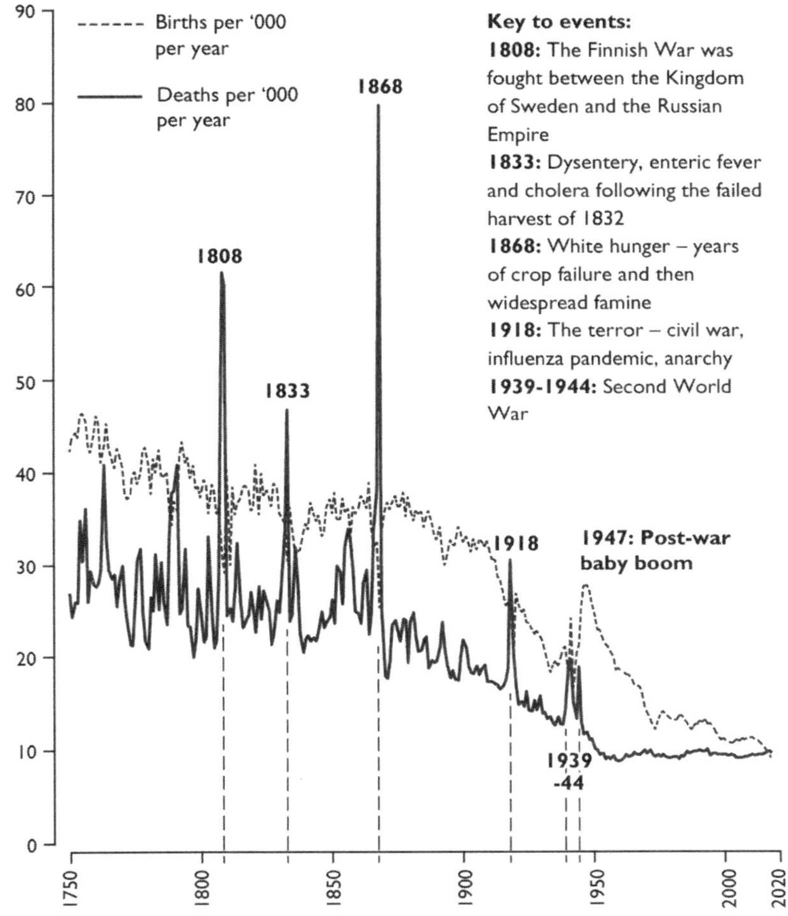

Source: Official Statistics Finland (OSF) (2019n).

first this was because there were relatively few old people in Finland in an era of high emigration, and deaths abroad are not counted. The fertility rate was also falling.

The crude mortality rate being discussed here does not take into account the age distribution of the population; it is simply deaths divided by population. By the year 2000, the crude mortality rate was able to remain at around 1 per cent of the population a year because mortality rates had continued to fall dramatically, and life expectancy was continuing to rise. Furthermore, more and more young people were entering the country as migrants, increasing the overall population and reducing the crude death rates. Without any inward or outward migration, a crude mortality rate of 1 per cent only happens when average life expectancy is 100 years. No country on earth is currently anywhere near that point (or is likely to be in future).

The population of Finland reached half a million people in 1761, 1 million in 1811, 2 million in 1879, and 4 million by 1950. It thus doubled initially in 50 years, then again in the next 68 years, and again in the next 71 years, with the rate of growth gradually slowing down each century. It did not reach 5 million until 1991, and 5.5 million in 2016 (it is 5.53 as we write in early 2020). It is very unlikely to double ever again (from 4 million in 1950 to 8 million at some point in the future) given this deceleration in growth. The principal reason for the slowdown is that far fewer children are being born, as is now common across all of Europe. What is being seen in Finland is part of a dramatic worldwide slowdown in births.

Ageing and population sustainability

Finland is not an anarchist Utopia or a socialist show-home. It is ordered and careful, at times conservative, but in many aspects well ahead of the game. This includes the attitudes of its people to the environment, to ageing and to sustainability. In late 2019, the Ministry of Education and Culture, with Ministers Andersson (Education, Left Alliance), Kosonen (Science and Culture, Centre Party), and Mikkonen (Environment and Climate Change, The Greens) attended a roundtable event with representatives of Finland's youth to discuss the climate crisis. The event was live-streamed, and three hours long. The discussion centred on how to include representatives of the younger population in policy-making in a respectful and effective manner (Ministry of Education and Culture 2019c).

Everything is connected, and so when we are looking at ageing and sustainability, we must also consider the changes in education that began decades ago. These changes in Finland have now had a widespread effect on the general level of knowledge and understanding and on the ability of young people in Finland to hold ministers to account. As one set of commentators from England has explained it: "Finland's definition of twenty-first century skills is unique in that it includes such themes as cultural identity and internationalism and responsibility for the environment. The Finnish National Board of Education expects teachers to incorporate broad cross-curricular themes such as active learning, technology and society, active citizenship and media skills into their instruction, without prescribing exactly how they are to be taught" (Creese *et al.* 2016; Lähdemäki 2018).

Figure 8.2: Total fertility rate in Finland, 1900–2018

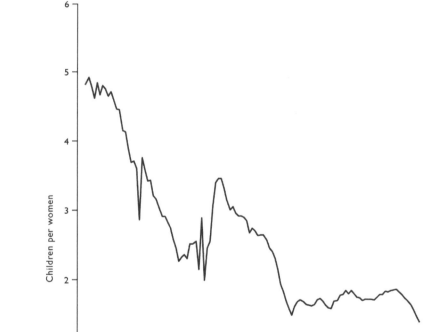

Source: Official Statistics Finland (OSF) (2019o).

197

Better education tends to be a precursor to lower fertility. Fewer children are born to each woman in Finland than in most of the rest of Europe. The graph in Figure 8.2 shows that relatively low fertility has been the norm in Finland since the 1970s and appears to be becoming even more common in recent years, with the Finnish statistical agency reporting that: "According to the birth rate of 2017, an average of 1.49 children would be born to each woman. The number is now the lowest ever" (OSF 2018e).

In 2018 the total fertility rate fell further, with women in Finland having an average of 1.41 children over their lifetime in Finland (Ervasti & Laitinen 2019). However, if the tempo-adjusted rate is considered, which allows for the later age at which younger women in Finland are now having children, then the actual rate might be somewhat higher because younger women are planning to have a child later (Human Fertility Database 2018).

Finland's demography has been (and in future will be) strongly affected by its education system, not only in terms of how good the system has become, but also in the lack of geographical variation between schools. In other countries, especially in areas of poor education, people tend to have more children, and have their first child earlier in life. In contrast, in areas where schooling is better and where the majority of children go on to higher education, adults tend to have far fewer children.

Sometimes a lower fertility rate can be explained by young women in more affluent areas being more likely to terminate unplanned pregnancies, because having a child when young is seen as almost impossible. In Helsinki, free-of-charge contraception is offered to everyone under the age of 25, including non-local students. Finland has almost no geographical variation in the teenage (15–19) pregnancy rate, which is 19 pregnancies per 1,000 women in most areas of the country (and almost all of those who fall pregnant are aged 19). Half of those 1.9 per cent then have an abortion, so only 0.95 per cent become mothers. In the UK the teenage pregnancy rate is almost three times higher, at 51 per 1,000 (with 42 per cent of pregnancies ending in termination). In the US, the rate is 86 per 1,000 (of which only 35 per cent are terminated). This implies that Finland, the UK and US have unwanted teenage pregnancy rates of at least 10, 21 and 30 respectively per 1,000 young women, with the variable quality of education in the three countries – including sex education – a key factor (Wikipedia 2019b).

Finland enjoys very low levels of variation in the quality of its schools, with almost all of them being seen as good (Sahlberg 2012; and see Figure 4.3 in Chapter 4). In 2013, the annual PISA report on the quality of education in OECD nations suggested that differences among schools in Finland accounted for just 7.7 per cent of the variation in student performance, while the OECD average was 42 per cent (OECD 2013). Across all OECD countries and regions, Finland's school system also has the least segregation of children of different socio-economic groups, according to the OECD 2013 report, which used data collected in 2009.

Because Finland's schools are not socially segregated, when new immigrants arrive in Finland they are more likely than immigrants in other countries to attend a school with a reasonable socio-economic cross-section of the Finnish population. Nevertheless, there are frequent reports of concerns in the news media and academic research whenever the children of immigrants appear to be clustered in particular schools, because the reduced social mixing that results is seen as problematic. It is widespread public awareness of even small changes in equity in education that will help prevent any rise in segregation in the future if politicians remain vigilant. Furthermore, although university fees for students who are not from the EU have been introduced from autumn 2017 onwards (Peltonen 2016) there are no fees for students who are officially resident in any EU country.

The official population projections of the government statistical office for Finland are conservative, and they assume that births will not fall much further and immigration will not rise at all in future. They are shown in Figure 8.3. In these projections, the death rate, which is the easiest variable to predict with accuracy, is set to keep falling. Despite that, the number of people dying each year in Finland will continue to rise right through to 2040 as the population as a whole ages. In contrast, the fall in births is projected to quickly abate and become far more gradual after 2020. However, there is no particular reason to think this will be so. These projections suggest that the net rise in immigration will cease after 2020; this is also very unlikely to be the case as people migrate more often and from further afield and migration is becoming easier (especially within the EU). Net immigration may well be higher than is predicted here, just as births may be lower in future. Finally, these projections suggest that after 2030 the population of Finland will fall overall. While populations are set to drop in many European countries over this timespan, will the same be true of such a successful, prosperous and equitable country?

Figure 8.3: Births, deaths and net migration, Finland, 1990–2040 (people per year)

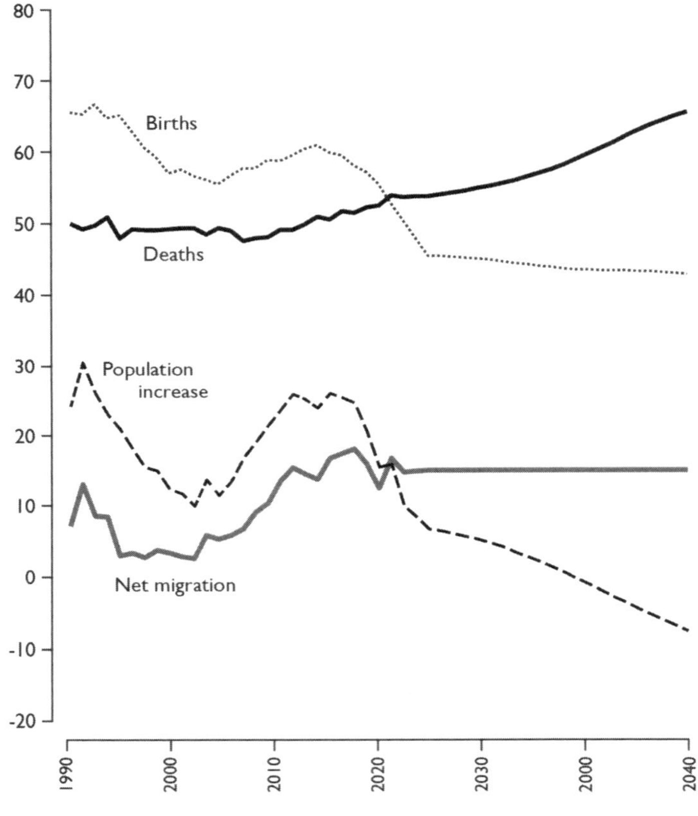

Source: Official Statistics Finland (OSF) (2019p).

In 2018, 19,141 Finns emigrated (in 2010 it was 11,905; in 2000 it was 14,311) (OSF 2019c). Net immigration in 2018 was 11,965 (2010: 13,731; 2000: 2,584). In 2015, the head of international affairs of a trade union confederation (Akava), Markus Penttinen, was surprised that the emigration of 10,000 Finns in the year 2015 was not larger, given the atmosphere of pessimism and the weak economy at the time (Orjala 2016). However, even in the 1990s depression there were no significant spikes in emigration.

Figure 8.4: Contributions to total population change, Finland, 1945–2017 (people/year)

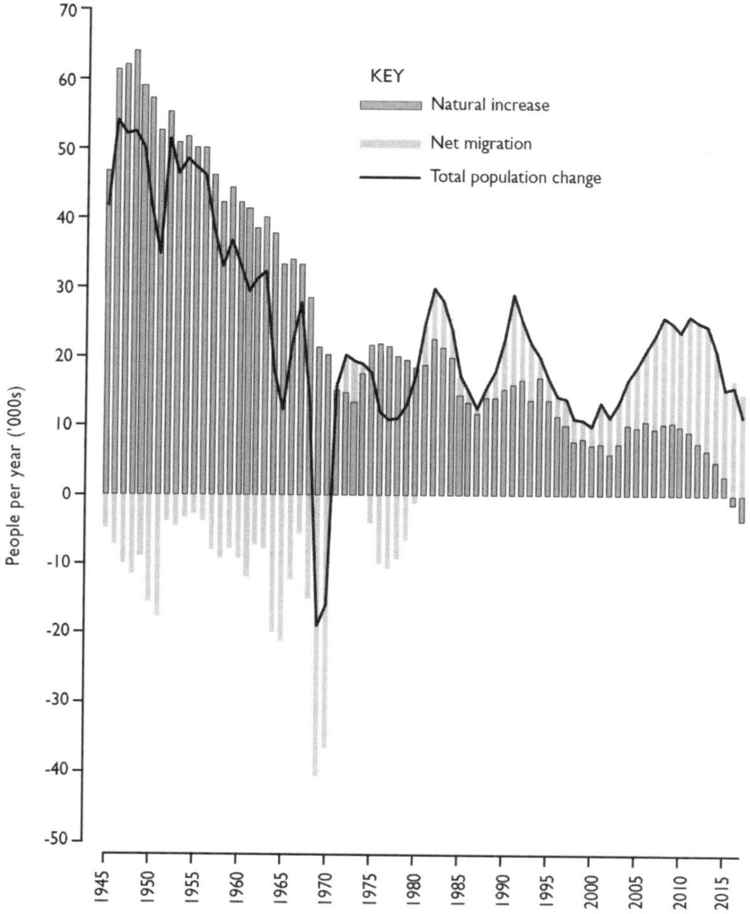

KEY

▨ Natural increase

▨ Net migration

— Total population change

Source: Official Statistics of Finland (OSF) (2019n).

The last great wave of outward-migration from Finland came in 1969 and 1970, when 40,000 people left for Sweden each year. In the same two years, 7,000 Finns moved back (see Figure 8.4). This was advantageous migration for Finland, as Finns returned with new skills and ways of thinking. Most commonly emigrants are young people seeking to build their career, gain experiences or language skills, or marry someone from another country. The most popular countries for emigrants have been Sweden, the UK, the US and

Germany – most likely because integration is easier, for reasons of language and working culture. Some may send money back to relatives in Finland; more are likely to save and then return and put down a large deposit on a mortgage or buy a home outright.

The role of migration in changing Finland

Emigration rates exceeded immigration rates in Finland until the 1980s. Thousands left to settle in Canada and the US following Finland's independence in 1917, and hundreds of thousands moved to Sweden in the 1960s (OSF 2007).

Migration can have far-reaching repercussions. For instance one person we spoke to when working on this book told us how, in Canada, it was Finnish immigrants from the losing side in the Finnish civil war who founded Canada's first large cooperative, and they were over-represented in left-wing organizations including the Communist Party of Canada, the Industrial Workers of the World (IWW), and the famed Mac-Paps (the Canadian Mackenzie–Papineau battalion in the Spanish Civil War). Other than from neighbouring and much more populous France, more volunteers on the republican side of the Spanish Civil War came from Canada than from any other country; this was partly as a result of Finnish emigration to Canada and the children of those emigrants.

From the 1920s through to the 1980s Finnish labour markets were unable to provide employment for the increasing numbers of working-age adults as health improved and more Finns survived through to adulthood. This, coupled with the postwar baby boom and a total fertility rate of 3.5 in 1947 and 1948, resulted in mass emigration of young adults from Finland in the 1960s (Figure 8.4). Because Sweden's economy was flourishing at the time, even Finnish migrants who did not speak Swedish were able to find work in its semi-automated, but still labour-intensive, industries.

Many of the group who went to Sweden in pursuit of work did, however, later move back to Finland. Finland's population has been rising by around 19,000 every year since the early 2000s, a growth rate that is now almost entirely due to immigration. It would have risen even more, were it not for the concurrent emigration rate of about 15,000 Finns annually since the year

2000. From 1998 to 2010, the working-age population increased steadily by 11,800 people a year. Since 2010 it has fallen steadily by 15,900 a year (Federal Reserve Bank of St. Louis 2019).

A further motivation for migration in the 1960s in particular was attributed to the introduction, in 1952, of a new passport union between Finland and the countries of the Nordic Council, which enabled people to cross borders without passports and later to apply for jobs and claim social security benefits in other Nordic countries. With Finnish wages and living standards lagging behind those of Sweden until the economic boom of the 1970s, many Finns opted to cross the border in search of better-paid jobs.

It was only from the late 1980s and then again for most of the 1990s that a significant upward trend began to be established of inward-migration dominating overall population growth in Finland. Net migration has remained positive since 1981, but at times has been almost insignificant.

In 2007, net immigration for the first time accounted for more than half of Finland's population growth. By 2015, over 80 per cent of its population increase was due to net immigration, and in the following two years the increase in population was entirely due to immigration, as birth rates dipped below death rates for the first time since 1940.

The number of immigrants arriving in Finland has doubled since the turn of the twenty-first century. As Figure 8.5 shows, a large number of immigrants (usually between 5,000 and 8,000 each year) are Finnish nationals returning home. Although the numbers have remained relatively stable, the proportion of all immigrants who are Finnish has declined from around 40–45 per cent between 1995 and 2005, to around 25 per cent today. Immigration from the rest of the EU, and also particularly from Asia, has grown in importance over the same period.

Whereas in 1990 Asian people represented just 9 per cent of all immigrants to Finland, by 2017 they accounted for 33 per cent of the total. In 2018, Iraq, China, Thailand, Vietnam, Iran, Afghanistan, India and Syria were the most common countries of origin of immigrants to Finland (OSF 2019c). Immigration from other EU states has increased significantly since 2004, when eight eastern and central European countries joined the EU and their citizens began emigrating in large numbers to more prosperous countries within Europe.

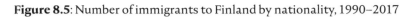

Figure 8.5: Number of immigrants to Finland by nationality, 1990–2017

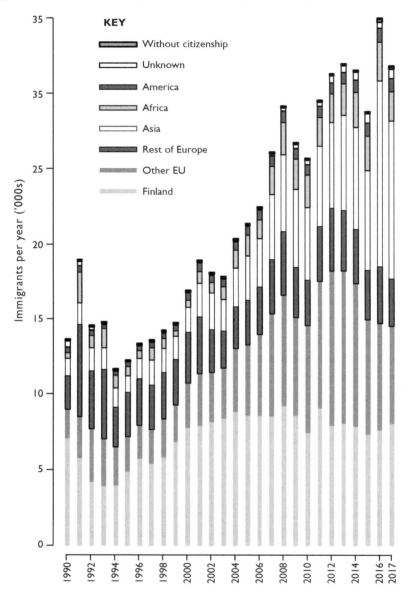

Source: Official Statistics of Finland (OSF) (2019q).

Perhaps because Finland is not very far west (and borders Russia), the Finns did not experience much of a rise in migration from eastern Europe. However, as immigration from many other countries has risen, there has been a decline in both the number and proportion of immigrants to Finland from the rest of Europe (outside the EU) – which principally means Russia and other countries of the former Soviet Union.

As the proportion of the Finnish population who are retirees grows, it is estimated that Finland will require around 34,000 immigrants of working age every year for the next decade, to fill vacancies in healthcare and social care in particular, but also for labour in the construction and video gaming industries (Bedhall 2018).

One of Finland's attractions for immigrants, once they obtain their residence permits and secure employment, is its policies aimed at a healthy balance in family and work life. This does not mean they are likely to have more children: as a rule, people have more children in more economically unequal countries. Migrants who move to Finland will tend to have fewer children than if they had remained at home. However, like most migrants worldwide, they are still likely to be poorer than the average established resident when they arrive and for many years afterwards. In Finland, the poor are still poor. The poorest 10 per cent of individuals in Finland in 2015 received 3.9 per cent of all income, on average slightly less than two fifths of mean national average income (World Bank 2018b).

When compared to a highly unequal country such as the UK, the proportion of national income that Finland's poorest inhabitants receive appears relatively high. In the UK, the income share of the poorest tenth of the population is 2.9 per cent, which means surviving on just less than 30 per cent of average income (World Inequality Database 2018). The poor in Finland also have access to far more services than do their counterparts in the UK. Furthermore, the official relative poverty rate for Finland in 2016 was 11.6 per cent, with men being fractionally (0.1%) more likely to be poor than women. In contrast, and using the same calculation, the rate in the UK was 15.9 per cent, and, unlike Finland, 38 women were poor for every 35 men who were poor (Eurostat 2018d).

In terms of income, households are even more equitable in Finland than are individuals. The UNDP income-quintile-ratio, the income of the best-off fifth of households as compared to the worst-off fifth, was 3.9 for Finland in 2010–15, whereas for the UK it was 5.3 (UNDP 2017). That is a huge difference. In the UK, well-off young people tend to pair up and marry, creating richer households; poor young people are more likely to have poor partners and so the inequality between households in the UK is even greater than that between individuals. Couples in Finland are far freer to pair up without unduly considering what each other earns (although they have access to that information, as individuals' tax returns are public documents!), or what wealth each may inherit, because the inequality gap is smaller across the population. It is notable that divorce rates in Finland have remained stable since the 1990s and have even reduced in the past decade, with the absolute number falling from 13,727 in 2009 to 13,145 in 2018 (OSF 2019h).

Finland has come a long way in many quality of life measures, but it ranks appallingly in metrics such as rates of violence against women, the fitness and effectiveness of its legislation on domestic violence and rape, and on acceptance of transgender individuals (Ministry for Foreign Affairs 2019b). Racism and problems with social integration might be regrettably predictable for a country that has only recently become more multicultural, but given the attention paid to gender equality, some of Finland's "antiquated" legislation is shocking (Amnesty International 2019).

Women and sexual minorities

Among matters of demography and the wider social environment, one area in which Finland does not do as well as might be expected is in the experiences of women and the treatment of sexual minorities. As was highlighted elsewhere in this book, significant gender inequality persists at most stages of life in Finland. Even so, the European Institute for Gender Equality ranked Finland fourth best (score 73.4) in its global 2017 Gender Equality Index (EIGE 2019). Sweden came first (83.6), Denmark came second (77.5) and France came third (74.6).

It was Finland's slightly lower scores in women's health and working conditions, pay and opportunities that have kept the country's overall score down. In the most recent assessment in 2019, women comprised just 34 per cent of board members in the largest listed companies, and 25 per cent of the

Finnish Central Bank's board members. Female participation in the work-place is higher in Finland than in most other European countries, but in other aspects of gender equity, Finland is not as advanced as it initially appears to be.

It is true that in 2019 female representation in the Parliament of Finland increased to 94 out of 200 MPs, or 47 per cent (Parliament of Finland 2019d). By mid-2019, 58 per cent of ministers, or 11 of 19, in Prime Minister Antti Rinne's 2019 cabinet were female (Finnish Government 2019). In contrast, in the US, only 25 per cent of seats in the Senate and 23 per cent in the House of Representatives are held by women (Hansen 2019). In the UK, the December 2019 election yielded a record high for female MPs, at just 34 per cent; it is unlikely to rise again for at least five years, as the next national poll is sched-uled for 2024.

The gender inequality index changes over time in terms of what is included. It was not until 2015 that violence was included in the index. Vio-lence is the only category in which a score closer to 100 does not indicate closer equality, but instead a higher incidence of the phenomenon. In 2017, within Europe, Finland had the fourth-highest record of violence against women (32.4), and the UK ranked eleventh (29.0) – however, we do not know the extent to which women in these two countries consider different physi-cal acts of aggression as violent, or are willing to report such acts in surveys (EIGE 2019). In 2019, Finland was the second least secure country in the EU for women and girls (Tolkki 2019a).

Areas in which Finnish women suffered significantly more than their male counterparts included not only in experiencing violence within rela-tionships, but also a higher poverty rate among the very elderly. Women are more likely to be in insecure employment, to have only temporary work, to be subject to greater racial harassment, and to receive the worst preventive healthcare with regard to cancer screening. A 2014 study by the EU Agency for Human Rights found that almost every second Finnish woman (47%) had experienced physical and/or sexual violence at some point since the age of 15, and almost one in three had been abused by their partner.

When the Council of Europe found that "Finland is failing survivors of rape", researcher Anna Blus at Amnesty International raised concerns over Finland's antiquated rape laws (Amnesty International 2019). A mere 209

convictions were made for rape in 2017, despite some 50,000 women reporting having experienced sexual violence in that year. In 2019, GREVIO (Group
of Experts on Action against Violence against Women and Domestic Violence) reported on the shortcomings of the Finnish legal system in addressing
sexual violence and domestic abuse, noting for example the limited legal
definition of rape. In 2020 the Ministry of Justice announced that the legal
definition of rape would be updated to include the lack of consent, among
other amendments.

Professionals in Finland's criminal justice system – prosecutors and law
enforcement officers – were found to be inadequately trained to identify and
understand the gendered nature of violence against women and its complex
forms, with some important areas of training remaining optional, including
honour-related violence, female genital mutilation, forced marriage, and
stalking (GREVIO 2019: 6). Factors such as these mean that women who
are immigrants are thus further disadvantaged in Finland's justice system.
There is limited capacity for public authorities to properly handle the cases
of immigrant women. Furthermore, as the GREVIO (2019: 7) report notes,
while the Finnish Aliens Act provides some basis for foreign women to access
an independent residence permit – in particular when their initial residence
permit was derived through sponsorship from an abusive spouse – the process to do so has not yet been fully or properly developed. Fear of deportation
and of having to leave their children behind means that foreign-born women
in Finland are more likely to remain with an abusive spouse.

Other demographic groups in Finland who might be less likely to relate
to Finland's ranking as the happiest country in the world include sexual
minorities. Homosexuality was decriminalized in Finland in 1971. Registered
same-sex partnerships were first allowed in 2002, and same-sex marriage
and joint adoption was approved in 2014 by the Finnish parliament following
a petition signed by 167,000 citizens (Seta 2017). The law came into effect on
1 March 2017. In 1995 discrimination based on sexual orientation was prohibited, and discrimination based on gender identity or gender expression
was prohibited in 2005 (Nybergh 2016).

In 2002, Finland's Trans Act gave people the right to legally change their
gender, but an individual had to be sterile or sterilized and have mental
health screening as a precondition. Despite calls by civil society (in particular

the Finnish Human Rights Centre, Amnesty International, the UN Human Rights Council, and the European Court of Human Rights) that the sterilization requirement is a violation of human rights, this condition remains in force. In June 2019, the Rinne government said it would remove the sterilization requirement for gender reassignment procedures. Other than in this one conspicuous policy area, Finland's recognition of LGBTQ rights and related policies are very good in the main (although outranked by Norway) and very much better than most countries in eastern, central and southern Europe.

The environmental successes and challenges of Finland

There are many things that Finland does well and many areas of life where it leads the rest of the world, which Finns are (usually quietly) proud of, and it is precisely these things that are likely to make the country an attractive place to live for outsiders. It may help at this point just to give some examples. For instance, according to a study of 200 countries published in *The Lancet* (Öhberg 2018b), Finland maintains very high food safety standards, with low use of chemicals such as pesticides and antibiotics in food production, and it has the world's largest area (7 million hectares) devoted to the production of wild organic crops such as blueberries (*Finland Today* 2018b).

Finland, along with its Nordic neighbours, leads the world when it comes to ambitious policies to tackle climate change. In January 2019, Finnish politicians agreed to work to achieve carbon neutrality quicker than politicians of any other nation, and have set a more ambitious target now – to do so by 2035 (Öhberg 2019). Reducing air travel will be key. Finland boasts the safest airline in the world, with Finnair regularly coming top in an annual safety ranking published by aviation experts comparing the largest 100 airlines on key safety parameters (*Finland Today* 2019b). Now Finland needs to have not only the safest planes in the world; but it must also try to have fewer of them. As we were finishing writing this book in February 2020 the Finnish parliament was planning to debate a new aviation tax.

The Finns have even been held up as exemplars of good forest management by none other than Donald Trump. The American president blamed the Californian wildfires of November 2018 on forest mismanagement, and noted in a tweet that Finns take good care of their forests by raking them regularly! The underlying reasons for forest fires in California are not a lack of raking. Trump's assertion inspired Finns to post a number of tongue-in-cheek videos involving garden rakes on social media (Öhberg 2018c).

More environmentally minded Finns do worry that their forests should be logged less often to provide a better carbon sink, and also campaign for better wetland protection than currently exists, and this is partly because Finland remains a beacon for what might be possible elsewhere. The awe-inspiring and magical landscapes of Finland regularly draw people to the country. Its lightness and greenness can come as a pleasant surprise to many new arrivals. One English woman who recently moved to the country was quoted as saying, "I'm stunned by the sudden explosion of life. I came at the end of May and was not expecting the greenness. A part of me thought blackness was just a part of the country; the constant light seems surreal" (Bouzas 2018b).

The government voted into office in 2019 has been particularly ambitious in trying to tackle the climate crisis. How it aims to achieve its goals, however, has been questioned. For example, the funding it pledged to halt the decrease in biodiversity in Finland by 2020, at €100 million a year, is only half as much as Professor Janne Kitoaho has estimated is needed (Paananen 2019). This goal is derived from the EU, but as the environmentalist Petri Alroth has further pointed out, the EU has not set up sufficient steps for reaching either its goal for biodiversity or sustainable agriculture. More will be needed than mere political will to tackle the climate crisis effectively.

Despite continual concerns, or perhaps partly because of them, Finland's recent environmental record is impressive – although state this to a green-minded Finn and you will be quickly reminded about the issue of carbon sinks! Greenhouse gas emissions produced by Finnish residents both in Finland and abroad (as a result of their travel to other countries) was 59 million tonnes in 2017, 5 per cent less than the previous year. The main reason for this drop was a reduction in emissions from the energy sector, which shrank by 10 per cent between 2016 and 2017.

In recent years the use of biofuels for transport has increased, leading to a reduction in greenhouse gas emissions, particularly from land transport, where emissions fell by 10 per cent from 2016 to 2017, and in household emissions, which fell by 2 per cent. However, the use of biofuels did lead to a rise in CO_2 emissions from the energy supply industry, thanks to the burning of more biomass (OSF 2019i). What's more, other sources suggest that there was an increase in emissions in 2018 of 2 per cent, exceeding Finland's internationally agreed allocation for the year, because of the greater use of natural gas and peat (OSF 2019j). These annual statistics are very closely monitored in Finland.

As you will know having read this far, Finland's statisticians produce enormous quantities of statistics on their country, and increasingly they are producing statistics related to monitoring the environment. Thus, when it comes to waste and recycling, we know that the total waste Finland produced in 2017 was 117,917,000 tonnes. The vast majority (92%) was mineral waste, some 95 per cent of which went into landfill. This waste comes mainly from mining and quarrying, and to a much lesser extent construction and manufacturing. Changes in the total amounts of waste generated, therefore, usually reflect changes in mining and quarrying production. Finnish reliance on peat has been identified as a key obstacle to reaching its 2035 carbon-neutrality aim. But peatlands, bogs, and marshes which are harmed by its extraction can also be restored into carbon sinks. Tero Mustonen, an author of IPCC reports, has successfully challenged Vapo, the state-controlled peat company, on this issue when peat extraction led to acidic discharge into his village's river (Gatehouse 2020). On the statistics for household waste in Finland, the figure for 2017 was 2,226,000 tonnes, of which 91 per cent was incinerated to recover energy, 5 per cent was recycled, and only 4 per cent went into landfill. All paper and cardboard waste was recycled in 2017 and a third of all plastic and rubber waste, the rest being incinerated to create electricity. Discounting mineral waste, about 65 per cent of Finland's waste is subject to energy recovery, 28 per cent is recycled and 6 per cent goes to landfill (OSF 2019k).

In terms of travel, Finnish residents made 8.2 million leisure trips abroad in 2018 – a drop from 8.5 million the year before, mainly because of a significant fall in the number of trips to Estonia, which is the Finns' most popular travel destination. Spain and Sweden are the second and third most popular. There has been a steady increase in the number of business trips abroad since 2013, from 1.7 million to 2.3 million in 2018 (OSF 2019l). The majority of the 19 million arrivals and departures per year at Helsinki Vantaa's airport are foreign tourists (Eurostat 2018e).

When it comes to counting Finland's cars, at the end of 2018 there were

6.6 million registered vehicles in the country, of which 5 million were in use on the roads (so just under one vehicle per resident which is a high ratio). The number of registered vehicles rose by 2.3 per cent from the previous year, and the number of vehicles on the road increased by 0.8 per cent. At the end of 2018 there were 3.5 million passenger cars registered in Finland, an increase of 2.1 per cent from 2017, and 2.7 million of them were on the road, a 1 per cent increase on the previous years. The average age of registered passenger cars in mainland Finland is 14.9 years, but the average age of those on the road is 12.1 years. New cars tend to pollute less (OSF 2019m).

The rising trend in car usage is at odds with the government's plans to curtail automobile emissions. Within the sustainable transport policies of the previous and current government, a key plank was to increasingly replace liquid fuels with biofuels in domestic transport (Särkijärvi *et al*. 2018). Lower-emission cars will help in the short term, as the take-up of zero-emission vehicles will be limited in the near future. The aim of the Transport Climate Policy working group is not for the absolute figure of biofuels used to increase from 2030 onwards, but for its overall share to rise, given the limited resources available for its production (Särkijärvi *et al*. 2018: 12). Use of hybrid and electric cars is rising, but in 2019 these vehicles comprised only 6.5 per cent of newly registered cars (2.9 per cent in 2017), and 17.6 per cent of used imported cars in 2018 (Traficom 2019). Plans to build faster railway connections to Helsinki from other large cities, such as Turku and Tampere, could have an even greater impact given the number of people who work in Helsinki but live elsewhere, and the opportunity to use train rides as working time (Vento 2020).

Housing and environment

Finland industrialized very much later than much of Europe. A huge proportion of Finns, 64 per cent of the population, were still working in forestry and agriculture in 1950 and loans for farm and rural housing still exceeded loans for urban housing in 1957 (Soininvaara 2017). Development of public housing policy and the welfare state grew following Finland's belated urbanization in the late 1960s and 1970s, which is often referred to as the "Great Migration" to the city (Ruonavaara 2003: 53).

Over time the differences between tenure patterns in rural and urban areas grew smaller. The proportion of rental dwellings shrank radically to 28 per cent of the nation's total housing stock by 1988, compared to 72 per cent in 1950 (Soininvaara 2017). Although rental housing was more common in the early twentieth century, the type of tenure was not a significant factor in social stratification as the middle classes usually lived in central city rental apartments, while the working class lived in suburban timber-framed houses which they often owned.

Although Finland is more rural than almost any other country in Europe (Lyytikäinen 2006), the population is concentrated in urban areas and the population growth in cities increases demand for apartments (Alho *et al.* 2018: 4). To be a little more precise, some 95 per cent of Finland's land area is still rural, but 75 per cent of the population live in towns and cities (Huotari 2018). However, according to one countryside indicator, only 40 per cent of Finnish people think of themselves as urban.

Growth in the Helsinki region is similar to the rate of urban population growth in other Nordic cities, such as Stockholm, Oslo and Copenhagen (Soininvaara 2017). The growth of big cities is no longer driven by people leaving the countryside, but now comes at the expense of small and medium-sized cities. More housing is required to accommodate this population growth, which in turn increases the measured productivity of Finland's largest city.

Some economists in Finland have argued for greater state investment in Helsinki. The Swedish government invests ten times as much in the growth of Stockholm as the Finnish government does in its capital. A weak economy in Finland has, at times, contributed to uncertainty over jobs and income. This has lessened the appeal of home ownership, with young people now seeing renting as a more flexible option.

Finnish municipalities have a monopoly on decision-making over their urban planning (Saarima 2018). Another important factor on where people locate within the country is the impact of the government's income tax and consumption tax on urban and regional populations; as well as housing prices being lower and often falling in small towns. The government's Institute for Economic Research argues that moving to larger cities generally increases people's gross income, but high taxes and housing prices can lessen its appeal. Taxation can therefore discourage people from leaving areas that might have lower productivity and income, but otherwise provide a good standard of living.

Rural areas typically have less traffic, cleaner air and greater proximity to nature. In a recent survey of Finns, almost two thirds of respondents said they preferred being closer to nature rather than being in an urban environment. Nevertheless, Finland is indeed undergoing urbanization, and economists working at the Institute for Economic Research argue it ought to be accelerated to improve the country's competitiveness (Loikkanen 2013). Urban living may also be more environmentally friendly living, as city dwellers use cars less often and use less fuel to heat homes that are not detached; but it may not be what great numbers of people want. Finnish urban areas can also look drably functionalist, with the insides of apartments generally much nicer than the view of them from the outside!

Renting, free-time residences, and city living

It is because of the lower carbon footprint of urban life that city living is greener. People tend to travel by public transport or by walking or cycling more often than by car. In Helsinki electric scooters are popular – although one suspects that they are mainly provided for tourists.

As Finland's population grows, and if that growth is to be concentrated in its cities (while occasionally renting in the countryside for a holiday), it could be greener growth. That outcome, however, will depend on what the people living in the city do in their free time. If they opt to fly abroad regularly for holidays, then the country as a whole is unlikely to become greener.

Second homes, or free-time residencies (kesämökit) as they are known in Finnish, are popular in Finland and facilitate access to Finnish nature and countryside. Only one third of such residences are currently suitable for year-round use. At the end of 2017 there were 507,200 free-time residences in total (OSF 2017d). Most of these, 431,000, were owned privately and 76,200 were owned by companies, foreigners or communities. Such residences are very traditional and important for Finns as a holiday destination that (most of the time) does not require air miles to reach. Often such residences are owned by the extended family.

A majority (290,700) of the owners of free-time residences in Finland do not live in the municipality in which the free-time residence is located. Around 819,000 people (15 per cent of the population) are members of what is technically described to be a "household-dwelling unit that owned a free-time residence" (Ministry of Agriculture and Forestry 2016). The average age of owners at the time of this survey was 62, only 12 per cent had children under 18, and roughly 60,000 worked remotely in them, with 100,000 occasionally commuting from them. On average, 79 days per year were spent in free-time residences during 2016. Of course, unlike in the UK and US where second-home and holiday-home ownership tends to result in more homelessness, the same is not true in Finland because, as we explained above, there is almost no homelessness in Finland.

Finland's second homes contribute to the local economy through services and employment and help to move a lot of money around the country. They play an important role in the development of the countryside and nine out of ten free-time residences have access to electric power. Of this, a seventh is generated by solar panels.

Spending on Finland's free-time residencies totalled approximately €6.3 billion in 2014, and indirectly or directly employed 60,000 people. Additionally, €1.7 billion was spent on repairs, €1.4 billion was spent on groceries, €1.2 billion was spent on travelling, and €700 million through property tradespeople annually.

Conclusion

In 2019, climate was the most important talking point of the Finnish general election, with the Finns Party alone in leaving climate change action off their agenda. The increased recognition of the importance of climate change and the environment was one of the reasons traditional parties saw their vote share shrink. Of particular interest is analysis that suggested that forest owners voted for parties with greener policies. With 600,000 forest owners in Finland, forestry features significantly in environmental policy and climate change debates.

The *New York Times*, in commenting on the 2019 election, said that the Finns Party had made climate change politics appear to be a concern of the political elite (Lemola 2019). The chairperson of the Finns Party is described in Finland as a climate-pessimist – someone who thinks what will be will be, and it just has to be accepted (Elonen & Mikkonen 2019).

The Finnish government, largely in step with the country's political elite as a whole, set out an extremely ambitious plan to become carbon-neutral by 2035. These plans were improved following protests inspired by young Swedish activist Greta Thunberg's campaigning in response to the climate crisis. Finnish protesters undertook mass climate strikes on 27 September 2019 along with the rest of the world. Estimates of the numbers of participants in Helsinki's demonstrations ranged from 16,000 to 18,000 – over 2.5 per cent of the city's population (Sequiera & Richardson 2019). According to police estimates, some 5,000–6,000 people gathered in front of the Finnish Parliament to make their demands heard; and they were listened to.

The banners of the protesters outside Parliament in the autumn of 2019 called attention to a range of concerns, such as the ongoing clear-cutting of forests in Finland. Clear-cutting is when every single marketable tree is cut down in an area; it is good for logging companies' short-term profit and bad for the environment, soil erosion and species diversity. On this issue, Sampo Soimakallio, the head of the Sustainable Use of Natural Resources unit of the Finnish Environment Institute, concluded that future political action would determine if and when the government would shift its position on forestry. The government is currently concentrating on the profits from wood production, and is being called on to understand better the capacity of forests to fight the climate crisis, and shift its policy. The petition to change legislation to prevent clear-cutting received significantly more than the 50,000 signatures required to proceed to parliament (Parliament of Finland 2019e).

The Research Institute of the Finnish Economy (Kaitila 2020) very recently published an assessment of Finland's capacity to meet the 2035 goal based on the development of greenhouse emissions and carbon sinks. There is no doubt that Finland has set itself an incredibly challenging goal, and Finland must go far further than simply planting more trees (and resisting cutting so many down to produce pulp). Most importantly, it must support and take advantage of Finnish technological innovation in energy production and other environmentally damaging industries, and promote measures that will change consumer and corporate behaviour, for which market mechanisms and price incentives can be useful.

Finland's success in so many international environmental rankings won't solve the climate crisis. As Greta Thunberg explained (on Instagram) when she declined the Nordic Council's environmental award on 29 October 2019:

> The Nordic countries have a great reputation around the world when it comes to climate and environmental issues. There is no lack of bragging about this. There is no lack of beautiful words. But when it comes to our actual emissions and our ecological footprints per capita – if we include our consumption, our imports as well as aviation and shipping – then it's a whole other story (Brito 2019).

Finnish postage stamp *c.* 1992, showing the main Moomin cartoon character overlooking a melting river during the winter, looking worried. Illustration by Tove Jansson. Olga Popova © 123RF.COM and reproduced with permission.

9

Success fatigue

"Child poverty increased more for Greece and Spain ... the latter especially showing an increasing trend at the end of the period. By contrast,
Finland had lower rates of child poverty with a diminishing trend during
the last years. Greece showed an increasing percentage of material deprivation in children from families with primary education level from the
year 2009 onwards, while Sweden showed the opposite trend."

Rajmil *et al.* (2018)

Finland has become the "by way of contrast" country, as the *British Medical
Journal* described it in 2018. Finland is the one place, above all other places
in Europe, that shows that something much better is possible than the status quo. That is a weighty responsibility. Of course, Finland is not Utopia, but
today it offers one of the closest approximations.

In 2018, when Finland first achieved its top placing in the UN's World
Happiness Report, a UK newspaper reported the news with the caveat:
"... even though its GDP is below that of the US and Germany" (Boseley 2018).
Finland shows why achieving a very high GDP is not necessary for great happiness as GDP is one of the measures where Finland does not top the tables.
When Finland overtook Norway to take first place in the World Happiness
Report, it did so with a GDP per capita that was more than a third lower
than that of Norway; and it held that top ranked position in both 2019 and
2020.

Finland is the country that shows how it is possible for happiness to be
achievable without becoming ever richer, and while having living standards

219

in terms of material wealth that are far below those in the most affluent parts of the world, including its more affluent Scandinavian neighbours. However, the publication in August 2018 of "In the Shadow of Happiness", a report on mental wellness, prompted some in the media to question the picture of Finland and its Nordic neighbours as happy places:

> The Nordic countries top the polls as the happiest in the world, but the assumption that life in Scandinavia is all bicycles and big smiles disguises the sadness of a significant minority of young people, it has emerged.
>
> Among those in Denmark, Finland, Norway, Sweden and Iceland who do not say that life is good, some of the largest numbers are among the young – and particularly young women. While the reasons will vary from one individual and one country to another, it is thought that stress, loneliness and feeling under pressure to succeed may be playing a large part in their unhappiness. (Boseley 2018)

The authors of the report (Andreasson & Birkjær 2018) had produced a graph to illustrate what the newspapers called "Nordic woes" (Figure 9.1). Respondents to their survey were asked how happy they were on a scale of 0 to 10, with a number of four or less interpreted as "suffering", and "struggling" defined by replies of 5 (average) or 6 (over-average). The inclusion of people who say that they are doing a little better than average as struggling was questionable. Nevertheless, the proportion of people reporting these levels are all relatively small, and the numbers provide only a snapshot of a person's sense of subjective well-being on a particular day. However, this does not mean they do not warrant attention; even though Finland turns out to have one of the lowest proportions of people in the world who report less than "7" in this measure of mental wellness.

In all Nordic countries combined, 12.3 per cent of the adult population was considered to be suffering or struggling, while for adults aged 18–23 the proportion was 13.5 per cent. In Finland, 11.5 per cent of all adults reported difficulties. However, for young Finnish women aged 18–23, the proportion was higher at 15 per cent, compared to 11 per cent for Finnish men in the same age group.

Figure 9.1: Proportion of adults by mental health, 2012–16

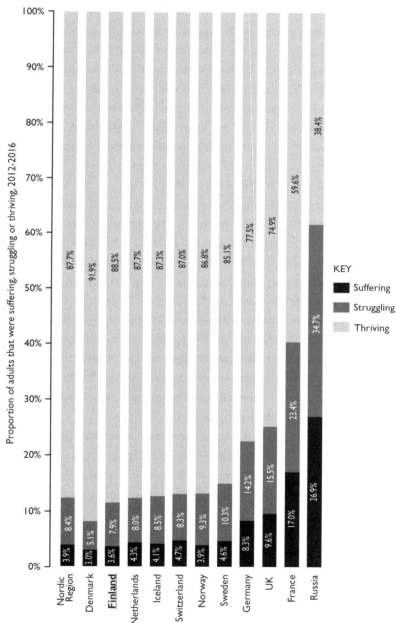

KEY
■ Suffering
■ Struggling
□ Thriving

Source: Andreasson & Birkjaer (2018).

Who is not happy?

Research conducted in Denmark suggests that a culture of perfectionism may be developing among some of the country's young adults there. The same, of course, is possible in Finland, even though the two countries are very different. Michael Birkjær of the Happiness Research Institute has suggested: "Young people feel they are expected to excel in exams – something referred to as 'the 12th grade culture' . . . It is a huge debate in Denmark and not something we can ignore. . . . We have seen these decreases in happiness in many countries since the financial crisis, even though countries *like* Denmark have regained economic growth" (emphasis added).

The very elderly in Nordic countries, including Finland, do well compared with very old people in other countries, but the proportion of them who say they are suffering is actually a fraction higher than for their young compatriots. This is because people with poor general health are those who most frequently report that they are struggling (Dorling 2016). Poor mental health was the second most important correlate that the Happiness Research Institute study found in predicting unhappiness. It was followed by respondents reporting that their understanding of inequality of income meant that they knew they were losing out. Next most important in predicting unhappiness was unemployment. Finally, respondents who reported that they had limited social contact were more likely to be unhappy, which was seen by the authors of this study as a good proxy for loneliness.

The researchers who produced the "In the Shadow of Happiness" report also discovered that: "Older men who were unhappy were less likely to see family and friends than older women". But for the young, it was not poor general health or loneliness that was key, but poor mental health. The report concluded:

Mental health problems among young people manifest themselves in the form of stress, depression, anxiety, self-harm, consumption of antidepressants and, in extreme cases, suicide. [This last] is a particularly big problem in Finland, which otherwise ranks as the happiest country according to the World Happiness Reports of 2018, 2019 and 2020. Here, suicide is responsible for one-third of all deaths among 15–24 year-olds.

Ulf Andreasson, senior advisor in the policy analysis and statistics unit of the Nordic Council of Ministers and an author of the report, said they wanted to look further because everybody knows people who are not happy, in spite of the image. "We also had a feeling that being unhappy in the Nordic countries perhaps comes with some kind of stigma", he said. "If everybody is happy and I'm unhappy, is it OK to give voice to that? We wanted to de-stigmatise being unhappy."

In Finland, children and young adults have one great advantage. This is that even when people there know they are living in the country that scores highest in the world for happiness, adults are still very concerned for the well-being of children – all children, and not just their own. And when those children become young adults, even though the levels of stress they show are some of the lowest in the affluent world, these difficulties are still of great concern to the wider population.

Finnish suicides decreased in the 1990s and 2000s, with a particularly rapid drop for men from around 1,193 in 1990 to 558 in 2015. However, since then levels have increased for both men and women, and remain above the EU average (Findikaattori 2018). It is not clear what led to the drop in suicide rates, but attributable factors include a national prevention campaign that began in the 1980s, increased research into psychiatric services, cultural change, and the normalization of depression in daily conversation (Isometsä 2019). There were also improvements in treatment, in particular via new medications with fewer side effects. After 2011, fewer anti-depressants were being prescribed, psychiatric outpatient care increased, and it became easier to access state (Kela) supported rehabilitative psychotherapy (Jaskari 2018). An online health network called Mental Health Hub was developed to address access issues, especially for Finns living in more rural areas (Johnson 2017; Kingsley 2019).

Professional development in psychiatry and increased specialization has also helped. The public sector Sote reforms, if successful, should help professionals to better address health problems related to social issues such as loneliness. The Finnish Psychological and Psychiatric Associations are lobbying the new more left-wing government to place even greater importance on mental health services. Fundamentally, they say that "every suicide is one too many", and access to services and professionals needs to be increased as only half the people in need of help seek it (Finnish Psycho-logical Association 2019).

Today's regional inequalities in mental health provision can be traced back to those budget cuts for mental health services that were made in the 1990s (Lindberg 2018). However, in 2017, Finland had the highest number of psychiatrists per person – 236 per million inhabitants – closely followed by Sweden, the Netherlands, France, Lithuania, Luxembourg, Germany and Greece (Eurostat 2017). Furthermore, Finnish social work practitioners find ways to enhance prevention through the creative use of mainstream resources being redirected to their client's benefit. In contrast, practitioners in countries such as the UK more often say that such actions would require them to go beyond accepted expectations, that such actions would be con-sistent with "going the extra mile" rather than being normal practice as they have now become in Finland (Stepney 2014).

Recent research conducted in Finland has established that "well-being is to a significant extent conditioned by the position one occupies in the social structure and by the welfare regime one lives in" (Kemppainen 2012). However, that research also found that Finland is unusual in one other way, namely when it comes to the thoughts and feelings of recent migrants to the country.

Welcoming strangers to stability

In affluent countries, immigrants usually tend to be more optimistic than the natives of their new country. When the UN measured the happiness of immi-grants for the first time in their 2018 report, Finland scored the highest of any country being compared (Collinson 2019b). However, in general in Nordic countries, including Finland, where people's well-being is generally so high, being of an immigrant background is an adverse factor, when all else is taken into account. Whether this is because native Finns who are equally poor are comparatively less miserable, or because immigrants in Finland are made to feel unusually unwelcome in a society that is so socially cohesive, is not yet known. It is possible that it is very hard for outsiders to fit into a society that is already so equal and cohesive.

If you turn up in London or New York as an immigrant, you are just one of many similar others in cities full of immigrants. What is more, you have just arrived in a society that is deeply divided. The rich do not trust the poor, and the poor have good reason not to trust the rich. Almost everyone is an outsider in one way or another. Many, if not most, people you meet will be migrants like you, or their parents were. The same cannot be said of Finland or of other countries that top the list of most happy or most politically stable places. In Chapter 2 of this book, a brief mention was made of the international index of political stability. Here, in Table 9.1, is the list of the most stable countries in the world today and the measures of the components to stability.

Table 9.1: The ten most politically stable countries in the world in 2019, stability measures

Country (the top 10 of all 178)	Rank (178th is the most stable)	Total (of scores to rank)	Security Apparatus	Factionalized Elites	Group Grievance	Economic Decline	Uneven Economic Development	Human Flight and Brain Drain	State Legitimacy	Public Services	Human Rights and Rule of Law	Demographic Pressures	Refugees & internally displaced	External Intervention
Finland	178	16.9	2.5	1.4	1.2	2.9	0.7	2.0	0.9	0.7	0.7	1.0	1.9	1.0
Norway	177	18.0	2.1	1.1	3.3	1.9	1.0	1.3	0.6	0.8	0.9	1.2	2.8	1.0
Switzerland	176	18.7	1.1	1.0	3.3	1.9	1.8	1.7	0.7	1.0	1.4	1.4	2.7	0.7
Denmark	175	19.5	1.3	1.4	4.3	1.6	1.2	1.9	0.9	0.9	1.7	1.6	2.0	0.7
Australia	174	19.7	2.7	1.7	3.3	1.6	1.6	1.0	1.0	1.5	1.7	1.2	1.7	0.7
Iceland	173	19.8	0.7	1.8	1.0	3.1	0.9	2.5	1.0	1.0	1.0	1.3	1.7	3.8
Canada	172	20.0	2.8	2.5	2.8	1.5	2.1	1.7	0.7	1.0	1.4	1.3	1.6	0.7
New Zealand	171	20.1	1.4	1.4	3.2	3.2	1.9	2.3	0.6	1.0	0.8	1.7	1.7	0.9
Sweden	170	20.3	2.7	1.8	1.7	1.5	1.5	1.1	0.8	0.9	0.9	1.6	4.9	0.9
Luxembourg	169	20.4	1.3	3.4	2.7	1.2	1.2	1.7	0.7	1.7	1.0	1.6	3.1	0.8

Source: Fragile States Index (2019b).

Note: 178th is "most stable" and low scores are better scores. For an explanation of the measures see: https://fragilestatesindex.org/indicators/.

The Fragile State Index (previously the "Failed State Index") has been published annually since 2005. It ranks 178 countries across 12 indicators that attempt to summarize the key risks and vulnerabilities faced by individual nations. Currently, Finland ranks highest overall in this index, as the least fragile state in the world. It also ranks highest on many components of the index, including on low group grievance, on high (as well as even) economic development, on good public services, and on low demographic pressures – all as compared with the other countries in the top ten shown in Table 9.1.

At first it appears quite remarkable that as well as performing very strongly on so many other international rankings, Finland ranks highest of all 178 countries for political stability. However, international rankings are very positively correlated with each other. It is easier for your people to be happy if your state is not fragile, your press is free and responsible, your schools are cohesive, the health of your infants is good and the health of the population as a whole is improving rapidly from what used to be quite a poor record.

The reason Finland ranks so highly on all these international comparisons is not simply because it is a particularly homogeneous nation. Among the countries with higher proportions of refugees than Finland (where they constitute just 0.22 per cent of the population) are a number of other "highly stable" states: Sweden (1.47%), Norway (0.91%), Switzerland (0.85%), Canada (0.42%) and Denmark (0.32%), with the figures in parenthesis reflecting the proportion of the total population who were refugees registered between 2007 and 2016. However, these countries' share of refugees are dwarfed by the figures, in these same years, for Lebanon (where refugees made up 21 per cent of the population), Jordan (9%) and Turkey (24%). Incidentally, internationally, when it comes to state stability, Sweden (where refugees make up 1.47 per cent of its population) ranked ninth, the UK (only 0.18%) 59th and the US (0.84%) 75th (Wikipedia 2019c).

It is possible to do well and have more migrants than Finland currently has; and also, for migrants to feel more at home more quickly than those in Finland currently do. Thus, even in the world's least fragile state, there is still much room for improvement.

Ancient lessons on equality, housing and hospitality

We are still in the infancy of our understanding of what makes large groups of people happy. This applies as much to current research focused on today's societies using household surveys and other sources to produce fragile state indices, as to research now being conducted into the most ancient of societies. All societies have rules of hospitality for greeting strangers. These developed over millennia and they can easily be suspended or quickly strengthened depending on the actions and perseverance of individuals. We sometimes forget that we or our ancestors were once strangers in a strange place. It can help to look back in time to see where, in the past, high equality has been successfully achieved and maintained for a long time.

Archaeologists have recently made some remarkable findings while studying the relics of people living in a harsh environment thousands of years ago, near Lake Turkana in the Kenyan Rift Valley at a time when the rains failed and it became much harder to subsist. What the archaeologists concluded, as Kate Grillo, the co-director of the excavations explained, was that "the burial of even small children with ornaments indicates that everyone in the society was valued. This was a supposedly terrible period, with much harder environmental conditions than earlier periods, but instead of the conflict you would expect we are seeing larger and tighter social networks." There are lessons here for us today (Burke 2018). And this is just one of many recent archaeological studies pointing to the ways that humans grew to respect each other when "war and rich elites were unknown more than 3,000 years ago" (Cushing 2018). No wonder equality is so good for us: we evolved to live as equals.

Finland today is one of the few environments on earth that replicates most closely the situation in which we are most content: when we are caring for each other and not competing; where we are each valued very similarly, and where no one is greatly elevated or diminished. In another affluent country that is in many ways Finland's opposite, in today's UK, 1 in every 200 people are homeless. In Finland the proportion is at least four times lower and almost no people are to be found actually sleeping on the streets anywhere in Finland.

Crude estimates by the UK government show that the number of people who were street homeless rose by 169 per cent between 2009 and 2018 in England (Ministry of Communities and Local Government 2018). In Finland homelessness fell by 35 per cent, and rough sleeping was eradicated in Helsinki, where only one 50-bed night shelter now remains (Henley 2019).

Every week on the streets of England, three people who have nowhere safe to sleep die. The BBC recently reported that Finland was "the only EU state not suffering from a housing crisis which is the result of Finland's Housing First initiative which started in 2008 ... in Finland housing is seen as a right, not as a reward, as it often is in other EU countries. The Finnish system is financed by public funds and Finnish slot machines" (BBC3 2018), and the government is considering using new (including on-line) gambling taxes and licences as well. Finland is abandoning transitional and temporary housing for the homeless. Instead, they are given a normal apartment, immediately.

As news spreads of Finland's success across so many areas of public life, there is a risk of success fatigue setting in, of Finns resting on their laurels, and of people who would like lower taxes proclaiming that enough has already been achieved. On the other hand, success also encourages success, and Finland has a reputation to maintain.

As a small nation, Finland inevitably pays a lot of attention to its high ranking on many international indices. The general populace is aware of the country's prominent position in such measures, and the Foreign Ministry shares its success frequently via social media. Some Finns are sceptical of the methods used, of course, and of the way things such as "happiness" are interpreted. For example, Finns know that Finland would not be the happiest country in the world if it were judged on how positive survey respondents said they felt on the preceding day to the day they are asked (Ervasti 2019). So Finns, or at least Finland's academics and journalists, do turn a critical eye on the research methods and metrics underpinning such rankings and don't accept their results without question.

Finland's high rankings appear to help draw attention to the value of Finnish institutions. The new government tends to speak of restoring honour to the Finnish education system (by investing once again, rather than cutting). In a more theoretical sense, happiness or achievement is always relative; you value good times more when you've had bad times. In one of his best-known works, Eino Leino, a pioneer of Finnish poetry in the late nineteenth and early twentieth century, wrote "he who has happiness, should hide it". Jukka Ukkola, whose columns in the weekly newspaper *Suomen Kuvalehti* are typically satirical, quoted this line when Finland was first proclaimed the world's happiest country, and joked that because Finns can no longer hide their happiness, they should learn to market it (Ukkola 2018). As with the PISA educational rankings, he suggested, perhaps researchers will soon start arriving to ask how Finland has become so happy.

The good news for the rest of the world is that Finland will not always be at the top of the rankings, because its achievements are not an unobtainable extreme. In Finland, as elsewhere, there are always things that could be better. And, as this book has made clear, Finland has only a fairly modest amount of natural resources, no unusual historical advantages, no innate national characteristic, no special trick or magic word (such as *sisu*) to account for its current position.

To treat each other with respect is to be human; not to do so is inhumane. Regrettably, all of us are capable of both. By choosing the right path more often when there was an option, Finland has shown that any nation could do as well. And by doing so well it achieves so much else as a by-product of greater equality.

The non-fake press, in and about Finland

Part of how Finland avoids fatigue is the robustness of its press. Ed Miliband, a former leader of the Labour Party in the UK, has been a passionate and early campaigner on climate change and helped steer his political party to becoming both greener and more democratic, with every party member having the opportunity to vote for the next party leader. As a result, Britain now has a far more Finnish-style party in its Labour Party than it would have had if it were not for Ed; but Ed was often subjected to personal attacks in place of criticisms of his policies. His successor, Jeremy Corbyn, was attacked even more relentlessly, and in particular during the 2019 election, where he was misrepresented and demonized by both privately owned media and the state-owned BBC. It is true that the Labour Party has recently proposed some policies that would be too left-wing for Finland. For instance, in November 2019 the Labour Party proposed nationalizing the largest broadband company in the

UK and providing free broadband for all (BBC 2019c). However, it is more often the case that Labour's policies are significantly to the right of Finnish public policy; in its 2019 election manifesto, the UK's Labour Party proposed raising spending on public services, but only to German levels, rather than those of Finland. You would know little of this from reading the British press.

Recently featured on Ed Miliband's podcast "Reasons to be Cheerful", Vesa Häkkinen, the director of current affairs communications at Finland's Ministry for Foreign Affairs, spoke of the anti-disinformation campaign that was launched in Finland in 2014. The campaign encourages critical thinking and awareness to increase people's ability to spot fake news, from training election officials to reforming the education curriculum. When Miliband asked at what age Finnish children were educated about identifying disinformation, Häkkinen mentioned seeing a children's television show featuring a teddy-bear that was critical of the news during its adventures. To prevent cynicism rising, a good press and an aware citizenry are both vital.

As well as the government and journalists taking action to increase media literacy and critical thinking, social media companies must also play their respective part to combat disinformation. During late 2019, Finland held the presidency of the European Union. It chose to set priorities for its presidency that included strengthening common values and the rule of law. This followed the success of May 2018 when the EU brought in the General Data Protection Regulation (GDPR), the most important change in European data privacy regulation in 20 years, and the Finnish presidency aimed to build on that momentum.

During its presidency Finland's goals included making the EU more competitive and more socially inclusive, strengthening the EU's position as a global leader in climate action, and helping to protect the security of citizens comprehensively, including protection from disinformation (Ministry of Economic Affairs and Employment 2019).

According to Reporters Without Borders, Finland rose back up the global freedom of the press ranking from fourth place in 2018 to second place in 2019 (Yle Uutiset 2019g). Finns typically see press freedom and responsibility as a more serious matter than citizens of other states do. Finland is in the minority of countries where freedom of the press is characterized as good – see Figure 9.2 (Reporters Without Borders 2019). The earlier drop in the

Figure 9.2: Trust in journalism, 2015–16, leading countries

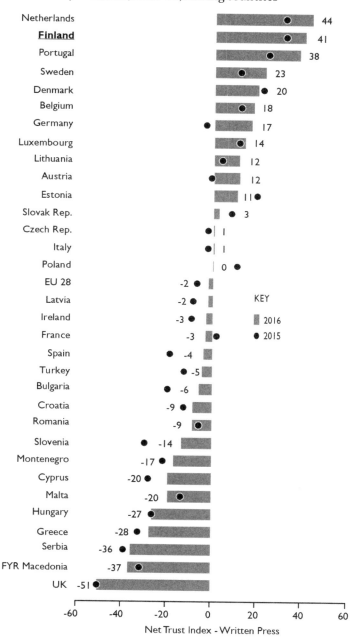

Source: Ponsford (2017).

rankings for Finland from first place in 2010 was attributed to "Sipilägate" – political interventions by former Prime Minister Juha Sipilä into the work of Yle, the state-owned but still very independent public service broadcasting company (Kauppinen 2016). Reporters Without Borders raised concerns after Yle altered its reporting on a conflict of interest involving funding provided to a state-owned mining company, Terrafame (now Finnish Minerals Group), in which relatives of the prime minister held ownership stakes (Reporters Without Borders 2016).

In 2018, two men, Ilja Janitskin and Johan Bäckman, were found guilty by the Helsinki district court of harassment and aggravated defamation of a journalist, Jessikka Aro, who was investigating Russian troll factories (offices that employ people to pretend to be members of the public and write comments on internet news stories and in social media). This was a significant case for defining the limits of what can justifiably be called freedom of speech, and when it is violated in cases of online harassment and defamation. Russian troll factories can expect to be exposed by Finnish journalists protected by Finnish courts. In 2018, Presidents Vladimir Putin and Donald Trump, arriving for a summit in Helsinki, were greeted with billboards and posters created by Finland's highest-circulation daily newspaper, *Helsingin Sanomat*, welcoming them to the "land of free press".

One concern raised by analyses such as the Centre for Media Pluralism and Media Freedom's annual *Media Pluralism Monitor* is the concentration of media ownership in Finland, and the lack of government regulation of that ownership. The centre's 2017 report found that the four largest companies in Finland's television-broadcasting sector together claimed a 92 per cent audience share and 72 per cent of revenues; in radio the figures were 94 per cent and 87 per cent respectively, and in the newspaper market it was 55 per cent and 71 per cent, respectively (Manninen 2018). Another concern raised by the report is the lack of proportional access to airtime by Finland's minorities. Media ownership concentration grew even further in February 2020 when media conglomerate Sanoma acquired another major media company, Alma Media. Although concerns were raised over the decreased media pluralism, the deal was not considered a significant risk to competition in the media market by the Finnish Competition and Consumer Authority.

Universal basic income

When we think of Finland as a role model for other countries, one initiative that comes up often is the idea of introducing a universal basic income (UBI). Universal basic income could represent a major shift in the current welfare state model of the West. Pilot experiments have recently been run in the city of Seattle and the Canadian province of Ontario, and in 2016 the Finnish government launched a basic income experiment involving 2,000 participants. UBI is not the only proposal for reforming social security in Finland. Most of the country's political parties have their own models, and the experiment itself was targeted rather than universal. Dutch historian and journalist Rutger Bregman stated that universal basic income "is all about freedom" at the 2019 World Economic Forum annual meeting in Davos (Klein 2019).

The Finnish Basic Income trial, which ran from 2017 to 2018, was initiated in response to the changing nature of work and the fact that a greater proportion of the population are now employed in temporary and part-time work (Muraja 2018). The participants, who were unemployed when they began the trial, received a basic income of €560 every month for two years regardless of any other income and regardless of whether they were actively seeking work. The trial aimed to assess whether the existing social security system could be simplified, and whether the alternative basic income system encouraged employability, since currently benefits diminish on starting paid employment or on receipt of other sources of income. The theory was that because basic income payments alone are not necessarily sufficient to cover all living costs in the long term (such as holidays), it therefore would not discourage recipients from finding work. One participant, journalist and writer Tuomas Muraja, responded to critics of the experiments saying:

> Concerns have been voiced about the high cost of the basic income model. But free school meals, free basic education and universal basic healthcare are expensive too... The system requires more investment to boost the minimum income level, to improve the level of financial incentives and to simplify it. Critics fear that basic income

233

will make people lazy. However, limited evidence from several basic-income trials from around the world prove that people use basic income to improve their quality of life and not as a license to do nothing.

The results published in 2019 showed that the intervention did not increase the number of people who found employment, but neither did it reduce it. Some attributed this to the design of the experiment; but even with these results, Rutger Bregman argued that other outcomes of the study warranted attention – namely, that participants reported higher levels of well-being, less stress, and greater overall happiness (Samuel 2019).

The experiment was criticized on the basis that in addition to including unemployed youth, the pool of participants was limited to primarily the long-term unemployed who would benefit more from services to help with health issues or outdated skills rather than from financial incentives. Additionally, taxation was not considered, and halfway through the experiment the "activation model" was introduced which skewed comparisons with the control group, that is, everyone else who was unemployed (Hiilamo 2019; Soininvaara 2019).

One thing worth bearing in mind about the early results of the trial is that increasing employment need not be a major aim of basic income. If people in Europe are to consume less, and pollute less, then they need to also produce less and learn to live on lower incomes than they currently do. A basic income makes it possible to live on a very low income and spend your time doing what you really want to do, including useful unpaid work. If you need a little more money, you can work, but it need not be high-paid work. If Finland is to remain one of the happiest countries in the world (Figure 9.3), it won't be because everyone works for as many hours as they can, for as much money as they can get. The World Happiness Report ranks countries according to GDP, life expectancy, generosity, social support, freedom, and corruption levels in each country to evaluate the quality of their current lives on a ladder scale ranging from 0 for the worst possible life to 10 for the best possible life. Figure 9.3 shows the ranking based on data collected between 2016 and 2018.

Figure 9.3: The happiest countries in the world, and selected others, 2016–18

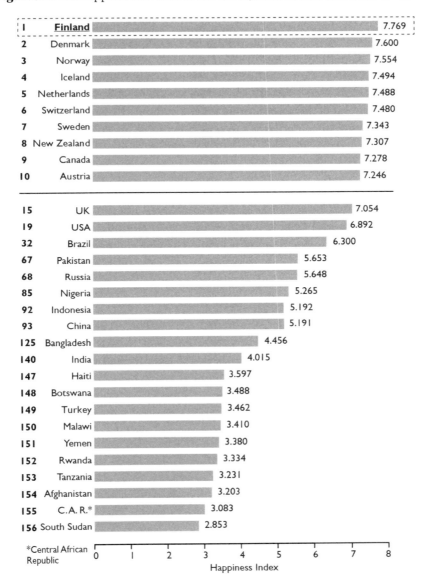

1	**Finland**	7.769
2	Denmark	7.600
3	Norway	7.554
4	Iceland	7.494
5	Netherlands	7.488
6	Switzerland	7.480
7	Sweden	7.343
8	New Zealand	7.307
9	Canada	7.278
10	Austria	7.246
15	UK	7.054
19	USA	6.892
32	Brazil	6.300
67	Pakistan	5.653
68	Russia	5.648
85	Nigeria	5.265
92	Indonesia	5.192
93	China	5.191
125	Bangladesh	4.456
140	India	4.015
147	Haiti	3.597
148	Botswana	3.488
149	Turkey	3.462
150	Malawi	3.410
151	Yemen	3.380
152	Rwanda	3.334
153	Tanzania	3.231
154	Afghanistan	3.203
155	C.A.R.*	3.083
156	South Sudan	2.853

*Central African Republic

Happiness Index

Source: Helliwell, Layard & Sachs (2019); as summarized at https://www.statista.com/chart/17428/happiest-countries-in-the-world/; and with additional data from https://en.wikipedia.org/wiki/World_Happiness_Report#2019_World_Happiness_Report

Promoting the Nordic model worldwide

Being held up as "best in class" is not an easy position to be in. For anyone who supports the aims of the Nordic model, this book should help confirm their understanding that, of all the systems currently running in Europe, its model is by far the most successful. But can it be translated to work elsewhere on that continent, or is there something intrinsic about the Nordic countries in general, and Finland in particular, that means that it would take two or three generations, possibly as long as a century, for somewhere else in Europe to "become Nordic", or even to do as well as Finland has done?

In contrast, any Finns who find fault with the Nordic model will doubtless find this book very annoying. They might well point out that until very recently Finland had been moving away from this model, and they might argue that this shift was for good reasons. The government in power in Finland until early 2019 had made changes intended to take Finland towards the British, or in some cases the US, model. These changes included the attempts to further privatize healthcare services, and levying fees for university tuition for non-EU students, unlike in Germany where university education remains essentially free for all. However, Finland is still to a very large extent the exemplar Nordic welfare state, even if the foundations of those ideals have been under recent attack.

In the past couple of decades, like acid rain eroding the façade of a once-beautiful building, neoliberal arguments and reasoning have etched scars deep into the surface of the body politic of Finland. This would not have happened had all been well in paradise, or if those outside of Finland had not wanted to change the direction in which it was going. In recent years right-wing think tanks in the UK and US have been targeting Finland, as have far-right parties and politicians who hate and fear the Nordic model. Many of those think tanks are almost certainly largely funded by American businesses and billionaires but they claim to present independent research and their funders hide behind a dark veil of anonymity (Ramsey & Geoghegan 2018).

In the not-so distant past, and still occasionally today, some far-right and extreme-right groups have lauded Scandinavia and its "white race". The notion of the true Aryan home of the white master-race is an extreme fantasy that never quite goes away. Because eugenic practices, including the steriliza-tion of those deemed unworthy to have children, were permitted in Sweden – right through to the 1970s – Scandinavians have partly lived up to their bit-part in this fantasy. Thankfully, however, Scandinavians and the Finns then looked out to the rest of the world. They saw the criticism of eugenics and reacted. Just as importantly, they saw how else society could be arranged, especially when children are not allocated to schools based on eugenic assumptions about inherent ability.

People in Finland were no doubt influenced greatly by what was occur-ring elsewhere in the world, not least the radicalism of the 1960s in the US and to a lesser extent in the UK, France and Germany at that time. Finland's most significant student protests in that era, which are not widely known outside of the country, occurred in 1968 when the Old Student House in Hel-sinki was occupied (Wikipedia 2019d). While it may be overstating the case to suggest that Finland had a "summer of love", nevertheless Finns travelled and brought home useful stories. From the 1960s onwards, a vision of what the greater welfare state could achieve became a widely shared dream. That dream became a reality through establishing common ground and common agendas between political left and right. This alliance helped all of Finnish politics to (in fits and starts) drift leftwards.

It was also during the 1960s that Finnish activists created the anti-authoritarian November Movement, which advocated for stigmatized peo-ples, among them the disabled, LGBTQ (referred to in Finland as "rainbow people"), prisoners, alcoholics, the mentally ill and the homeless (Alapuro 1997). The movement's goal was to reduce the pressure for uniformity in society. Today Finland is arguably the antithesis of what the world's political right admires, and the government elected in 2019 is moving Finland again in the direction of greater equality.

When viewed from a British or American standpoint, a Finnish con-servative today is likely to look very much like a socialist. Finland avoided the alternative that often arises when Social Democrats are dominant for a time, introduce a more wishy-washy welfare state, one that could have been more easily eroded. Instead, the left in Finland in the 1960s and 1970s man-aged to establish in the national mindset the idea of social investments and from there, the idea of investing in people entered the normal practice of the

National Coalition Party, the country's moderate right. In this sense, Finland's practice of investing in universally good schooling, health insurance, and the only genuinely comprehensive safety-net housing system in Europe, were not conceived of as social transfers from rich to poor, but as sound macroeconomic policy. The Finns are, above all, pragmatic.

One key question of great importance remains: why is Finland so rarely mentioned as an example by the left and Greens on the world political stage? Why aren't its pragmatic, consensus-driven, day-to-day demonstrations of the benefits of investing in people and communities not more often cited by people elsewhere who want to build a better future? Why are the eye-opening statistics about the human, environmental and fiscal benefits of the Finnish approach not wheeled out more often? To help in this we have listed a summary of how well Finland does, below, as an appendix.

The struggle for equality against forgetting

Progress, it is often said, is the battle to remember in a time of forgetting, including remembering some lessons learnt over a century ago (Anttonen & Sipilä 2012; Kananen 2014). Finland's equality was not a gift given by the profits from natural resources, or the spoils of an empire. Finland does not have Sweden's larger population and legacy of imperial wealth, nor does it have the petroleum riches of Norway. It cannot use geothermal activity to smelt aluminium as in Iceland, or use its proximity to the rest of Europe to its advantage, as Denmark does. Nor did Finland have equality imposed upon it, as was the case in Japan, and to a lesser extent in Germany, after 1945.

Improving competitiveness in world markets is currently high on the Finnish political agenda, just as it was in the postwar reconstruction era. As this book has made clear, Finland is not just aiming for international competitiveness in economic terms, but achieving it with due concern for its social values and institutions. Ideas such as transfers from the rich to the poor being beneficial to all don't necessarily sell as well abroad to a set of people who have yet to encounter the results of such choices. But political campaigns that promote social policies as ones that will benefit the entire society, and not merely one sub-group, are much more effective. This is easier to achieve in a parliamentary democracy where compromise and consensus are essential, than it is in countries where two-party systems prevail.

Wealth inequality has been increasing in Finland and is higher than income inequality, which has remained relatively low and stable after a rise at the end of the 1990s (Törmälehto 2018). Wealth inequality is probably greater than official measurements indicate given the wealth that is hidden in tax havens, and it has become more difficult to measure accurately since the abolition of the wealth tax. But if inequality is considered from the perspective of post-tax national income, then the share of the top 1 per cent decreased from the year 2002 (when it was 7.2%) to 2016 (6.11%). This latest number for 2016 was released in February 2020 and is a rise from 5.54 per cent the year before, representing an average rise of 10 per cent in the incomes of the top Finnish 1 per cent as far as the 1 per cent themselves are concerned. It is nevertheless important to consider within a broader global context, as is illustrated in Figure 9.4.

Figure 5.5, shown earlier in this book, uses exactly the same data as Figure 9.4, but highlights how the recent slight increase in the take of the top 1 per cent in Finland has been largely absorbed by a slight fall in the average incomes of other people in the top half of the income distribution (but not in the top tenth). With significantly higher taxes, but little wage stagnation and much lower income inequality than, say, the UK, Finnish political parties rarely emphasize social transfers from the rich to the poor as their fundamental aim. Instead, they focus on how health, housing, education, financial security and much more are of benefit to the whole community, not just the present recipients.

In 2019 the National Coalition Party (NCP) built their electoral platform on continuing Finland's success story by increasing individual freedom (Kansallinen Kokoomus 2019); the Left Alliance focused its message on social justice; the Green League emphasized securing the future by a process of "fair change" (Vihreät 2012); and the Social Democratic Party presented a manifesto that stressed Finns' shared interests, the benefits of democratic control of the market and the need to uphold the values of freedom, solidarity, and peace (SDP 2019). The Centre Party's 2019 election programme stated that "Finnishness is finding reconciliation" (Centre Party 2019). The Swedish People's Party emphasized individual freedom, a bilingual Finland, and support

Figure 9.4: The take of the 1% in the US, UK, Sweden and Finland, 1910–2019

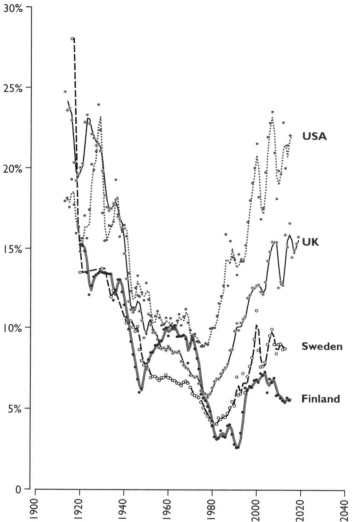

Source: World Inequality Database for the US, Finland and Sweden; for the UK, the data series detailed in Dorling (2019a).

Note: fiscal data for tax units in the US (1913–2015) and Sweden (1916–2013). For Finland tax units 1920–69, individual from 1970–79, and post-tax 1980–2016. For the UK the data is for 1910–2019, pre-tax, however estimated rates of tax evasion and avoidance by the top 1 per cent are so high in the UK that this is a comparable time series to the post-tax Finnish data since 1980.

for a Nordic welfare state and equality (SFP 2019). The post-election alliance formed by five of these six parties (all bar the NCP), in order to pull together a majority of members of parliament, was a pragmatic arrangement.

The Finnish welfare state developed through consensus politics in a parliamentary democracy; it has never been an idea owned by a single party (Kettunen 2019: 225). However, in the past few decades political parties on the right (by Finnish norms), such as the National Coalition Party and the Centre Party, have advocated for greater privatization. They have called for greater choice and decision-making capabilities being given to citizens with regard to public services; this would represent a partial move towards the US model for healthcare and other services that is in marked contrast to the aims and norms of welfare state provision.

Due in part to recent policy proposals running counter to established Finnish practice, such as the previous government's plans for privatization, the more left-wing parties now in power have become steadily more vocal in their opposition to conservative economic policies. Their positions are far more critical than those heard from, for example, today's UK Labour Party, and are emphatically far to the left of the US Democratic Party.

Figure 9.4 compares the share taken by the very richest people in four countries: the US, the UK, Sweden and Finland. A century ago, the most unequal nation was Sweden, where the best-off 1 per cent received 28 per cent of all income, leaving the other 99 per cent to share just 72 per cent, most of which went to those who were just below the top 1 per cent. All affluent countries at that time were very unequal, and it was an era when inequalities began to be forced down, first in Europe and then in North America and Japan, by concerted political action including the redistribution of both land and wealth following defeat in war. The rich did not readily give up their huge share.

By 1976 the richest 1 per cent were claiming just 9 per cent of all income in the US; by 1978 just under 6 per cent in the UK; by 1981 just 4 per cent in Sweden; and by 1984 just 3 per cent in Finland. It was in each of these years that these four countries were most equal. In contrast, the latest data on how much the 1 per cent take is 22 per cent and rising in the US, 16 per cent and rising more slowly in the UK, under 9 per cent and falling in Sweden, and under 6 per cent and falling in Finland. Thus, Finland's least-equal phase is currently as equal as the UK was at its most equal, and when the best-off

241

1 per cent took just six times the mean average salary home each year (four times after tax).

Cross-country comparisons and new norms

Trying to understand the various factors that have led to Finland being so equitable today is not easy. Chance will have played a part as well as many other minor factors that we cannot fully evaluate. For example, in the 1980s, social psychologists Sybil Eysenck and Jaana Haapasalo undertook a study of almost 1,000 Finnish adults and concluded: "In attempting a cross-cultural comparison of norms, the extremely unusual situation arose that the Finnish sample, especially the males, scored lower than the English one on Social Desirability. This has not occurred before in our cross-cultural studies and is hard to explain" (Eysenck & Haapasalo 1989: 125).

The Social Desirability scale (that was popular in 1980s psychology) was a measure of the extent to which individuals tended to tick "yes" to statements that they might think would make them appear to be more sociable than they actually were. Psychologists debated the issue amongst themselves and attempted to determine "whether this tendency is attributed to a need for approval, deliberate lying, or unconscious defensiveness" (McCrae & Costa 1983: 883). Whatever it was, people in Finland, as long ago as in the 1980s, and especially Finnish men, did not appear to feel the need to deceive themselves or others as much as people did in places such as England.

Finland's high levels of happiness and contentment can be understood partly in relation to the accepted social norms and expectations of what is possible in Finnish society. These norms are good due to excellent public services and low levels of inequality, particularly in comparison to the conditions prevailing today in all other countries, including most other affluent societies. We know that Finns are happy and contented with their lives, although they are often disinclined to show it. Public displays of emotion of any kind are rare. This may be part historical, reflecting the former dominance of Russia and Sweden, and has now become cultural (as revealed by Eysenck and Haapasalo's study). It is also possible that both Finns' reserve and their contentment makes funding excellent public services easier, as higher taxes are more accepted.

Today employees in Finland still contribute some of the highest proportions of their personal income in tax. In 2016, when, as Figure 9.4 shows, the take in income of Finland's 1 per cent was less than 6 per cent of the country's total, the tax collected from personal incomes in Finland made up 13 per cent of GDP. In Chile, one of the developed world's most unequal countries, it amounts to just 1.8 per cent of GDP by OECD estimates (Whiting 2018). As the mass protests (and police repression) of late 2019 demonstrated to the rest of the world, the toll taken by Chile's economic travails have for many years been falling most heavily on its badly paid, indebted and politically voiceless majority. When income is more evenly spread, overall taxation is far more effective, public services can be far better, and civil unrest is very rare.

A huge proportion of Finns, 79 per cent, say they are "happy to pay their taxes". An astonishing 96 per cent, when asked, agree that "it's important to collect tax to maintain the welfare state" (Whiting 2018). The tax bills of everyone in Finland are public documents, although individuals earning above €100,000 ($119,000) a year can, as of 2019, request to opt out of their tax information being released on the list of high-income earners provided to the media (4,400 such requests were successful in 2020). Individual tax records remain public and can be found, but this list facilitates the media's commentary on income and wealth distribution. This publicity has made it harder to hide corruption and tax evasion. In an equitable country with well-run public services, tax avoidance is rightly seen as no different from shop-lifting.

One day, a country will provide a universal basic income (UBI) to everyone. Finland may not be the first to do so, but it will experiment further and remains very open to similar new ideas. Many people say that UBI is unaffordable. But how much more unaffordable is it than the practice in the UK and especially the US of keeping large numbers of people in overcrowded prisons, with plans to build more prisons and calls for more and longer sentences? A universal basic income would not be compatible with wasting money on antisocial activities such as locking so many people up. It would, however, be compatible with massive reductions in carbon emissions, as those who chose to consume less would be able to. They would not have to drive to work if they chose not to work, and a basic income means exactly what it says – basic.

One day, a country will have no need for prisons; and Finland already has very few prisoners. People find the idea of no prisons strange, because when it is suggested they think of a future society that is just like their current society, but without jails. However, as a journalist based in the Bronx in the United States, Alice Speri, explains: "in a society that is tackling things like white supremacy, economic deprivation, toxic masculinity, and that is providing connections between people, and where communities are responsible for each other, I actually don't think it would be weird at all. You wouldn't even need the things that we now think of as elemental parts of our society, like the local jail." (Speri 2019).

One day, a country will have no homeless people. Finland is very nearly that country. One day, no one will die prematurely. This utopian vision is at least two centuries old. In western countries it is best remembered through the words of mill owner Robert Owen, and his address to the inhabitants of New Lanark in Scotland on New Year's Day 1816: "What ideas individuals may attach to the term 'Millennium' I know not; but I know that society may be formed so as to exist without crime, without poverty, with health greatly improved, with little, if any misery, and with intelligence and happiness increased a hundredfold; and no obstacle whatsoever intervenes at this moment except ignorance to prevent such a state of society from becoming universal." (New Lanark Trust 2019).

A universal basic income is only unaffordable if you think it is necessary for some to go hungry, cold and homeless to keep many of the rest of us at the grindstone of paid employment, much of which is of little ultimate benefit to society. Finland is in its current position because it often made the right choices; choices that frequently reduced the stresses and increased the happiness of the majority. It will continue to have to make choices; some will be the right ones, and others the wrong ones. As our societies make choices that we hope will build a better future, we all need to look at what has been done elsewhere – badly, or well.

Lessons from Finland

Many of the policies that are fundamental to Finland's success have come out of compromise. One of the first major interventions by the state into social and health services was accomplished many decades ago in 1937 with the Maternity Grants Act by a government made up of the Social Democratic Party and Agrarian League (now the Centre Party) – the country's first left–right coalition since the civil war (and dubbed a "red–mud coalition"). Even before this, land reforms passed into law in 1918 which enabled the rural proletariat to purchase small holdings of land immediately after the civil war, required the Social Democratic Party to approve private ownership which it had previously opposed, and the bourgeois parties to accept that parts of larger estates would have to be sold off. By no means had Finns put civil war acute tensions behind them this soon after the bloody national conflict, but as author Kjell Westö explains, Finns were pragmatic and worked together despite their history (Yle Uutiset 2019h). Policies that emerge from compromise between parties of different ideological stripes can also become policies that are broader, more innovative and stronger than those forged by any single political party. Problematic elements of how a society is organized, such as maintaining segregation in education, can then be discarded later when empirical support emerges for action.

Although education reforms were primarily the work of Finland's left, the importance of the Centre Party, the old Agrarian Party, in advancing them has also been highlighted in this book. The political debates over education went on for decades and were implemented gradually from the north to the south. Thankfully, the parties on the left and of the countryside, along with teachers and researchers, never gave up. They continue to stand their ground today, with the national trade union for Finnish teachers emphasizing that the high levels of respect afforded to the country's teaching profession is closely connected to Finnish teachers' freedom and ability to teach and assess, and arguing that more national examinations and inspections result not in better education but in counter-productive competition between schools. A "socialist nanny state" would hardly give this much freedom to teachers.

Finland's hosting of the 1975 conference on security and cooperation, that led to the Helsinki Accords, cemented its place in international relations and its role in promoting international peace and security. We have no space left in this book to itemize the long list of Finland's international achievements, but we cannot end without at least mentioning Kari Cantell's development of interferons and his international generosity in promoting health biotechnology in the global south (Reid-Henry 2010). Some people know of these aspects of Finland, but few outside of the country are aware of the ongoing complex debates within the country as to where progress is next to be found.

Improving competitiveness in a global economy while ensuring workers are paid fair wages has been a particularly intense area of debate. Arguably, Juha Sipilä's government's competitiveness reforms were crucial for Finland's ability to recover from the combined hit of the global recession, the fall of Nokia, and the domestic impact of the EU economic sanctions imposed on Russia. It is notable that his government ruled in a significantly different economic era than the more generous, Social Democratic Party-led government that followed it. Today, Finland continues to innovate economically. As climate scientists have now reached a consensus that economic focus must shift away from GDP growth (Carrington 2019), Finnish entrepreneurs are already far more focused on climate change and adaptation than their counterparts in almost any other country.

Finnish corporatist traditions, including collective bargaining, continue to play an integral role in making sure workers' demands and needs are heard in particular as new forms of work emerge, and in keeping wage stagnation at bay. One way in which Finland's economic development progressed in the past was through implementing policies that freed individuals, especially women, to enter the workforce if they so wished. Finland is now facing a new challenge over its need for a larger workforce, and it has known the answer for a long time: greater immigration. Yet its political climate can be both hostile and disenfranchising to the newcomers who have already contributed so much to Finnish society and diversity. Trade unions and employer organizations must work to meet new challenges including accommodating a more diverse population of workers.

Of course, Finland has had failures, too, but its capacity to learn from them has, in most cases, led to eventual success. Not all societies will have to make the mistakes that Finland has made in order to learn from their important lessons. For instance, the Finns now know that penalizing the unemployed does not work; instead, it humiliates them, and can push them deeper into other problems that are even harder to escape. A recent report by Kela, the VATT Institute for Economic Research and the University of Turku provides justification for widespread criticisms that increased employment under Sipilä's government cannot be conclusively sourced back to the "activation model". Furthermore, Sweden's recent experience has also led to research showing that reducing unemployment benefits for the longer-term unemployed does not give them the "nudge" they are widely supposed to be lacking (Kolsrud *et al.* 2018: 985).

Conclusion

Finland is the happiest country in the world, but only when its people are asked to answer a very specific question. Henry Cantril's self-anchoring striving scale ladder was devised in 1965 and is used in the annual world happiness reports. Those reports rely on surveys in which each survey respondent is asked to think of a number from 0 to 10. Each person is then asked to "place the status of their lives" on a ladder. Try it yourself. Record 0 if you think you are living the worst possible life, and 10 if you consider that what you have is the best possible life. You will almost certainly choose a number in between. Here is how the question is often worded and presented, usually including a picture of a ladder itself:

> Please imagine a ladder with steps numbered from zero at the bottom to 10 at the top.

> The top of the ladder represents the best possible life for you and the bottom of the ladder represents the worst possible life for you.

> On which step of the ladder would you say you personally feel you stand at this time?

The question being asked is as much about what you think is possible and how you think your life compares to those of others, as it is about the happiness you might feel right now. In fact, someone could record a very high score, because they think that for them they have a life as near as it can be to the best that is possible, but they may not actually be very happy. However, other measures are also included in the annual global surveys, and these tend to be strongly correlated with the Cantril ladder score. These include "positive affect", which is a combination measure of the reporting of the average frequency of happiness, laughter and enjoyment the respondent can remember from the previous day, and negative affect, which records the average frequency of worry, sadness and anger (also as remembered from the day before). Clearly the extent to which you think you are living a good life depends on what you think is possible – and the extent to which you are happy or sad, worried or angry also depends on that. Finns, in general and compared to all other states, think they are living lives that are nearest to the best that is possible, given the world in which they live.

Finland is not Utopia and its people are well aware that there is much that could still be better. However, they also know that they live under a flexible system in a pragmatic country that will permit better ways to be found and further improvements to be made. Knowing that things are going to get better, especially for the less well-off, is often more important than how the situation is today. We will always worry, but we also need to be able to hope. Finland's recent history can give us all hope. On 20 March 2020 it was announced – for the third year in succession – that Finland was once again the happiest country in the world. The report in which this was declared included a chapter dedicated to the Nordic countries which concluded: "... there seems to be no secret sauce specific to Nordic happiness that is unavailable to others. There is rather a more general recipe for creating highly satisfied citizens: Ensure that state institutions are of high quality, non-corrupt, able to deliver what they promise, and generous in taking care of citizens in various adversities" (Martela *et al.* 2020). And then on 20 March 2021 Finland was again ranked the happiest country in the world for a fourth term with the BBC reporting that Finland "ranked very high on the measures of mutual trust that have helped to protect lives and livelihoods during the pandemic" (BBC 2021). We hope that in these pages we have given you some of the details as to how and why the Finnish recipe works in practice and what it is – because it urgently needs to be made more widely available.

Appendix: Finland among
the best in the world

Statistics Finland produces a handy annual list of areas in which Finland is deemed to excel. It was last fully updated on 5 December 2018, although a few more items were added on 6 December 2019. The source for all the claims found below can be found in the update: http://www.stat.fi/tup/ tilastokirjasto/itsenaisyyspaiva-2019_en.html, and in the original list: http:// www.stat.fi/tup/satavuotias-suomi/suomi-maailman-karjessa_en.html.

Finland is a small country on a global scale. It accounts for just 0.07 per cent of both the world's total population and exactly the same global share of its total land area. But even a small country can jump to the top of the world, and this is what Finland has done: in international country comparisons of positive things, Finland is often among the top countries next to other Nordic countries.

In honour of Finland's centenary celebrations, Statistics Finland collected a list of comparisons in which Finland is one of the best in the world. The list was last updated on 5 December 2018, when Finland was for the last day one hundred years old.

Society

- Finland is the most stable country in the world.
- Finland is the safest country in the world.
- Finland is the fourth "best" country in the world. (The Good Country Index).

- Finland had the best governance in the world in 2018 (and ranked second best in 2019).
- Finland's police and internal security as a whole are the second best in the world.
- Finland has the lowest level of organized crime in the world.
- Next to Norwegians and Icelanders, Finns are the second least insecure-feeling people in the world.
- Finland's judicial system is the most independent in the world.
- After the Danes, Finns' elections are the freest and most reliable in the world.
- Finland has the third lowest level of corruption in the world.
- Finland is the third most prosperous country in the world.
- Protection of property rights in Finland is the best in the world.
- Access to official information in Finland is the best in the EU.
- Finnish banks are the soundest in the world.
- Finland's pension system is the third-best in the world (in a field of 34 countries).
- Finland has the third highest levels of personal freedom and choice in the world.
- Finland had the fourth greatest press freedom in the world in 2018 (rising to second best in 2019).
- After Denmark and Sweden, Finland is the most socially just EU country.
- Of the world's richest countries, Finland ranks third highest in its dedication to policies that benefit people living in poorer nations.
- Finland is the best country in the world in a comparison of human well-being.
- Finland is the third best country in the world in adhering to the rule of law.
- Finland is the world's highest-ranked country for the protection of fundamental human rights.

Satisfaction and trust

- Finland is the happiest country in the world.
- In 2018, Finns were the second most satisfied with their life among Europeans (and the most satisfied in 2019).

- Of all EU citizens, Finns are the most satisfied with their accommodation.
- Among EU citizens, Finns are the second most likely to have someone to rely on in case of need.
- Finns' trust in the police is the highest in Europe, and second-highest in Europe in their trust in their political and legal systems (in 2018, then rising to the top in 2019).
- Worldwide, Finns have the highest level of trust in the news media.
- Finns' trust in other people is the highest in Europe.
- In Finland, consumers' confidence in the economy is the second strongest in Europe.

Equality

- Finland is the third most gender equal country in the world (dropping to fourth in 2019).
- Participation of different genders in working life in Finland is the second most equitable in the EU.
- Finnish women's gender equality in working life is the fourth best in the world.
- In Finland, power is divided between genders the third most equally in the EU.
- Finland had Europe's third largest number of female MPs in 2018 (and the second largest by 2019).
- Finland has the second lowest poverty rate amongst OECD countries.
- Finland has the fifth lowest income differences amongst OECD countries.

Environment and energy

- The air in Finland is the cleanest in the world.
- Finland is the most water-rich country in the world.
- The risk of exposure to natural disasters is lowest in the world in Finland, together with Bahrain, São Tomé and Príncipe, and Singapore.
- Finland has the most forests in Europe.
- Finland has the third largest area of wetlands in Europe.

- The share of total energy consumption accounted for by renewable energy in Finland is the second greatest of all EU countries.

Education and human capital

- Finland has the most human capital in the world.
- Finland in 2019 ranked first of all OECD countries in education.
- Education in Finland in 2018 when measured by its ability to answer to future needs, ranked the third best in the world (and it was in first place by that score in 2019).
- Finland was third in a qualitative comparison of lifelong learning in EU countries in 2018 (and rose to the number one spot in 2019).
- Finnish adults have the third highest levels of numeracy of all OECD countries.
- Finland is the most literate country in the world.
- Finns are the second biggest library users in Europe.

Information society and competitiveness

- Finland is the second best in the world in using information and communication technologies to boost competitiveness and well-being.
- Finland has the EU's best digital public services.
- Finland has the strongest human capital in digital knowledge in Europe.
- Finland has the second largest number of wireless mobile broadband subscriptions per inhabitant in OECD countries.
- Finns use most mobile data per subscription of all users in all OECD countries.
- Finnish enterprises are more likely than in any other OECD country to have their own website.
- Finland was the third best country for business in Europe in 2018 (and the best in the world in 2019).
- Finland has the third best economic environment for business growth.
- Corporate ethics in Finland are the second best in the world.
- Finland is the second-best country in the field of clean technology.

- Finland's sustainable competitiveness is the fourth best in the world.

Children's well-being and school attendance

- Finland has the second lowest inequality among children in the world.
- Finland is the second-best country in the world to be a girl.
- Finnish children had the fifth most secure childhood in the world in 2018 (up to third spot in 2019).
- Young people (aged 11 to 15) in Finland in 2018 were the fourth most satisfied with their life (rising to third in 2019).
- Finns aged 15 are the third most satisfied with their lives among young people of the same age in OECD countries.
- Finnish fourth graders' knowledge of science is the second best in OECD countries.
- Finns aged 15 are the second best in literacy and the third best in science among OECD countries.

Health

- Finland is among the world's top 25 countries in life expectancy at birth. The differences among the countries at the top of this table are small.
- Finland has the fewest underweight (under 2,500 g) newborns of all OECD countries.
- Mothers' and children's well-being in Finland are the second best in the world.
- Finland in 2018 had the world's third lowest infant mortality rate, which records deaths at the age of under one year, and by 2019 it had the lowest.
- Maternal mortality is the lowest in the world in Finland, together with Greece, Iceland and Poland.
- Finland has the second lowest total mortality from cancer in EU countries.
- Finnish adults are the second least likely to smoke of EU countries.
- The proportion of inhabitants of Finland who actively exercise is greater than in any other EU country.

Capital city

- Helsinki is the third best city to live in (of many compared in one global survey).
- People living in Helsinki have the world's highest satisfaction with the place where they live, along with residents of Stockholm.
- Helsinki is the second most appealing city in the world for start-ups.
- Helsinki is the most equal city in Europe.
- Helsinki is the fifth best city worldwide in terms of the availability of a talented workforce.
- Helsinki is the third best city in Europe in terms of technology, innovation and entrepreneurship.
- Among European cities, Helsinki is the fourth best in supporting digital enterprises and entrepreneurs.
- Of European big cities, Helsinki is the easiest and most pleasant to get around in.
- People living in Helsinki are the second most satisfied with cultural facilities, of all EU capital cities' inhabitants.
- Helsinki is the most honest city in the world.
- The Helsinki-Vantaa airport is the best in the world (according to Lonely Planet).

And in these Finland is also at the top of the world

- Finland has the third most space per person in Europe.
- Finns drink most coffee per person in the world (although the Dutch contest this claim).
- Finns drink the most milk per capita in the world.
- Finland has the most Summer Olympics medals per capita.
- Finnish adults' English skills are the sixth best in a comparison of 80 countries.
- In 2018, the Finnish passport had the third greatest influence in the world (rising to second in 2019).
- Finland has the second largest number of islands in the world.
- Finland has the greatest number of heavy metal bands per inhabitant in the world.

And, as updated in December 2019
in addition to the above:

- Finland is the second most just country for children among the world's developed countries.
- Finland has the second most skilled workforce in the world.
- Finland is the third best country in the world for women.
- Finland is the most advanced country in the EU in the use of digitalisation.
- Finland is the third most innovative country in the world.
- Among EU citizens, Finns have the greatest trust in their defence forces.
- Finland is third best in the world at achieving progress on the United Nations' Sustainable Development Goals (SDG).
- Compared to its size, Finland generates the most good for humanity.
- Finland is the country in the world where people are the most free* (tying, in 2018, with Sweden and Norway for first place).

---

* And, we might add, free to do what they want, any old time, as The Soup Dragons sang in their 1990 cover of the 1965 Rolling Stones song "I'm free". Or, as it was a little more prosaically put by the 2018 and 2019 Freedom in the World reports – when measuring the degree of civil liberties and political rights that people enjoy – Finns are free to think what they want, and say what they want, and achieve what they want to achieve. Equality is freedom, freedom is equality, and today of any country in the world, it is in Finland that people are the freest.

References

An online copy of these references, along with URLs where available, can be found at: http://www.dannydorling.org/books/Finntopia/.

Aho, J. (2016). "Given the different levels of phonemicity of languages, are there fewer dyslexics in Finland than in English-speaking countries?" Answer given on *Quora*, 23 June, based on an article by Heikki Lyytinen.

Alho, E. *et al.* (2018). "Vuokra-asuntosijoutusalan kannattavuus, kilpaulutilanne ja kehittämistarpeet" [Profitability, competition, and development needs in the private rental housing market]. Helsinki: Prime Minister's Office.

Alapuro, R. (1997). "Ylioppilasliike ja sosiologia 60-luvulla – eli miten sosiologia auttoi opiskelijoita löytämään kansandemokraattisen liikkeen" [The student movement and sociology in the 60s – how sociology helped students find a people's democratic movement]. *Tieteessä tapahtuu* 15(4).

Amnesty International (2019). "Finland: International body condemns outdated definition of rape as Amnesty calls for rape law reform". Amnesty International press release, 2 September.

Andreasson, U. & M. Birkjær (2018). *In the Shadow of Happiness*. Copenhagen: Nordisk Ministerråd.

Anttonen, A. & J. Sipilä (2012). "Universalism in the British and Scandinavian social policy debates". In A. Anttonen, L. Häikiö & K. Stefánsson (eds), *Welfare State, Universalism and Diversity*, 16–41. Cheltenham: Elgar.

Anttosen, V. (2015). "Uskontotiede, pyhä ja poikkeavat rationaliteetit. Kuinka natiivit ajattelevat?". *Uskonnontutkija: religionforskaren* 1/2, 1–13.

ARA (2013). "ARA implements Finland's housing policy". The Housing Finance and Development Centre of Finland (ARA). Updated 14 June 2017; http://www.ara.fi/en-US/About_ARA.

ARA (2018). "Asunnottomuus väheni edelleen – nuorten asunnottumuus kasvusuunnassa" [Homelessness continued to decline – youth homelessness rising]. Helsinki: ARA.

Arkko, S. (2018). "Kotihoidon tuki leikkuriin? Asiantuntijat haluavat maahanmuuttajataustaiset lapset päiväkoteihin" [Home care support into the shredder? Experts want children with an immigrant background in kindergartens]. *Suomen Kuvalehti*, 19 October.

Asthana, A. (2018). "Health department 'ignoring UK life expectancy concerns': academics call for investigation into effects of NHS underfunding and austerity politics". *The Guardian*, 21 February.

Asunto ensin (2018). "Asunnottomuus väheni edelleen – nuorten asunnottomuus kasvusuunnassa" [Homelessness decreased in Finland in 2017]. Helsinki: Apartment First, 7 March.

Aulasmaa, M. (2017). "Miksi isät eivät käytä enemmän perhevapaita? – Katso tästä tärkeimmät syyt" [Why don't fathers use more family leave? – Here are the main reasons]. Yle Uutiset, 21 March.

Bäck, M. & E. Kestilä-Kekkonen (eds) (2019). "Poliittinen ja sosiaalinen luottamus: polut, trendit ja kuilut" [Political and social trust: paths, trends and gaps]. Helsinki: Valtiovarainministeriö [Ministry of Finance].

Balkelis, T. (2015). "War, revolution and terror in the Baltic States and Finland after the Great War". *Journal of Baltic Studies* 46(1), 1–9.

Bank of Finland (2019a). "Historia, Suomen Pankki on maailman neljänneksi vanhin keskuspankki" [History, the Bank of Finland is the fourth oldest central bank in the world].

Bank of Finland (2019b). "Opintolainoja nostettiin ennätysmäärä tammikuussa" [A record amount of student loans was withdrawn in January].

Bank of Finland (2019c). "Velat mitoitettava takaisinmaksukyvyn mukaan" [Debts should be sized according to their repayment capacity]. *Euro & Talous* 27(2), 9 May.

BBC News (2015). "Finland: speeding millionaire gets 54,000-euro fine". BBC News, 3 March.

BBC (2019a). "Quite interesting facts from the team behind the BBC TV show QI". @quikipedia tweet, 6 October; https://twitter.com/qikipedia/status/1180830065560444928?s=09.

BBC (2019b). "Finland college attack: sword attacker kills woman in Kuopio". BBC News, 1 October.

BBC (2019c). "General election 2019: Labour pledges free broadband for all". BBC News, 14 November.

BBC (2021). "Finland ranked happiest country in the world – again". BBC News, 20 March.

BBC Three (2018). "Homelessness in the UK versus Finland". BBC Three, 10 October; https://youtu.be/yKrZIYBF7ks.

Bedhall, R. (2018). "Top of the world in happiness report but how is Finland integrating immigrants?". *Finland Today*, 10 April.

Bennike, C. (2019). "New data reveals serious problems with the EU's official public opinion polls". *Dagbladet Information*, 3 December.

Bernelius, V. & M. Vaattovaara (2016). "Choice and segregation in the 'most egalitarian' schools: cumulative decline in urban schools and neighbourhoods of Helsinki, Finland". *Urban Studies* 53(5), 3155–71.

Berner, A.-S. (2019). "Kirjeenvaihtajan kommentti: Miksi Antti Rinne sai lähteä muutamassa päivässä, mutta Donald Trump on yhä presidentti?" [Correspondent's comment: why Antti Rinne was able to leave in a few days but Donald Trump is still president?]. *Helsingin Sanomat*, 4 December.

Bernstein, L. (2018). "U.S. life expectancy declines again, a dismal trend not seen since World War I". *Washington Post*, 29 November.

Björksten, T. (2016). "Uudet Pisa-tulokset: Suomen tytöt maailman toiseksi parhaita, vaikka ei edes huvita" [New Pisa results: Finnish girls second best in the world, even though they are not even interested]. Yle Uutiset, 6 December.

Blanden, J. (2009). "How much can we learn from international comparisons of intergenerational mobility?". LSE Paper No. CEEDP0111, London School of Economics: Centre for Economic Performance.

Böckerman, P. & R. Uusitalo (2006). "Erosion of the Ghent system and union membership decline: lessons from Finland". *British Journal of Industrial Relations* 44(2), 283–303.

Boffey, D. (2019). "Plan to sell 50m meals made from electricity, water and air". *The Guardian*, 29 June.

Bolt, J. *et al.* (2018). "Rebasing 'Maddison': new income comparisons and the shape of long-run development". GGDC Research Memorandum Vol. GD-174. Groningen: Groningen Growth and Development Center.

Boseley, S. (2018). "Nordic countries' 'happy' reputation masks sadness of young, says report". *The Guardian*, 25 August.

Bouzas, P. (2018a). "The struggle to find a job in Finland". *Finland Today*, 23 April.

Bouzas, P. (2018b). "The constant light, magical atmosphere, snow – *Finland Today*'s readers share reasons for moving here". *Finland Today*, 24 June.

Branch, H. (2019). "Where does Finnish come from?". This is Finland blog; https://finland.fi/life-society/where-does-finnish-come-from/.

Brenner, A.-K. (2019). "Jussi Halla-ahon tytär osallistui nuorten ilmastolakkoon isän vastustuksesta huolimatta – Perussuomalaisten puheenjohtaja ei usko, että pelastumme ympäristötuholta" [Jussi Halla-aho's daughter participated in a youth climate strike despite her father's opposition – The Finns Party's chair does not believe we will be saved from the environmental scourge.]. Yle Uutiset, 28 February.

Brimblecombe, N., D. Dorling & M. Green (2019). "Who still dies young in a rich city? Revisiting the case of Oxford". *Geographical Journal*. https://doi.org/10.1111/geoj.12336. Published online 12 November.

Brink, S. & K. Nissinen (2018). "Challenge for equity and excellence: evidence for future successful action in bilingual Finland". Finnish Institute for Educational Research Reports 54, University of Jyväskylä.

Brito, C. (2019). "Greta Thunberg turns down environmental award and $51,000 in prize money". *CBS News*, 30 October.

Burke, J. (2018). "Kenya burial site shows community spirit of herders 5,000 years ago: large-scale cemetery in Africa points to shared workload without social hierarchy". *The Guardian*, 20 August.

Böckerman, P. & J. Kiander (2006). "Talouspolitiikka" [Political economy]. In J. Saari & P. Böckerman (eds), *Suomen malli – murroksesta menestykseen* [*The Finnish Model: From Transition to Success?*], 135–72. Helsinki: Helsinki University Press.

Carrington, D. (2019). "Climate crisis: 11,000 scientists warn of 'untold suffering'". *The Guardian*, 5 November.

Center for High Impact Philanthropy (2015). "High return on investment". University of Pennsylvania.

Central Connecticut State University (2019). "World's most literate nations". https://www.ccsu.edu/wmln/rank.html.

Centre Party (2019). "Parliamentary election programme" [eduskuntavaaliohjelma]. https://www.keskusta.fi/Suomeksi/Ohjelmia-ja-politiikkaa/Vaaliohjelmia.

Chang, H.-J. (2002). *Kicking Away the Ladder: Development Strategy in Historical Perspective*. London: Anthem.

Chang, H.-J. (2008). *Bad Samaritans: The Guilty Secrets of Rich Nations and the Threat to Global Prosperity*. London: Random House.

Chang, H.-J. (2012). "Austerity has never worked". *The Guardian*, 4 June.

Chinchilla, N. & C. León (2005). *Female Ambition: How to Reconcile Work and Family*. Basingstoke: Palgrave Macmillan.

Christian Democrats (2019). "KD:n aakkoset: kristillisdemokratiaa selkokielellä" [Christian Democrats' alphabet: Christian democracy in plain language]. https://www.kd.fi/politiikka/ohjelmat/kd-asta-ohon/.

Chzhen, Y., A. Gromada & G. Rees (2019). "Are the world's richest countries family friendly?". Florence: UNICEF Office of Research – Innocenti.

City of Helsinki [Helsingin kaupunki] (2018). "Kiirrettömään hoitoon pääsyn toteutuminen" [Realization of access to urgent care]. Helsinki local authority website.

City of Helsinki [Helsingin kaupunki] (2019). "What and how do schools teach? Language studies". Helsinki local authority website.

Collinson, P. (2019a). "Danish bank launches world's first negative interest rate mortgage". *The Guardian*, 13 August.

Collinson, P. (2019b). "Finland is the happiest country in the world, says UN report, Nordic nations take top four places in happiness rankings, with annual study also charting the decline of the US". *The Guardian*, 14 March.

Corbyn, J. (2019). "This is our last chance to keep the NHS as it was entrusted to us". *The Guardian*, 7 December.

Country Economy (2019). "Finland – Life expectancy at birth". https://countryeconomy.com/demography/life-expectancy/finland.

Country Life (2017). "Is Ikigai the new Hygge? This Japanese concept might be the secret to finding longevity and purpose in life". 10 October.

Craveiro, D. *et al.* (2019). "Back to replacement migration: a new European perspective applying the prospective-age concept". *Demographic Research* 40(45), 1324–44.

Creese, B., A. Gonzalez & T. Isaacs (2016). "Comparing international curriculum systems: the international instructional systems study". *Curriculum Journal* 27(1), 5–23.

Criminal Sanctions Agency [Rikosseuraamus] (2018). "Vangit" [Prisoners]. http://www.rikosseuraamus.fi/fi/index/rikosseuraamuslaitos/tilastot/vangit.html.

Cushing, J. (2018). "Letters: peace and equality in the bronze age: the evidence from Dartmoor suggests that war and rich elites were unknown more than 3,000 years ago". *The Guardian*, 24 August.

de Fresnes, T. (2019). "How will millennial leaders change the world? Finland will give us a clue". *The Guardian*, 11 December.

Department for Work and Pensions (UK) (2017). "Proposed new timetable for state pension age increases". London: DWP.

Deutsche Schule Helsinki (2019). "Tietoa koulusta" [About the school]. https://www.dsh.fi/fi/tietoa-koulusta/tietoa-koulusta.

Dickinson, K. (2019). "How does Finland's top-ranking education system work?". *World Economic Forum*, 15 February.

Dinkin, E. (2018). "40% of the American middle class face poverty in retirement, study concludes". *CNBC*, 12 October.

Donner, J. (2017). "Mannerheim and Finnish independence". Speech given at the Finnish Institute, London, 28 September.

Dorling, D. (2006). "Prime suspect: murder in Britain". *Prison Service Journal* 166 (July), 3–10.

Dorling, D. (2011). "Roads, casualties and public health: the open sewers of the 21st century". Publication of PACTS' 21st Westminster Lecture. London: Parliamentary Advisory Council for Transport Safety.

Dorling, D. (2014). *All That Is Solid: How the Great Housing Disaster Defines Our Times, and What We Can Do About It*. London: Penguin.

Dorling, D. (2015). *Injustice: Why Social Inequality Still Persists*. Bristol: Policy Press.

Dorling, D. (2016). *A Better Politics*. London: London Publishing Partnership.

Dorling, D. (2017). *The Equality Effect: Improving Life for Everyone*. Oxford: New Internationalist.

Dorling, D. (2019a). *Inequality and the 1%*. Third edition. London: Verso.

Dorling, D. (2019b). "Kindness: a new kind of rigour for British geographers". *Emotion, Space and Society* 33 (Nov), 100630.

Dorling, D. & B. Hennig (2010). "Angles, Saxons, inequality, and educational mobility in England and Germany". *Social Europe Journal*, contribution to on-line debate, http://www.dannydorling.org/?page_id=598.

Dorling, D. & J. Rigby (2019). "Recession, austerity and life expectancy". *Irish Medical Journal* 112(2); see http://imj.ie/recession-austerity-and-life-expectancy/

Duxbury, C. (2019). "Finland's Social Democrats win close election victory". Politico, 15 April.

Economic Policy Council (2019). "Economic Policy Council Report 2018". https://www.talouspolitiikanarviointineuvosto.fi/en/reports/report-2018/.

Eerola, P. & J. Lammi-Taskula (2019). "Kuinka saada isät kotiin?" [How to get fathers home?]. *Alusta!* E-publication by the Faculty of Social Sciences, Tampere University, 4 November.

Eerola, P. *et al.* (2019). "Fathers' leave take-up in Finland: motivations and barriers in a complex Nordic leave scheme". *Sage Open* 9(4), 1–14.

EIGE (European Institute for Gender Equality) (2019). "Gender Equality Index 2017: Comparing in Violence".

Elinkeinoelämän keskusliitto (EK) (2018). "Tuotanto ja investoinnit" [Production and investment]. Helsinki: Elinkeinoelämän keskusliitto.

Elonen, P. & M. Mikkonen (2019). "HS vertaili: Näin puolueiden ilmastokannat eroavat toisistaan – Suuri ilmastotentti tänään Sanomatalossa kello 16" [A HS comparison: how party climate policies differ – a big climate exam today at 4 pm]. *Helsingin Sanomat*, 3 April.

Elovainio, P. (1999). *Facts About Finland*. Helsinki: Otava Publishing.

Environmental Administration (2018). "Rented housing". Environment: the joint website of Finland's environmental administration; http://www.ymparisto.fi/en-US/Housing/Rented_housing.

Ervasti, A.-E. (2019). "Kansainvälinen vertailu: Suomi on edelleen maailman onnellisin maa" [International comparison: Finland is still the happiest country in the world]. *Helsingin Sanomat*, 20 March.

Ervasti, A.-E. & J. Laitinen (2019). "Suomen syntyvyys putoaa jopa synkkiä ennusteita nopeammin, tällaisen vauvakadon piti olla edessä vasta 2045" [The birth rate in Finland will drop even faster than the gloomy forecasts predict, such a baby loss was only meant to come in 2045]. *Helsingin Sanomat*, 26 September.

European Systemic Risk Board (ESRB) (2019). "Follow-up report on countries that received ESRB warnings in 2016 on medium-term vulnerabilities in the residential real estate sector". Frankfurt: European Systemic Risk Board.

European Casino Association (2019). "Finland, country by country report".

European Commission (2016). "Lessons learnt and ways forward in a post-crisis context". Institutional Paper 31. Brussels: European Commission.

European Commission (2017). "CAP in your country: Finland". Brussels: European Commission.

European Commission (2019). "Commission opinion of 20 November 2019 on the Draft Budgetary Plan of Finland". Brussels: European Commission.

Eurostat (2017). "Mental health: how many psychiatrists in the EU". Brussels: European Commission.

Eurostat (2018a). "Share of young adults aged 18–34 living with their parents by age and sex, last updated 19 July 2018". Brussels: European Commission.

Eurostat (2018b). "Hospital beds by type of care per hundred thousand inhabitants". Brussels: European Commission.

Eurostat (2018c). "In-patient average length of stay (days)". Brussels: European Commission.

Eurostat (2018d). "At-risk-poverty rate by sex". Brussels: European Commission.

Eurostat (2018e). "Air passenger transport in the EU: record number of air passengers carried at more than 1 billion in 2017". Eurostat news release, 6 December. Brussels: European Commission.

Eurostat (2019a). "Statistics explained: migration integration statistics – education, May". Brussels: European Commission

Eurostat (2019b). "Life expectancy at birth by sex". Brussels: European Commission.

Eurostat (2019c). "Frequency of being happy in the last 4 weeks by age, sex and educational attainment level". Brussels: European Commission.

Evon, D. (2019). "Did the president of Finland post a video response to his White House visit?" *Snopes*, 7 October.

Eysenck, S. & J. Haapasalo (1989). "Cross-cultural comparisons of personality: Finland and England". *Personality and Individual Differences* 10(1), 121–5.

Financial Action Task Force (FATF) (2019). "Anti-money laundering and counter-terrorist financing measures – Finland". Fourth round mutual evaluation report. Paris: FATF.

Federal Reserve Bank of St Louis (2019). "Working age population: aged 15–64: all persons for Finland". https://fred.stlouisfed.org/series/LFWA64TTFIQ647S.

Findicator (2018). "Suicides". https://findikaattori.fi/en/table/10.

Findicator (2019). "Employment rate". https://findikaattori.fi/en/41.

Findicator (2020). "Unemployment rate". https://findikaattori.fi/en/34.

Finland Today (2018a). "Significance of labor migration increases". 23 May.

Finland Today (2018b). "Low use of antibiotics and pesticides prove the strengths of Finnish food production in international comparison". 13 June.

Finland Today (2019a). "Government takes action to prevent sexual offences in general and crimes by immigrants". 20 February.

Finland Today (2019b). "Finnair is the safest airline in the world". 5 January.

Finlex (1999). *Suomen perustuslaki* [The Finnish Constitution]. https://www.finlex.fi/fi/laki/ajantasa/1999/19990731.

Finnish Centre for Pensions [Työeläke] (2018). "Different pensions".

Finnish Centre for Pensions [Työeläke] (2019). *Statistical Yearbook of Pensioners in Finland 2018*.

Finnish Government [Valtioneuvosto] (2019). Pääministeri Antti Rinteen halitus [Government of Prime Minister Antti Rinne], "Government information page listing minsters first appointed".

Finnish Migration Service (2019). "Citizenship application". https://migri.fi/en/citizenship-application.

Finnish Psychological Association (2019). "Jokainen itsemurha on liikaa" [Every suicide is too much]. 10 September.

Fleetwood, B. (2013). "If you want the American dream, go to Finland". *Washington Monthly*, 18 November.

Fragile States Index (2019a). "Finland (country dashboard)". https://fragilestatesindex.org/country-data/.

Fragile States Index (2019b). "Global data". https://fragilestatesindex.org/data/.

Frank, R. (2016). *Success and Luck: Good Fortune and the Myth of Meritocracy*. Princeton, NJ: Princeton University Press.

Fransham, M. & D. Dorling (2017). "House prices can keep rising only if the Government backs mass buy-to-let". *The Telegraph*, 8 April.

Finnish Union of University Researchers and Teachers (FUURT) (2019). "Academic of the Year – Researcher Nafisa Yeasmin". 25 October.

Gillin, J. (2018). "Gambling in Finland: vice to national virtue". Yle Uutiset, 1 June.

Global Property Guide (2019a). "Square metre prices in United Kingdom compared to Europe".

Global Property Guide (2019b). "Square metre prices in United States compared to North America".

Good News from Finland (2019). "Solar Foods 2". Blog post, 9 September.

Government Communications Department (2017). "Report: Sámi people's rights should be reinforced to comply with the Constitution and international law". Finnish Government report, 25 January.

Government of Finland (2017). "Reply to Report of the Working Group on the Universal Periodic Review: Finland". Human Rights Council thirty-sixth session, UN General assembly, 8 September.

Group of Experts on Action against Violence against Women and Domestic Violence (GREVIO) (2019). "Baseline Evaluation Report Finland". Brussels: Council of Europe.

Gugushvili, D. & D. Hirsch (2014). "Means-testing or universalism: what strategies best address poverty?". University of Loughborough: Centre for Research and Social Policy.

Häkkinen, A. & H. Forsberg (2015). "Finland's 'famine years' of the 1860s: a nineteenth-century perspective". In D. Curran, L. Luciuk & A. Newby (eds), *Famines in European Economic History: The Last Great European Famines Reconsidered*, 99–123. New York: Routledge.

Hallberg, P. & T. Martikainen (2018a). "Suomen Politiikan pitkä kaari: Valtiopolitiikan vakaantuminen ja paluu arkeen 1946–1956" [The long arc of Finnish state politics: stabilization of state politics and return to everyday life 1946–1956]. E-publication on the Parliament of Finland website.

Hallberg, P. & T. Martikainen (2018b). "Suomen Valtiopolitiikan pitkä kaari: Valta keskityy – ja lopulta hajoaa" [The long arch of Finnish state politics: power concentrates – and eventually disintegrates]. E-publication on the Parliament of Finland website.

Hall, W. (1953). *Green, Gold and Granite: A Background to Finland*. London: Max Parrish.

Halla-aho, J. (2006). "Problems of Proto-Slavic Historical Nominal Morphology".

Doctoral dissertation, University of Helsinki, Department of Slavonic and Baltic Languages.

Halla-aho, J. (2019). "Finns Party's 'Workmen's Discussion Hour'". Perussuomalaiset website, 22 February.

Halme, K. *et al.* (eds) (2014). *Finland as a Knowledge Economy 2.0: Lessons on Policies and Governance*. Washington, DC: World Bank Publications.

Hämäläinen, V.-P. & M. Rautio (2019). "'Ei se ihan näin mene' – kokoomus älähti Halla-ahon halpatyöväitteestä" ["It does not quite work like that" – the National Coalition Party responds to Halla-Aho's claim about cheap labour]. Yle Uutiset, 21 September.

Hansen, C. (2019). "116th Congress by party, race, gender, and religion". *US News*, 3 January.

Happonen, P. (2019). "Miksi 10 vuoden takaisista koulusurmista ei otettu riittävästi oppia? – Nuoria voidaan auttaa, jos ihan oikeasti halutaan" [Why didn't we learn enough about the school murders 10 years ago? – Young people can be helped if they really want to]. Yle Uutiset, 7 October.

Harjula, M. (2019). "Kun kansalainen kohtasi Kelan virkailijan: hyvinvointivaltio kokemushistoriana" [When a citizen encountered a Kela official: the welfare state as an experience]. *Alusta!* E-publication by Faculty of Social Sciences, Tampere University.

Hassel, A. (2006). *Wage Setting, Social Pacts and the Euro: A New Role for the State*. Amsterdam: Amsterdam University Press.

Hatzfield-Rea, M. (1969). *Finland Fantasies*. Ilfracombe: Arthur H. Stockwell.

Hearst, W. (1939). "Let Stalin keep his blood-stained hands off Finland". *San Francisco Examiner*, 13 October.

Heikkinen, P. (2017). "Kiinniottajasta kiinniotettavaksi: Suomen taloudellisesta kehityksestä 1870–2015" [From the catcher to the catch: economic development in Finland 1870–2015]. *Kansantaloudellinen Aikakauskirja*, 113(3), 293–311.

Heikkinen, P. & A. Kuusterä (2001). "Finnish economic crises in the 20th century". In J. Kalela *et al.* (eds), *Down From the Heavens, Up From the Ashes: The Finnish Economic Crisis of the 1990s in the Light of Economic and Social Research*. Government Institute for Economic Research Publications, 27(6).

Heiskanen, M. (2019). "For the 7th consecutive year, Finland is the number one foreign direct investment target in the Nordic countries". *Nordic Business Forum*, 11 October.

Helliwell, J., R. Layard & J. Sachs (2019). World Happiness Report 2019. New York: Sustainable Development Solutions Network.

Helminen, M.-L. (2017). "Maahanmuutto kasvattaa nuorten määrää" [Immigration increases the number of young people]. *Tilastokeskus* [*Statistics Finland*], 8 March.

Henley, J. (2019). "'It's a miracle': Helsinki's radical solution to homelessness". *The Guardian*, 3 June.

Herkman, J. (2018). "Old patterns on new clothes? Populism and political scandals in the Nordic countries". *Acta Sosiologica* 61(4), 341–55. Doi: 10.1177/0001699317737816

Herva, V. (2018). "Understanding the cultural impacts and issues of Lapland mining: a long-term perspective on sustainable mining policies in the north". University of Oulu, on-online research project description. https://www.oulu.fi/archaeology/node/48198.

Hetemaa, T. *et al*. (2018). "Social and health care client fees: allocation, effects and fairness". Helsinki: Prime Minister's Office.

Hiam, L., D. Dorling & M. McKee (2020). "Things fall apart: the British health crisis 2010–2020". *British Medical Bulletin*, March.

Hickel, J. (2020). "The sustainable development index: measuring the ecological efficiency of human development in the Anthropocene". *Ecological Economics* 167, 106331.

Hiilamo, E.-A. & P. Ala-Risku (2019). "Miehet ansaitsevat naisia enemmän lähes puolessa ammattiryhmistä – Katso, millaiset erot ovat eri ammateissa" [Men earn more than women in nearly half of occupations – See the differences between occupations]. *Helsingin Sanomat*, 7 September.

Hiilamo, H. (2019a). "Vähäisen syntyvyyden syitä ei tunneta tarpeeksi" [The causes of low birth rates are not sufficiently known]. *Helsingin Sanomat*, 12 October.

Hiilamo, E.-A. (2019b). "Jussi Halla-ahon blogikirjoituksista ja 'ihmiskäsityksestä' tuli hidaste perussuomalaisten hallitustielle – Näin Halla-aho kirjoitti vähemmistöistä vuosikymmen sitten" [Jussi Halla-aho's blog posts and 'people's concept' became a retardation of the Finns' government – this is how Halla-aho wrote about minorities a decade ago]. *Helsingin Sanomat*, 17 April.

Honkanen, P. (2018). "Aktiivimallin karikoita" [Pitfalls of the activation model]. *Kela tutkimusblogi* [Research blog of Kela], 8 January.

Honkapohja, S. & V. Vihriälä (2019). *Suomen kasvu: Mikä määrää tahdin muuttuvassa maailmassa* [Finland's growth: what determines its pace in a changing world]. Helsinki: Taloustieto Oy.

Human Fertility Database (2018). "Tempo-adjusted total fertility rate in Finland".

Huotari, M. (2018). "Isot syövät pieniä" [Big fish eat little fish]. *Suomen Kuvalehti*, 25 May.

IFS (2019). "Universal free school meals are back on the table". London: Institute for Fiscal Studies, 5 December.

Ilkka, J., T. Heikki & N. Väinö (2012). "The variability of winter temperature, its impacts on society, and the potential use of seasonal forecasts in Finland". *Weather* 67(12), 328–32.

Info Finland (2018). "Financial support for disabled persons".

Info Finland (2019a). "The Finnish education system".

Info Finland (2019b). Your rights and obligations in Finland".

Infopankki (2019a). "Taking care of a child".

Infopankki (2019b). "Preschool education".

Inman, P. (2018). "Social mobility in richest countries 'has stalled since 1990s'". *The Guardian*, 15 June.

International Monetary Fund (2018). World Economic Outlook Database.

International School of Helsinki (2019). "Fee schedule".

Isometsä, E. (2019). "Professori Erkki Isometsä: 'Itsemurhien ehkäisy on tärkeää, mutta hyvä tarkoitus ei riitä – tarvitsemme tietoa'" [Professor Erkki Isometsä: 'Suicide prevention is important, but good intentions are not enough – we need information']. Mieli: Suomen Mielenterveys ry [Mental Health Finland].

Isotalo, V. *et al.* (2019). *The Finnish Voter*. Helsinki: Finnish National Election Studies.

Jacobson, M. (1957). *Finland: Myth and Reality*. Keuruu: Otava Printing.

Järvinen-Tassopoulos, J. (ed.) (2017). *Suomalaisen rahapelaamisen tilannekatsaus 2017* [A review of the situation of Finnish gambling in 2017]. Helsinki: Terveyden ja hyvinvoinnin laitos [Finnish Institute of Health and Welfare].

Järvinen, E. (2015). "Voiko maahanmuuttaja kotoutua puolen vuoden pätkissä?" [Can immigrants integrate in half a year's time?]. *Suomen Kuvalehti*, 17 December.

Jaskari, K. (2018). "Luulitko, että Suomi on edelleen maailman synkimpiä itsemurhamaita? – Ei ole, vaan eurooppalaisen keskitason tuntumassa" [Did you think that Finland is still one of the world's darkest suicide countries? – No, but close to the European average]. Yle Uutiset, 26 July.

Jefferies, T. (2019). "Are these the best retirement destinations in Europe? Spain tops the league, Finland is a surprise second . . . and Britain lags in 17th place". *Daily Mail*, 31 October.

Johnson, S. (2017). "What can the UK learn from Finland's approach to mental health?". *The Guardian*, 5 April.

Jokinen, M. (2018). "Suomessa jokainen saa hoitoa, maksoi mitä maksoi – Kun lääketiede kehittyy, lupaus voi käydä liian kalliiksi" [Everyone in Finland gets treatment, whatever it costs – As medicine advances, the promise can become too expensive]. *Suomen Kuvalehti*, 18 June.

Jonker-Hoffrén, P. (2019). "Finland: goodbye centralised bargaining? The emergence of a new industrial bargaining regime". In T. Müller, K. Vandaele & J. Waddington (eds), *Collective Bargaining in Europe: Towards an Endgame*. Brussels: European Trade Union Institute.

Juntto, A. (1992). "Post-industrial housing crisis: Finland as a case study". *Scandinavian Housing and Planning Research* 9(2), 47–59.

Kaarenoja, V. (2019). "Näin Antti Rinteen hallitus tuhoutui viikossa" [This is how Antti Rinne's government fell apart in a week]. *Suomen Kuvalehti*, 3 December.

Kaitila, V. (2020). "Suomen CO_2-päästöt 2019–2023 ja hiilineutraalisuustavoitteen saavuttaminen". [CO_2 emissions in Finland 2019–2023 and the carbon neutrality objective]. ETLA Muistio no. 84.

Kallio, J. (2008). "Yksityisen lääkäripalvelujen käyttö ja ideologiset tekijät" [Use of private medical services and ideological factors]. *Yhteiskuntapolitiikka* 73(5), 477–93.

Kananen, J. (2014). *The Nordic Welfare State in Three Eras: From Emancipation to Discipline*. Farnham: Ashgate.

Kangas, O. & L. Kalliomaa-Puha (2018). "Finland: the government's social and healthcare reform is facing problems". European Social Policy Network Flash Report 2018/2.

Kansallinen Kokoomus (2019). "Kokoomuksen eduskuntavaaliohjelma 2019" [The National Coalition Party's parliamentary election program 2019].

Kantola, A. & H. Kuusela (2019). "Wealth elite moralities: wealthy entrepreneurs' moral boundaries". *Sociology* 53(2), 368–84.

Karvonen, S. & M. Salmi (2016). *Lapsiköyhyys Suomessa 2010-luvulla* [Child poverty in Finland in the 2010s]. Terveyden ja hyvinvoinnin laitos [Finnish Institute for Health and Welfare].

Katsui, H., T. Kröger & K. Valkama (2018). "Finland fact sheet on social care & support services sector for persons with disabilities". Helsinki: Helsinki Institute of Sustainability Science (HELSUS).

Kauppinen, J. (2016). "Ylen musta viikko: Näin Yleisradion uskottavuus ajautui kriisiin" [Yle's black week: This is how the credibility of Yleisradio went into crisis]. *Suomen Kuvalehti*, 8 December.

Kestilä-Kekkonen, E. & I. Vento (2019). "Poliittinen luottamus – käsitteet, teoriat ja mittaaminen" [Political trust – concepts, theories, and measurement]. In M. Bäck & E. Kestilä-Kekkonen (eds), *Poliittinen ja sosiaalinen luottamus: Polut, trendit ja kuilut* [Political and social trust: paths, trends and gaps], 18–34. Helsinki: Valtionvarainministeriö [Ministry of Finance].

Kela (2017). "Private day care allowance". Kela (Kansaneläkelaitos) [Social Insurance Institution of Finland].

Kela (2018a). "Benefits for families with children". Kela (Kansaneläkelaitos) [Social Insurance Institution of Finland].

Kela (2018b). "Kela benefits in euros 2018". Kela (Kansaneläkelaitos) [Social Insurance Institution of Finland].

Kela (2018c). "Kela as an organization". Kela (Kansaneläkelaitos) [Social Insurance Institution of Finland].

Kela (2019a). "Äitiysavustuksen historia" [History of maternity assistance]. Kela (Kansaneläkelaitos) [Social Insurance Institution of Finland].

Kela (2019b). "Äityispakkaus" [The maternity package]. Kela (Kansaneläkelaitos) [Social Insurance Institution of Finland].

Kela (2019c). "Opintolainan määrä" [Amount of student loan]. Kela (Kansaneläkelaitos) [Social Insurance Institution of Finland].

Kela (2019d). "Vanhempainpäivärahat" [parental allowances]. Kela (Kansaneläkelaitos) [Social Insurance Institution of Finland].

Kela (2019e). "Sateenkaariperhe" [Rainbow family]. Kela (Kansaneläkelaitos) [Social Insurance Institution of Finland].

Kela (2019f). "Työttömän perusturvan menot ylittivät vuonna 2018 ansioturvan menot ensimmäistä kertaa" [For the first time in 2018, expenditure on basic social security for the unemployed exceeded expenditure on unemployment benefits]. Kela (Kansaneläkelaitos) [Social Insurance Institution of Finland].

Kela (2019g). "Takuueläke, määrä ja maksaminen" [Guaranteed pension, amount and payment]. Kela (Kansaneläkelaitos) [Social Insurance Institution of Finland].

Kela (2021). "Student loan compensation". Kela (Kansaneläkelaitos) [Social Insurance Institution of Finland].

Kelly, C. (2018). "'Make America rake again': confusion in Finland over Trump's wildfire comments". *CNN*, 20 November.

Kemppainen, T. (2012). "Well-being in socio-political context: European welfare regimes in comparison". Studies in Social Security and Health, Working Paper 123. Helsinki: Kela Research Department.

Kerry, B. (2019). "I walk past people dying on the streets. And so do you". Guest blog. London: Equality Trust, 13 November.

Kettunen, P. (2001). "The Nordic welfare state: Finland". *Scandinavian Journal of History* 26(3), 225–47.

Kettunen, P. (2019). "The conceptual history of the welfare state in Finland". In N. Edling (ed.), *The Changing Meanings of the Welfare State: Histories of a Key Concept in the Nordic Countries*, 225–75. Oxford: Berghahn.

Kingsley, S. (2019). "Finland: from suicide hotspot to world's happiest country". *Jakarta Post*, 13 April.

Kivimäki, T. (2017). "Suomen terveydenhoitojärjestelmä on EU:n epätasa-arvoisimpia" [The Finnish health care system is one of the most unequal in the EU]. *Sosiaalivakuutus*, 16 May.

Kiviranta, V. (2016). "Suomen Pankki linjaa: Suomi on jättänyt taantuman taakseen" [According to the Bank of Finland, the recession is in the past]. Yle Uutiset, 13 December.

Klein, E. (2019). "The case for a universal basic income, open borders, and a 15-hour workweek". Vox, 26 July.

Koivulaakso, D., M. Brunila & L. Andersson (2012). *Äärioikeisto Suomessa* [The Far Right in Finland]. Helsinki: Into.

Kokkinen, A. (2011). *On Finland's Economic Growth and Convergence with Sweden and the EU15 in the 20th Century*. Florence: European University Institute.

Koljonen, A. & D. Dorling (2018). "Life expectancy is rising in Finland – unlike in the UK. What's going right?". *The Guardian*, 17 October.

Kolsrud, J. *et al.* (2018). "The optimal timing of unemployment benefits: theory and evidence from Sweden". *American Economic Review* 108(4/5), 985–1033.

Konttinen, M. (2019). "Naisia nousi kansanedustajiksi historiallisen paljon – 85 prosenttia vihreiden edustajista naisia" [A historic amount of women have become MPs – 85 per cent of the Green League representatives are women]. Yle Uutiset, 14 April.

Kontula, K. (2018). "Maailman sairaanhoidon laadun uusi ranking-lista" [World health care new ranking]. Faculty of Medicine blog, University of Helsinki, 11 June.

Korpela, S. (2006/2019). "Finland's Parliament: pioneer of gender equality". This is Finland.

Korpi, W. & J. Palme (1998). "The paradox of redistribution and strategies of equality: welfare state institutions, inequality, and poverty in the Western countries". *American Sociological Review* 63(5), 661–87.

Krugman, P. (2018). "Are the Danes melancholy? Are the Swedes sad?". *New York Times*, 27 October.

Kumpulainen, T. (2017). "Opettajat ja rehtorit Suomessa 2016" [Teachers and principals in Finland 2016]. Opetushallitus Raportit ja selvitykset [Finnish National Agency for Education Reports and Reviews].

Kupianen, S., J. Hautamäki & T. Karjalainen (2009). "The Finnish education system and Pisa". Ministry of Education Publications, Finland 2009:46.

Lähdemäki, J. (2018). "Case study: the Finnish national curriculum 2016 – a co-created national education policy". In J. Cook (ed.), *Sustainability, Human Well-Being, and the Future of Education*, 397–422. London: Palgrave Macmillan.

Lahelma, E. (2019). "Koulututkimuksen konkari Elina Lahelma neuvoo kuuntelemaan nuoria. Ei pidä olettaa, pitää kysyä" [Elina Lahelma, an educational researcher, advises to listen to young people: don't assume, you have to ask]. *Helsingin Yliopisto Y/01/19*, 29–32.

Lång, L. *et al.* (2019). "See how the parties rank in the political quadrilateral". Yle Uutiset, 11 April.

Laurent, H. (2017). "Asiantuntijuus, Väestöpolitiikka, Sota: Lastenneuvoloiden kehittyminen osaksi kunnallista perusterveydenhuoltoa 1904–1955" [Expertise, demography, war: the evolution of child health counseling as part of municipal primary health care 1904–1955]. *Valtiotieteellisen tiedekunnan julkaisuja 61/2017* [Faculty of Social Science Publications 61/2017].

Lee Hogg, A. (2008). "Timeline: Somalia, 1991–2008 – from troubled to dire". *The Atlantic*, December.

Lehtinen, V. & V. Taipale (2001). "Integrating mental health services: the Finnish experience". *International Journal of Integrated Care* 1(26). doi: 10.5334/ijic.30.

Lemola, J. (2019). "The Finns Party campaigned against climate action. It came in second". *New York Times*, 14 April.

Lemola, T. (2014). "Background: evolution of Finland's knowledge economy policy". In K. Halme *et al.* (eds), *Finland as a Knowledge Economy 2.0. Lessons on Policies and Governance*, 33–48. Washington, DC: World Bank.

Lewis, R. (2005). *Finland: Cultural Lone Wolf*. Boston, MA: Intercultural Press.

Liiten, M. (2019). "Sitran selvitys: Perussuomalaisten kannattajia tulevaisuus pelottaa eniten – paitsi yhdessä suhteessa" [Sitra's analysis: supporters of the Finns party are the most afraid of the future – except in one measure]. *Helsingin Sanomat*, 1 March.

Lindberg, N. (2018). "Mistä muodostuu suomalaisen psykiatrian menestystarina?" [What led to the success story of Finnish psychiatry?]. Suomen psykiatriyhdistys [Finnish Psychiatric Association], 9 January.

Lingdren, K.-O. (2011). "The variety of capitalism in Sweden and Finland: continuity through change". In U. Becker (ed.), *The Changing Political Economies of Small West European Countries*, 45–72. Amsterdam: Amsterdam University Press.

Linna, V. (2003). *Under the North Star 3: Reconciliation*. [Translation of *Täällä Pohjantähden alla 3* (1962)]. Ontario: Aspasia Books.

Liukas, C. (2017). "The Nordic welfare state has disappeared from the Finnish government programme". Nordic Welfare News, University of Helsinki, 15 May.

Loikkanen, H. (2013). "Kaupunkialueiden maankäyttö ja taloudellinen kehitys – maapolitiikan vaikutuksista tuottavuuteen sekä työ- ja asuntomarkkinoiden toimivuuteen" [Urban land use and economic development – the impact of land policy on productivity and the functioning of labour and housing markets]. VATT Working Papers 17. Helsinki: Valtion taloudellinen tutkimuskeskus [Government Institute for Economic Research].

Londen, M., J. Enegren & A. Simons (2008). *Come to Finland: Posters and Travel Tales 1851–1965*. Second edition. Helsinki: Otava Book Printing.

Lukacovic, F. (2018). "School debt and the need for universal programs". Medium, 29 December.

Luukka, T. (2019a). "Kommentti: Rinteen hallitus on käyttänyt jo lähes kaikki pysyvät rahalliset panokset, joita se jakoi itselleen" [Comment: The government has already used up almost all of the permanent financial contributions it has distributed to itself]. *Helsingin Sanomat*, 18 September.

Luukka, T. (2019b). "Valtiovarainministeriön budjettiehdotus julki: Lisää rahaa saavat muun muassa kunnat, väylät ja puolueet" [Ministry of Finance budget proposal unveiled: municipalities, fairways, and political parties get more money]. *Helsingin Sanomat*, 16 August.

Luukka, T. (2021). "Miksi taistelu koronavirusta vastaan on hallitukselle nyt niin paljon vaikeampaa kuin vuosi sitten?" [Why is the fight against coronavirus so much harder for the government now compared last year?]. *Helsingin Sanomat*, 8 March.

Lyytikäinen, T. (2006). "Rent control and tenant's welfare: the effects of deregulating rental markets in Finland". VATT Discussion Papers 385. Helsinki: Valtion taloudellinen tutkimuskeskus [Government Institute for Economic Research].

Määttänen, N. (2019). "Unlocking housing wealth to foster the silver economy". *ETLA News*, 9 July.

MacDougal, D. (2018). "Nazis, vigilantes and swastikas reveal the dark side of Independence Day". *News Now Finland*, 7 December.

Malin, T. (2019). "Invalidiliiton vammaispalvelut syyniin" [Disabled people's disability services under inspection]. *Suomen Kuvalehti*, 27 November.

Malinen, A. (2008). "Työelämän toteutumaton murroskohta? Tarkastelussa 1960- ja 1970- lukujen yritysdemokratiavisiot" [An unrealistic turning point in working life? Looking at the corporate democracy vision of the 1960s and 1970s]. *Työelämän tutkimus* 6(1), 82–93.

Manninen, V. (2018). "Monitoring media pluralism in Europe: application of the media pluralism monitor 2017 in the European Union, FYROM, Serbia & Turkey Country Report: Finland". Florence: Centre for Media Pluralism and Media Freedom, European University Institute.

Mantsinen, T. (2018). "The Finnish Pentecostal Movement: an analysis of internal struggle as a process of habitual division". In J. Moberg & J. Skjoldli (eds), *Charismatic Christianity in Finland, Norway, and Sweden*, 109–36. Cham: Palgrave Macmillan.

Mäntylä, J.-M. (2019). "Opintotuki on tänään suurimmaksi osaksi velkaa – ja sitä otetaan ennätystahtia" [Student support is today mostly debt – and it is taken up at record pace]. Yle Uutiset, 13 May.

Mäntylä, J.-M. (2021). "Iskeekö konkurssiaalto helmikuussa? Verottaja ja eläkeyhtiöt hakevat yrityksiä useimmin konkurssiin – ja heillä on rauhoittava viesti" [will a bancruptcy wave hit in February? The tax administration and pension funds most often petition for bankruptcy, and they have a calming message]. Yle Uutiset, 16 January.

Markkola, P. (2015). "The long history of Lutheranism in Scandinavia: from state religion to the people's church". *Perichoresis* 13(2), 3–15.

Marklund, B. (2017). *The Nordic Guide to Living 10 Years Longer*. Translated by Stuart Tudball. London: Little Brown.

Martela, F., B. Greve, B. Rothstein and J. Saari (2020) The Nordic exceptionalism: what explains why the Nordic countries are constantly among the happiest in the world, Chapter 7 in J. Helliwell et al. (Eds), *World Happiness Report 2020*, New York: Sustainable Development Solutions Network.

Martineau, G. (1953). *Nagel's Finland Travel Guide*. Paris: Nagel Publishers.

Martineau, G. (1980). *Nagel's Encyclopaedic Guide – Finland*. Geneva: NTC/Contemporary Publishing.

Matthijs, M. (2015). "The eurozone's 'winner-take-all' political economy: institutional choices, policy drift, and diverging patterns of inequality". Paper prepared for biennial EUSA meeting, Boston, 5–7 March.

McCrae, R. & P. Costa (1983). "Social desirability scales: more substance than style". *Journal of Consulting and Clinical Psychology* 51(6), 882–8. Doi: 10.1037/0022-006X.51.6.882.

Mead, W. & H. Smeds (1967). *Winter in Finland*. London: Hugh Evelyn.

Medium (2019). "The growth of Maria 01 will be massive. People are not really aware of the scope we are talking about, says Ville Simola – CEO at Maria 01". *Medium*, 21 November.

Meinander, H. (2010). "Kekkografia: historiaesseitä" [Kekkography: history essays]. Helsinki: Siltala.

Meinander, H. (2011). *A History of Finland*. London: Hurst.

Meinander, H. (2013). *Kansanvallan pitkä tie* [Democracy's long road]. Parliament of Finland.

Merikanto, T. (2019). "Analyysi: Rinteen sote-pakasta pullahti voitto keskustalle, demarit näyttivät yksityisille firmoille kaapin paikan" [Analysis: Rinne's *sote*-plan led to a win for the Centre Party, Social Democrats show private firms their place in a locker]. Yle Uutiset, 23 May.

Miettinen, L. (2018). "Emeritusprofessori varoittaa, että sote-keskus voi kiertää kustannuksia passittamalla kalliit potilaat muualle" [Emeritus Professor warns that *sote*-centres can garner expenses by sending expensive patients elsewhere]. Yle Uutiset, 12 January.

Migri [Finnish Immigration Service] (2019). "Residence permit application for an employed person (TTOL)".

Mikkonen, S. & V. Korhonen (2018). "Työläistaustaiset yliopisto-opiskelijat ja koulutusmahdollisuuksien tasa-arvo" [University students from working-class backgrounds and equal opportunities for education]. Helsinki: Ministry of Education and Culture.

Milne, R. (2017). "True Finns split holds lesson for Europe's populists". *Financial Times*, 16 June.

Milne, R. (2019). "Nordea hit by new money-laundering allegations". *Financial Times*, 4 March.

Ministry for Foreign Affairs, Finland (2019a). "Suomen tie jäsenyyteen, Eurooppatiedotus" [Finland's path to membership, Europe information].

Ministry for Foreign Affairs, Finland (2019b). "The Council of Europe evaluates violence against women and domestic violence in Finland". Press release, 2 September.

Ministry of Agriculture and Forestry, Finland (2016). "Free-time residence barometer: growth in popularity and more common remote work". 17 March.

Ministry of Agriculture and Forestry, Finland (2019). "Forests and the economy".

Ministry of Communities and Local Government (UK) (CLG) (2018). "Rough sleeping statistics Autumn 2017, England (revised)". London: CLG.

Ministry of Economic Affairs and Employment, Finland (2019). "Finland's Presidency of the Council of the EU and the Ministry of Economic Affairs and Employment". 1 July.

Ministry of Education and Culture, Finland (2018). "Finnish education in a nutshell".

Ministry of Education and Culture, Finland (2019a). "OECD comparison: In Finland, competition for higher education places is fierce". 10 September.

Ministry of Education and Culture, Finland (2019b). "Finnish education system".

Ministry of Education and Culture, Finland (2019c). "Nuoret ja ilmastokriisin ratkaisu" [Young people and the solution to the climate crisis]. YouTube video, 1 November.

Ministry of Finance, Finland (2019). "Economic growth continues at a steady rate". Press release, 17 June.

Ministry of Finance and Ministry of Social Affairs and Health, Finland (2018). "Government's joint opinion: the regional government, health and social services reform is for all of Finland". Press release, 11 May.

Ministry of Justice, National Offender Management Service, HM Prison Service, and HM Prison and Probation Service (UK) (2017). "Prison population figures 2017". Population monthly bulletin, December.

Ministry of Social Affairs and Health, Finland (2018). "Comprehensive reform of Alcohol Act".

Ministry of Social Affairs and Health, Finland (2021). "Covid-19 cases on the rise again in Finland – infections reported particularly among Euro 2020 football fans returning from Russia". Press release, 1 July.

Ministry of the Environment, Finland (2013a). "Housing". Helsinki: Ministry of the Environment's Department of the Built Environment.

Ministry of the Environment, Finland (2013b). "Housing programmes and strategy". Helsinki: Ministry of the Environment's Department of the Built Environment.

Ministry of the Interior, Finland (2018). "Sisäministeriön tulevaisuuskatsaus: Suomesta maailman turvallisin maa" [Futures Review of the Ministry of the Interior: Finland to be the safest country in the world]. Valtioneuvoston julkaisusarja [Government Publication Series] 12/2018, 4 June.

Ministry of the Interior, Finland (2019a). "Property and traffic offences the most common types of crime".

Ministry of the Interior, Finland (2019b). "Hunting and target practice popular recreational activities in Finland".

Ministry of the Interior, Finland (2019c). "Migration and asylum Policy".

Ministry of the Interior, Finland (2019d). "Suomi vastaanottaa 850 pakolaista vuoden 2020 pakolaiskiintiössä" [Finland will accept 850 refugees in the 2020 refugee quota]. Press release, 17 September.

Mogi, K. (2017). *The Little Book of Ikigai: The Secret Japanese Way to Live a Happy and Long Life*. London: Quercus.

Morris, T., D. Dorling & G. Davey Smith (2016). "How well can we predict educational outcomes? Examining the roles of cognitive ability and social position in educational attainment". *Contemporary Social Science* 11(2/3), 154–68.

Muhonen, T. (2019a). "HS-analyysi: Kulmunin vaatimukset ajoivat vasemmistolaisen Sanna Marinin heti ahtaaseen rakoon" [HS Analysis: Kulmuni's demands drove left-wing Sanna Marin into a narrow slot]. *Helsingin Sanomat*, 10 December.

Muhonen, T. (2019b). "Rinteen eläkelupaus on vaarassa pienentyä lisää: 'Tämä yhtälö ei toimi', sanoo Kelan päämatemaatikko [Rinne's pension promise risks falling further: 'This equation doesn't work', says Kela's chief mathematician]. *Helsingin Sanomat*, 20 June.

Muhonen, T. & P. Sajari (2019). "EU:n komissio huolestui Rinteen hallituksen rahankäytöstä – valtiovarainministeri Lintilä: Pitää suhtautua vakavasti" [EU Commission became concerned about spending by the Rinne government – Minister of Finance Lintilä: this must be taken seriously]. *Helsingin Sanomat*, 22 October.

Muraja, T. (2018). "Universal basic income hasn't made me rich. But my life is more enriching". *The Guardian*, 7 August.

Myllyntaus, T. (2016). "Matkustajia, puutavaraa ja vallankumouksellisia unelmia: Rautatieliikenne Suomen historiankirjoituksessa" [Travellers, timber, and revolutionary dreams: rail transport in historical writing]. *Tekniikan Waiheita* 3(4), 32–42.

Nagesh, A. (2019). "Finland basic income trial left people 'happier but jobless'". BBC News, 8 February.

Nenonen, J. & A. Portaankorva (2009). *The Geology of the Lakeland Finland Area*. Helsinki: Geological Survey of Finland.

New Lanark Trust (2019). "Robert Owen and New Lanark: a man ahead of his time".

News Now Finland (2019). "Police suspect five Finnish men in violent child sex abuse case". *News Now Finland*, 28 March.

Nickels, S. (1965/1977). *Travellers' Guide: Finland*. London: Jonathan Cape.

Nicol, G. (1975). *Finland*. London: Batsford.

Niemelä, M. (2019a). "Sote tappoi Sipilän hallituksen – Ja se on Sipilän hallituksen oma syy" [*Sote* killed the Sipilä government – and that's the Sipilä government's own fault]. *Suomen Kuvalehti*, 8 March.

Niemelä, M. (2019b). "Sote-suunnitelmat kaivettu jälleen esiin" [*Sote* plans were dug up again]. *Suomen Kuvalehti*, 3 October.

Niemi, M. (2015). "Perussuomalaiset jahtaavat sopivaa vihollista" [The Finns Party is chasing a suitable enemy]. *Suomen Kuvalehti*, 14 August.

Niskakangas, T. & M. Nalbantoglu (2019). "Näin budjettiin kaavaillut muutokset vaikuttavat sinuun: HS listasi hyötyjiä ja häviäjiä" [This is how the speculative changes in the budget affect you: HS listed the winners and the losers]. *Helsingin Sanomat*, 15 August.

Noack, R. & S. O'Grady (2019). "'Circus Trump': what that White House news conference looked like to the Finns". *Washington Post*, 3 October.

Norum, R. & J. Proctor (2010). *The Rough Guide to Finland*. London: Rough Guides.

Nybergh, T. (2016). "We're not done yet: LGBT rights in Finland aren't perfect". *Ink tank*, 6 July.

Nygård, M. (2015). "Hyvinvointivaltiosta kilpailuvaltioon?" [From welfare state to competition state?]. In J. Autto & M. Nygård (eds), *Hyvinvointivaltion kulttuurintutkimus* [A cultural study of the welfare state], 136–66. Rovaniemi: Lappi University Press.

O'Hara, M. (2015). "Which are the best countries in the world to grow old in? America compared". *The Guardian*, 3 March.

O'Shaughnessy, H. (2013). "Chilean coup: 40 years ago I watched Pinochet crush a democratic dream". *The Guardian*, 7 September.

OECD (2010). *Strong Performers and Successful Reformers in Education: Lessons from PISA for the United States*. Paris: OECD.

OECD (2013). "Does it matter which school a student attends?". PISA in Focus. Paris: OECD.

OECD (2017a). *Pensions at a Glance 2017: OECD and G20 Indicators*. Paris: OECD Publishing.

OECD (2017b). "Pensions at a Glance 2017. How does the United Kingdom compare?". Paris: OECD.

OECD (2017c). "Affordable housing database, HC3.1: Homeless population". Paris: OECD.

OECD (2018a). *A Broken Social Elevator? How to Promote Social Mobility*. Paris: OECD Publishing.

OECD (2018b). "Revenue Statistics 2018: Finland". Paris: OECD.

OECD (2019a). "Income Inequality". Paris: OECD.

OECD (2019b). *Negotiating Our Way Up: Collective Bargaining in a Changing World of Work*. Paris: OECD.

OECD (2019c). "Education at a Glance 2019: OECD Indicators". Paris: OECD.

OECD.Stat (2018a). "Teachers' statutory salaries".

OECD.Stat. (2018b). "Social expenditure (SOCX), public, old age".

OECD.Stat (2018c). "Doctors: total per 1,000 inhabitants, 2017 or latest available".

OECD.Stat (2019a). "Time use, social protection and well-being".

OECD.Stat (2019b). "Trade unions".

OECD/European Observatory on Health Systems and Policies (2017). "Finland: country health profile 2017". State of Health in the EU. Paris: OECD/Brussels: European Observatory on Health Systems and Policies.

Öhberg, T. (2018a). "Here's what it was like to witness the march of neo-Nazis on Finland's 101st Independence Day". *Finland Today*, 8 December.

Öhberg, T. (2018b). "Finland has the best public health care system in the world, according to a study". *Finland Today*, 27 June.

Öhberg, T. (2018c). "Finnish forest professor about Trump's comments on Finnish forestry: raking is real forest management in the United States". *Finland Today*, 19 November.

Öhberg, T. (2019). "Nordic countries agree to achieve carbon neutrality quicker than anyone else". *Finland Today*, 26 January.

Ohisalo, M. & J. Saari (2014). *Kuka seisoo leipäjonossa? Ruoka-apu 2010-luvun Suomessa.* [Who stands in the breadline? Food aid in Finland in the decade of 2010]. Helsinki: Kunnallisalan kehittämissäätiö.

Office for National Statistics UK (ONS) (2017). "UK drops in European child mortality rankings". 13 October.

Office for National Statistics UK (ONS) (2018). "Changing trends in mortality: an international comparison: 2000 to 2016". 7 August 2018.

Opetusalan Ammattijärjestö (OAJ) [Trade Union of Education in Finland] (2011). "Opetusalan eettisen neuvottelukunnan kannanotto 10.11.2011" [Statement of the ethical advisory board for teachers 10.11.2011].

Opetusalan Ammattijärjestö (OAJ) [Trade Union of Education in Finland] (2019). "Opettajana varhaiskasvatuksessa ja esiopetuksessa" [Teaching in early childhood education and pre-school education].

Opetushallitus (OPH) [Finnish National Agency for Education] (2019). "Perusopetuksen arvioinnin periaatteet uudistuvat – luonnos avattu kommentoitavaksi" [Criteria for comprehensive education to be reformed – draft open for comments]. 16 September.

Orjala, A. (2016). "Lähes 10 000 suomalaista muutti ulkomaille viime vuonna – tässä suosituimmat maat" [Almost 10,000 Finns moved abroad last year – these are the most popular countries]. Yle Uutiset, 23 May.

Orjasniemi, S. (2019). "Sipilän Hallituksen Talous- Ja Budjettipolitiikka" [Economic and Budget Policy of Sipilä's Government]. *Politiikasta*, 13 April.

Official Statistics Finland (OSF) (2007). "Väestönkehitys itsenäisessä Suomessa – kasvun vuosikymmenistä kohti harmaantuvaa Suomea" [Demographic development in an independent Finland – decades of growth towards a greyish Finland]. 5 December.

Official Statistics Finland (OSF) (2016). "Migration, immigration rose to a new record level in 2016".

Official Statistics Finland (OSF) (2017a). "Isät tilastoissa 2017" [Dads in statistics 2017].

Official Statistics Finland (OSF) (2017b). "Asuntokunnat ja asuinolot 2017" [Households and living conditions 2017].

Official Statistics Finland (OSF) (2017c). "Rents increased by 2.2 per cent in 2016".

Official Statistics Finland (OSF) (2017d). "Buildings and free-time residences, Free-time residence usually owned by a person from out-of-town".

Official Statistics Finland (OSF) (2018a). "Accommodation statistics 2018".

Official Statistics Finland (OSF) (2018b). "Tohtorintutkintojen määrä väheni seitsemän prosenttia edellisvuodesta" [Doctoral degrees decreased by 7% compared to the previous year].

Official Statistics Finland (OSF) (2018c). "Isät tilastoissa 2018" [Dads in statistics 2018].

Official Statistics Finland (OSF) (2018d). "Vuokra-asuminen yleistyy – pienet asunnot useimmiten vuokralla" [Rental housing is becoming more common – small homes are mostly rented].

Official Statistics Finland (OSF) (2018e). "Syntyvyys kaikkien aikojen matalin" [Total fertility rate at an all-time low].

Official Statistics Finland (OSF) (2019a). "Wages, salaries and labour costs".

Official Statistics Finland (OSF) (2019b). "Educational finances (current expenditure on education has decreased in real terms since 2010)".

Official Statistics Finland (OSF) (2019c). "Väestö: väestörakenne 31.12" [Population: population structure].

Official Statistics Finland (OSF) (2019d). "Steep decline in the birth rate continued".

Official Statistics Finland (OSF) (2019e). "Vapaarahoitteiset vuokrat nousivat eniten pääkaupunkiseudulla ja Turussa" [Non-subsidized rents rose the most in the Helsinki metropolitan area and in Turku].

Official Statistics Finland (OSF) (2019f). "Työtaistelutilasto" [Labour dispute statistics].

Official Statistics Finland (OSF) (2019g). "Parliamentary elections 2019".

Official Statistics Finland (OSF) (2019h). "Solmittujen avioliittojen määrä väheni huomattavasti" [The number of marriages decreased significantly].

Official Statistics Finland (OSF) (2019i). "Greenhouse gas emissions in energy supply and land transport declined in 2017".

Official Statistics Finland (OSF) (2019j). "Greenhouse gas emissions increased, emission allocation exceeded".

Official Statistics Finland (OSF) (2019k). "Total amount of waste decreased in 2017".

Official Statistics Finland (OSF) (2019l). "Finnish residents' travel to southern Europe increased in 2018".

Official Statistics Finland (OSF) (2019m). "Vehicle stock grew in 2018".

Official Statistics Finland (OSF) (2019n). "Vital statistics and population 1749–2017".

Official Statistics Finland (OSF) (2019o). "Total fertility rate 1776–2018".

Official Statistics Finland (OSF) (2019p). "Births, deaths, net immigration and population change 1990–2018".

Official Statistics Finland (OSF) (2019q). "Migration by year, nationality and language 1990–2017".

Official Statistics Finland (OSF) (2021). "Number of employed persons decreased from the year before".

Øvretvei, J. (2003). "Nordic privatization and private healthcare". *International Journal of Health Planning and Management* 18(3), 233–46.

Oxford Economics (2019). *Assessing the Macroeconomic Impact of EU Membership for Finland: A Report on Behalf of Akava*. Oxford: Oxford Economics.

Paananen, K. (2019). "Rinteen hallitus lupasi pysäyttää luonnon monimuotoisuuden tuhon – Tutkijan tyly arvio: tavoite oikea, mutta keinot eivät riitä" [Rinne's government pledged to halt biodiversity loss – scientist's blunt assessment: the goal is right, but the means are insufficient]. *Suomen Kuvalehti*, 31 October.

Pallaste, T. (2019). "Ahvenanmaan kuningas Anders I" [Åland's king, Anders I]. *Helsingin Sanomat*, 7 September.

Palonen, W. (2019). "Yhä pidempi koulutaival" [An even longer school path]. *Suomen Kuvalehti*, 9 August.

Palvelukeskus Helsinki (2019). "Leikkipuistoruokailu" [Playground meals]. Palvelukeskus [City of Helsinki Service Centre].

Pantsu, P. (2017). "Soten valinnanvapauden nykyversio on palveluseteli – sitä käytetään ällistyttävän vähän" [The current version of Sote's freedom of choice is the service voucher – it is used staggeringly little]. Yle Uutiset, 13 July.

Pantzar, K. (2018), *Finding Sisu: In Search of Courage, Strength and Happiness the Finnish Way*. London: Hodder & Stoughton.

Parkkinen, P. (2019). "Suomi nousi lehdistönvapausindeksissä toiselle sijalle, edellä vielä Norja" [Finland ranks second in the press freedom index, Norway still ahead]. Yle Uutiset, 18 April.

Parliament of Finland (2019a). "Eduskunnan lyhyt historia – autonomian ajalta EU-Suomen parlamentiksi" [A short history of the parliament – from autonomy to the EU-Finland Parliament].

Parliament of Finland (2019b). "Aloitteet eduskuntakäsittelyn käynnistäjinä 1962–1963" [Initiatives as initiators of the parliamentary process 1962–1963].

Parliament of Finland (2019c). "Vaalit ja äänestäminen" [Elections and voting].

Parliament of Finland (2019d). "Women as Members of Parliament: The Parliament's number of women has ballooned in a little over a century".

Parliament of Finland (2019e). "Kansalaisaloite avohakkuiden lopettamisesta valtion metsissä luovutettiin eduskuntaan" [*A citizens' initiative to stop logging in state forests was passed to Parliament*].

Parliament of Finland (2020) "Perhevapaauudistus" [Parental leave reform].

Partanen, A. (2018). "The Nordic theory of love: everything you need to know". *Financial Review*, 2 February.

Parviala, A. (2019). "Uusiutuva polttoaine on Nesteen kultakaivos – Etumatka alkaa olla niin pitkä, että maailmasta ei löydy kunnon vastusta suomalaisyhtiölle" [Renewable fuel is Neste's gold mine – Its lead is such that there is no good opposition to this Finnish company in the world]. Yle Uutiset, 6 February.

Pekkarinen, T. & R. Uusitalo (2012). "Peruskoulu-uudistuksen vaikutukset" [The effects of the comprehensive education reform] *Kansantaloudellinen aikakausikirja* 108(2), 128–39.

Pekkonen, S. (2017). "Sipilä: Hallitusyhteistyö Halla-ahon kanssa kaatui arvojen eroihin ja johtamistapaan" [Sipilä: Government cooperation with Halla-aho fell due to differences in values and leadership style]. *Kauppalehti*, 12 June.

Peltomäki, T. *et al.* (2019). "Uutisraportti podcast 12.12.2019: Al-Hol, Trumpin virkarikossyytteet, Sanna Marin – supertähti" [Al-Hol, Trump's impeachment, Sanna Marin – superstar]. *Helsingin Sanomat*, 12 December.

Peltonen, M. (2016). "University of Helsinki to introduce fees for new non-EU/EEA students as of autumn 2017". University of Helsinki, 29 January.

Peltonen, S. (2018). "Maahanmuuttajat ovat aliedustettuina yliopistoissa – uusi neuvontapalvelu SIMHE auttaa hakijoita" [Immigrants are underrepresented in universities – new advisory service SIMHE helps applicants]. University of Helsinki, 22 October.

Penzel, M. (2019). "The next start-up cities that will transform the global economy". World Economic Forum, 23 July.

Petäjä, J. (2017). "Yhtenäistä Suomea ei ole olemassakaan, sanoo tutkija – 'Suomi on aina ollut monien kulttuurien maa'" [There is no homogenous Finland, says researcher – 'Finland has always been a country of many cultures']. *Helsingin Sanomat*, 2 May.

Petri, A. (2019). "Some feedback from the Finnish president on his visit to the United States". *Washington Post*, 3 October.

Piccoli, S. & E. Harris (2017). "New York City offers free lunch for all public school students". *New York Times*, 6 September.

Pirie, M. (2018). "The Continental Telegraph". Adam Smith Institute blog, 27 February.

Pleace, N. *et al.* (2015). *The Finnish Homelessness Strategy: An International Review*. Helsinki: Ministry of the Environment.

Ponsford, D. (2017). "Survey finds that UK written press is (by some way) the least trusted in Europe". *Press Gazette*, 26 May.

Poropudas, O. (1996). "Suomen taloudellisen menestystarinan tulkinnat" [Interpretations of Finland's economic success story]. *Kansantaloudellinen aikakauskirja* 92(3), 352–63.

Poulter, S. & A. Kallioniemi (2014). "Uskonto, kansalaisuus, ja kansalaiseksi kasvaminen: kohti katsomustietoista kansalaiskasvatusta" [Religion, citizenship, and citizenship growth: towards a view of conscious education]. *Kansalaisyhteiskunta* 1, 29–48.

Pöysä, S. & S. Kupiainen (eds) (2018). "Girls and boys in school – how can boys' weak performance be defeated in comprehensive school?". Helsinki: Prime Minister's Office.

Puttonen, M. (2019). "Hyötyvätkö vähätuloiset perheet varakkaista naapureista? Näin naapurusto voi vaikuttaa lapsesi elämään" [Do low-income families benefit from wealthier neighbours? This is how your neighbourhood can affect your child's life]. *Helsingin Sanomat*, 11 November.

Rae, A. & E. Nyanzu (2019). *An English Atlas of Equality*. London: Nuffield Foundation.

Rajmil, L. *et al.* (2018). "Trends in social determinants of child health and perinatal outcomes in European countries 2005–2015 by level of austerity imposed by governments: a repeat cross-sectional analysis of routinely available data". *British Medical Journal Open* 8(10); https://bmjopen.bmj.com/content/8/10/e022932.

Ramsey, A. & P. Geoghegan (2018). "Revealed: how the UK's powerful right-wing think tanks and Conservative MPs work together". Open Democracy, 31 July.

Rankola, T. (1997). "Winter maintenance of highways in Finland". *Proceedings of the Institution of Civil Engineers: Municipal Engineer* 121(3), 135–41.

Rasila, V. (1970). "Torpparikysymyksen ratkaisuvaihe: Suomen torpparikysymys vuosina 1909–1918" [The solution of the crofter problem: the crofter problem in Finland, 1909–1918]. Historiallisia tutkimuksia, no. 81. Helsinki: Kirjayhtymä.

Raunio, T. (2005). "Finland: one hundred years of quietude". In M. Gallagher & P. Mitchell (eds), *The Politics of Electoral Systems*, 463–90. Oxford: Oxford University Press.

Reaktor (2019). "Finland's bold AI experiment, 'Elements of AI'". https://www.reaktor.com/elements-of-ai/.

Reid-Henry, S. (2010). *The Cuban Cure: Reason and Resistance in Global Science*. Chicago, IL; University of Chicago Press.

Reinborth, S. (2019). "'Vakavan pohdinnan paikka', sanoo sisäministeri Maria Ohisalo Suomen saamasta ihmisoikeustuomiosta" ['A place for serious reflection', says the Interior Minister, Maria Ohisalo, on Finland's human rights sentence]. *Helsingin Sanomat*, 14 November.

Reporters Without Borders (2016). "Reporters Without Borders (RSF) remains concerned about actions taken by national broadcaster Yle". 15 December.

Reporters Without Borders (2019). "2019 World Press Freedom Index".

Reuters (2019). "Long-delayed Finland nuclear reactor to start July 2020 – TVO". Reuters News, 17 July.

Richardson, H. (2018). "At least '320,000 people homeless in Britain'". BBC News, 22 November.

Risku, M. (2014). "A historical insight on Finnish education policy". *Italian Journal of Sociology of Education* 6(2), 46–68.

Rosendahl, J. (2015). "Finnish parliament will debate next year leaving euro zone". Reuters, 16 November.

Rotko, T. *et al.* (2011). "Kapeneeko kuilu? Tilannekatsaus terveyserojen kaventamiseen

Suomessa 2007–2010" [Narrowing the gap? Review of the narrowing of health differences in Finland 2007–2011]. *Terveyden ja hyvinvoinnin laitos* 8/2011.

Ruffini, K. (2018). "Universal access to free school meals and student achievement: evidence from the community eligibility provision". IRLE Working Paper No. 102–18.

Ruonavaara, H. (2003). "Finland". In J. Doling & J. Ford (eds), *Globalisation and Home Ownership: Experiences in Eight Member States of the European Union*. Delft: Delft University Press.

Saarenheimo, T. (2019). "Finland – reply to the European commission". Helsinki: Ministry of Finance, 16 October.

Saarikoski, S. (2019). "Nainen voi lähteä idästä" [A woman can leave East Helsinki]. *Helsingin Sanomat*, 7 December.

Saarima, T. (2018). "Vauhditetaanko kaupungistamista" [Should we accelerate urbanization?]. *Suomen Kuvalehti*, 15 June.

Sahlberg, P. (2011). "PISA in Finland: an education miracle or an obstacle to change?" *Center for Educational Policy Studies (CEPS) Journal* 1(3), 119–40.

Sahlberg, P. (2012). "A model lesson: Finland shows us what equal opportunity looks like". *American Educator* 36(1), 20–27.

Sahlberg, P. (2015). *What Can the World Learn from Educational Change in Finland?* New York: Teachers College Press.

Sahlberg, P. & W. Doyle (2019). *Let the Children Play: How More Play Will Save our Schools and Help Children Thrive*. Oxford: Oxford University Press.

SAK [Central Organization of Finnish Trade Unions] (2019a). "Sopimukset" [Agreements].

SAK [Central Organization of Finnish Trade Unions] (2019b). "Activation model neither activates people nor helps in finding a job, it simply cuts unemployment benefits". *SAK News*, 4 January.

Salmi, V. (2019). "Entiset Pihit: Suomalaiset olivat nuukia, kun lainarahaa piti ruinata hattu kourassa. Mutta nyt sitä saa" [Former Misers: Finns were stingy when loans had to be begged for cap in hand. But now they can get it]. *Suomen Kuvalehti*, 23 August.

Salminen, J. (2010). "Millaista on suomalainen ääriajattelu? Edustavatko perussuomalaiset sitä?" [What is Finnish extremism like? Do the Finns represent it?]. *Suomen Kuvalehti*, 28 October.

Salo, J. (2018). "Yhdenvertaisuutta perusopetuksen arviointiin" [Equality in comprehensive school evaluation]. OAJ [Trade Union of Education in Finland].

Salo, S. & J. Rydgren (2018). "Politicisation of the eurozone crisis in Finland: adaptation toward the radical right?". *Journal of International and Comparative Social Policy* 34(3), 234–57.

Salovuori, S. (2016). "Kahden laman kasvatit" [Children of two depressions]. *Mielenterveys-lehti* 4/16.

Saltman, R. & J. Teperi (2016). "Health reform in Finland: current proposals and unresolved challenges". *Health Economics, Policy and Law* 11(3), 303–19.

Sambrook, C. & S. Ryan (2017). "Connor Sparrowhawk: how one boy's death in NHS care inspired a movement for justice". Open Democracy, 29 November.

Samuel, S. (2019). "Finland gave people free money. It didn't help them get jobs – but does that matter?" Vox, 9 February.

Sandell, M. (2016). "Kirkkoon kuuluu yhä vähemmän suomalaisia – moni uskoo silti Jumalaan ja rukoilee" [Fewer Finns remain members of the church – many still believe in God and pray]. Yle Uutiset, 21 November.

Sandell, M. (2018). "Väitöstutkimus: Taloudellinen eliitti saa sisäpiiritietoa, lobbaa lait ja hallitsee Suomea" [Doctoral dissertation: Economic elite get insider information, lobby laws and rule Finland]. Yle Uutiset, 28 March.

Sandell, M. & T. Tebest (2016). "Aseiden määrä Suomessa vähenee – katso, missä ovat maan 1,5 miljoonaa asetta" [The number of weapons in Finland is decreasing – look at where the country's 1.5 million weapons are]. Yle Uutiset, 18 January.

Sarapää, O. *et al.* (2013). "Rare earth exploration potential in Finland". *Journal of Geochemical Exploration* 133 (Oct), 25–41.

Sarhimaa, J. (2017). "Kansanedustaja Ozan Yanarilla on talousosaamista ja haluja vihreiden johtoon, mutta kukaan ei kuuntele, koska rasismi ja maahanmuutto nousevat jatkuvasti otsikoihin" [Ozan Yanar MP has the economic know-how and the will to lead the Greens, but nobody listens because racism and immigration are constantly in the headlines]. *Helsingin Sanomat*, 7 March.

Särkijärvi, J., S. Jääskeläinen & K. Lohko-Soner (eds) (2018). "Toimenpideohjelma hiilettömään liikenteeseen 2045. Liikenteen ilmastopolitiikan työryhmän loppuraportti" [Action programme for carbon-free transport 2045. Final report by the Transport Climate Policy working group]. Liikenne- ja viestintäministeriön julkaisuja 13/2018 [Ministry of Transport and Communications publications 13/2018].

Saure, M. (2019). "Laki ja sukupuoli" [Law and gender]. *Yliopisto/Helsingin Yliopisto* Y/08/19.

Scandinavian Homes (2019). "Self-build homes in the UK".

Scheinin, M. (2021). "Finland: soft measures, respect for the rule of law, and plenty of good luck: overview of legal and political response and adaptation to COVID-19". *Verfassungsblog*, 23 February.

SDP (2019). "Principles: the principles of social democracy as adopted by the 38th Party Congress held in Turku, 1999". https://sdp.fi/en/learn/principles/.

Seta (2017). "Avioliittolaki" [The marriage Act]. https://seta.fi/avioliittolaki/.

Sequeira, T. & E. Richardson (2019). "Finnish youth strike for climate action". Yle Uutiset, 27 September.

SFP (2019). "SFP Election Platform 2019". https://riksdagsval.sfp.fi/en/sfp-election-platform-2019/.

Shilliam, R. (2018). *Race and the Undeserving Poor: From Abolition to Brexit*. Newcastle upon Tyne: Agenda.

Siddique, H. (2018). "UK life expectancy growth falls faster than other leading nations". *The Guardian*, 7 August.

Silliman, M. (2017). "Targeted funding, immigrant background, and educational outcomes: evidence from Helsinki's 'positive discrimination' policy". VATT working papers 91.17. Helsinki: Valtion taloudellinen tutkimuskeskus [Government Institute for Economic Research].

Silliman, M. & H. Virtanen (2019). "Labor market returns to vocational secondary education". ETLA Working Paper No. 65.

Simula, M. (2014). "Kristillisdemokraatit – puolue lähellä tiukkaa herätyskristillisyyttä" [Christian Democrats – party close to strict Christian revivalism]. *Suomen Kuvalehti*, 2 July.

Simula, M. (2019). "Kiplailua kikyn jälkeen" [Competition after the Competitiveness Pact]. *Suomen kuvalehti*, 22 March.

Sipilä, J. (2011). "Hyvinvointivaltio sosiaalisena investointina: älä anna köyhälle kalaa vaan koulutus" [A welfare state as a social investment: do not give the poor fish but education]. *Yhteyskuntapolitiikka* 76(4), 359–72.

Sipinen, J. (2019). "Luottamuksen verkostot ulkomaalaistaustaisten ehdokkaiden rekrytoinnissa" [Networks of trust in the recruitment of candidates with foreign backgrounds]. In M. Bäck & E. Kestilä-Kekkonen (eds), *Poliittinen ja sosiaalinen luottamus: Polut, trendit ja kuilut* [Political and social trust: paths, trends and gaps], 174–98. Helsinki: Valtiovarainministeriö [Ministry of Finance].

Sivonen, J., A. Koivula & A. Saarinen (2018). "Asiantuntijaluokan uusi jako perussuomalaisten vaalimenestysten taustall". *Politiikka* 60(3), 192–207.

Sletholt, E. (1951). "Finland today". *International Journal* 6(2), 118–26.

Social Services and Healthcare Division (2020). "Fees". https://www.hel.fi/sote/en/services/fees.

Soini, T. (2015). "Välikysymys eurokriisin hoidosta ja Kreikan tilanteesta" [Intermediate question on the management of the euro crisis and the situation in Greece]. Perussuomalaiset, 2 January.

Soininvaara, O. (2016). "Syntyisi älämölö, jos vaikkapa Wahlroos ehdottaisi köyhien siirtämistä omiin taloihinsa" [Protests would follow should Wahlroos suggest moving the poor into their own houses] *Suomen Kuvalehti*, 9 December.

Soininvaara, O. (2017). "Helsingin asuntopula on tehokas este Suomen talouskasvulle" [Helsinki's housing shortage is a powerful obstacle to Finland's economic growth]. *Suomen Kuvalehti*, 28 May.

Solla, K. & A. Palmén-Väisänen (2017). "Kuntavaalit – 10 kiinnostavaa faktaa" [municipal elections – 10 interesting facts]. Yle Uutiset, 27 March.

Speri, A. (2019). "The criminal justice system is not broken. It's just doing what it was designed to do". *The Intercept*, 9 November.

Stepney, P. (2014). "Prevention in social work: the final frontier?" *Critical and Radical Social Work* 2(3), 305–20.

Stoet, G. & D. Geary (2018). "The gender-equality paradox in science, technology, engineering, and mathematics education". *Psychological Science* 29(4), 581–93.

Strömberg, J. (2019). "Yksinkertainen opas sote-finaaliin: Tätä vuosikausia kestäneellä hankkeella tavoitellaan, ja näin se voisi vielä edetä" [Guide to the sote-finale: what years of planning have been aiming for and how it could progress]. Yle Uutiset, 26 February.

Studyinfo (2020). "Finnish education system".

Sturge, G. (2019). "UK prison population statistics". House of Commons Briefing Paper CBP-04334, 23 July.

Suomenash (2019). "Kulutus" [Consumption]. Helsinki: ASH Association of Finland.

Sutela, H. & L. Larja (2015). "Yli puolet Suomen ulkomaalaistaustaisista muuttanut maahan perhesyistä" [Over half of foreign-born people in Finland moved here due to family reasons]. Official Statistics Finland (OSF).

Sutinen, T. (2019). "Uusimaa on jatkossa Helsinki ja neljä maakuntaa – hallituksen lupaama soten erillisratkaisu etenee" [Uusimaa will in the future be Helsinki and four regions – and the government promises that a separate solution is progressing]. *Helsingin Sanomat*, 1 November.

TAF (2019). Veronmaksajat [Taxpayers Association of Finland] "Palkansaajan veroprosentit 2020" [Wage earners' tax rates 2020].

Teittinen, P. (2019). "HS selvitti: Enemmistö puolueista haluaa kiristää turvapaikka-politiikkaa" [Most parties want to tighten up asylum policy]. *Helsingin Sanomat*, 13 March.

Terveyden ja hyvinvoinnin laitos (THL) [Finnish Institute for Health and Welfare] (2017). "Suomen alhaisella imeväiskuolleisuudella on monta syytä" [Finland's low infant mortality has multiple contributing factors]. 27 January.

Terveyden ja hyvinvoinnin laitos (THL) (2018a). "Vähemmistöt ja erityisryhmät" [Minorities and special groups].

Terveyden ja hyvinvoinnin laitos (THL) (2018b). "Suomalaisten alkoholinkulutus on vähentynyt, mutta edelleen yli puoli miljoonaa juo yli riskirajojen" [Alcohol consumption in Finland has decreased, but over half a million are still at risk from excessive drinking]. 5 September.

Terveyden ja hyvinvoinnin laitos (THL) (2019a). "Hyvinvointi- ja terveyserot: toimeentulo" [Well-being and health inequality: livelihood].

Terveyden ja hyvinvoinnin laitos (THL) (2019b). "Saamelaiset" [The Sami people].

The Economist (1994). "European telecoms: lessons from the frozen north". 8 October.

The Economist (2000). "Survey online finance: Scandinavian models". 20 May.

The Economist (2016). "Helsinking". 12 May.

The Economist (2019). "Gambling addiction in Finland". 3 October.

The Finns Party [Perussuomalaiset] (2019). "Perussuomalainen Talouspolitiikka" [The Finns Party's Economic Policy]. 21 January. https://www.perussuomalaiset.fi/wp-content/uploads/2019/02/P.

The Guardian (2019). "Finland's Social Democrats declare general election victory". 4 April.

This is Finland (2019). "Things you should and shouldn't know".

Thornhill, T. & L. Kjellsson (2020). "Best cities for families in 2020 revealed: Helsinki ranks No 1 out of 150, London a lowly 55th and Los Angeles is best for kids' activities". *Daily Mail*, 22 January.

Tikkala, H. & A. Pilke (2019). "Hallitus käynnistää sote-kokeilun kunnissa, rahaa jaossa 1000 uuden lääkärin palkkaamiseen – 'Jos tällä ei palkata lääkäreitä, niin millä sitten'" [The government will begin the *sote*-experiment in counties, money available to hire 1,000 new doctors] Yle Uutiset, 15 October.

Tiihonen, A. (2019). "Yhteiskuntaluokat ja poliittinen luottamus" [Social classes and political trust]. In M. Bäck & E. Kestilä-Kekkonen (eds), *Poliittinen ja sosiaalinen luottamus: Polut, trendit ja kuilut* [Political and social trust: paths, trends and gaps], 156–73. Helsinki: Valtiovarainministeriö [Ministry of Finance].

Tolkki, K. (2019a). "5 syytä, miksi maailman paras maa ei ole naisten ja tyttöjen onnela: Suomi on yhä Euroopan toiseksi väkivaltaisin maa naisille" [5 reasons why the best country in the world is not for women and girls. Congratulations: Finland remains Europe's second most violent country for women]. Yle Uutiset, 3 March.

Tolkki, K. (2019b). "Ylen mittaus: Perussuomalaiset jyristelivät taas eteenpäin, keskustalle kaikkien aikojen murskaluvut" [Yle's assesment: The Finns Party gains popularity, Centre Party faces an all time low]. Yle Uutiset, 5 December.

Törmälehto, V.-M. (2018). "Varallisuuserot kasvussa, tuloerot vakaat?". [Wealth inequality on the rise, income inequality stable?]. *Tilastokeskus* [*Statistics Finland*], 28 August.

Traficom (2019). "Ladattavien hybridien ja sähköautojen osuus käytettyinä maahantuoduista autoista ennätyskorkea" [Rechargeable hybrid and electric cars reach their highest share within the total number of imported cars]. 24 June.

Tram, V. (2018). "Onko suomalainen tasa-arvo osin myytti? Työläistaustainen opiskelija on yhä yliopistossa kuin vieraalla maalla: Minun piti perustella olemistani täällä" [Is Finnish equality in part a myth? Students with working-class backgrounds are as common in universities as those studying abroad"]. Yle Uutiset, 2 September.

Tulla, S. (1999). "Securitisation and finance for social housing in Finland". *Urban Studies* 36(4), 647–56.

Turun Sanomat (2017). "Åbo Akademi tutki: arabiankielisiä miehiä syrjitään asuntomarkkinoilla" [Åbo Akademi researched: Arab-speaking men are discriminated against in the housing market]. 31 August.

TUURF [Finnish Union of University Researchers and Teachers] (2019). "Academic of the Year – Researcher Nafisa Yeasmin". 25 October.

UK Government (2019). "The new state pension". https://www.gov.uk/new-state-pension/how-its-calculated.

Ukkola, J. (2011). "Mitä pitää tietää?" [What do you need to know?]. *Suomen Kuvalehti*.

Ukkola, J. (2018). "Onnen maa" [The land of happiness]. *Suomen Kuvalehti*.

United Nations Development Programme (UNDP) (2017). *2016 Human Development Report*. New York: United Nations.

United Nations High Commission for Refugees (UNHCR) (2017). *Global Trends: Forced Displacement in 2016*. Geneva: UNHCR.

United Nations Population Division (2001). "Replacement migration: is it a solution to declining and ageing populations?".

United Nations Office on Drugs and Crime (UNODC) (2017). "Global study on homicide".

Utti, O. (2006). "J. V. Snellman, without him where would Finland be?". This is Finland.

Uusitalo, P. (1984). "Monetarism, Keynesianism and the institutional status of central banks". *Acta Sociologica* 27(1), 31–50.

Vartiainen, J. (2011). "The Finnish model of economic and social policy – from Cold War primitive accumulation to generational conflicts?". In L. Mjøset (ed.), *The Nordic Varieties of Capitalism*, 52–87. Bingley: Emerald.

Veikkaus (2019). "Veikkaus prepared for major changes in the operating environment". Veikkaus Newsroom, 2 February 2019.

Vento, H. "Radat vaarassa menettää EU-rahoja" [Railways at risk of losing EU-finding]. *Suomen Kuvalehti*, 29 January 2020.

Venesperä, R. (2018). "Moving to Finland as a disabled expat: what you need to know". Expatfocus, 5 September.

Vero Skatt [Finnish Tax Administration] (2017). "Pääomatulon veroprosentti" [Tax rate of capital income].

Vihreät (2012). "The Greens of Finland's Statement of Principles, Responsibility, Freedom, Caring, Resolutions adopted at the party conference on 20.5.2012 in Lappeenranta". https://www.vihreat.fi/files/liitto/Greens_principle_programme.pdf.

Vilkama, K. (2012). "Kantaväestön ja maahanmuuttajien alueellinen eriytyminen pääkaupunkiseudulla" [Native population and immigrants' regional segregation in the Helsinki metropolitan area]. *Helsingin Seudun Suunnat* 3/2012, 8–10.

Visit Finland (2019). "Boosting the Finnish travel industry".

Von Schoultz, Å. (2019). "Kansalaisten näkemykset demokratian prosesseista ja legitimiteetistä" [Citizens' views on democratic processes and legitimacy]. In M. Bäck & E. Kestilä-Kekkonen (eds), *Poliittinen ja sosiaalinen luottamus: Polut, trendit ja kuilut* [Political and social trust: paths, trends and gaps], 174–98. Helsinki: Valtiovarainministeriö [Ministry of Finance].

Wahlbeck, Ö. (2018). "To share or not to share responsibility? Finnish refugee policy and the hesitant support for a common European asylum system". *Journal of Immigrant & Refugee Studies* 17(3), 299–316.

Wainwright, D. (2017). "Renting a home: how much space will £100 buy you?". BBC News, 19 December.

Walker, A. (2016). "Finland: the sick man of Europe". BBC News, 29 February.

Wall, D. (2014). "Best-selling economist Thomas Piketty: 'Time to start worrying about inequality'". Yle Uutiset, 15 June.

Wall, T. (2019). "The battle to save Lapland". *The Guardian*, 23 February.

Whiting, K. (2018). "Finland recently published everyone's taxes on 'National Jealousy Day'". World Economic Forum Blog, 2 November.

Wikipedia (2019a). "List of countries by traffic-related death rate".

Wikipedia (2019b). "Prevalence of teenage pregnancy".

Wikipedia (2019c). "List of countries by refugee population".

Wikipedia (2019d). "Vanhan valtaus" [The occupation of the Old Student House].

Wilde, O. (1891). "The soul of man under socialism". *Fortnightly Review* (February).

Wilkinson, A. (2017). "Labour must be bold – universal benefits offer a popular way forward". *The Guardian*, 7 April.

Wilkinson, R. & K. Pickett (2009). *The Spirit Level: Why More Equal Societies Almost Always Do Better*. London: Allen Lane.

Wilson, C. *et al.* (2013). "Migration and intergenerational replacement in Europe". *Population and Development Review* 39(1), 131–57.

Wilson, W. & C. Barton (2019). "Households in temporary accommodation (England)". Commons Briefing papers SN02110. 15 October.

Wood, J. (2019). "These are the best cities for work–life balance in 2019". World Economic Forum, 27 September.

World Bank (2018a). "Exports of goods and services (% of GDP) – Finland".

World Bank (2018b). "Income share held by lowest 10%".

World Bank (2019a). "Annual percentage growth rate of GDP per capita based on constant local currency: calculated without making deductions for depreciation of fabricated assets or for depletion and degradation of natural resources". World Bank data series: NY.GDP.PCAP.KD.ZG.

World Bank (2019b). "Share of youth not in education, employment or training, total (% of population aged 15–24 or 15–29)". World Bank data series: SL.UEM.NEET.ZS.

World Economic Forum (2018). "Finland performance overview 2018". Global Competitiveness Report. Geneva: World Economic Forum.

World Inequality Database (2018). "United Kingdom".

World Inequality Database (2019). "Net personal wealth: top 10% share – adults equal split".

World Population Review (2019). "Gun deaths by country 2019".

World Prison Brief (2019). "Finland".

Worstall, T. (2019). "The new – very expensive – Finnish food made from electricity, air and water". *Continental Telegraph*, 29 June.

Y-Foundation (2017). *A Home of Your Own: Housing First and Ending Homelessness in Finland*. Keuruu: Otava Book Printing.

Y-säätiö [Y-Foundation] (2018). "*Asunnottomuus Suomessa*" [Homelessness in Finland].

Ylä-Anttila, T. (2017). "Familiarity as a tool of populism: political appropriation of shared experiences and the case of Suvivirsi". *Acta Sosiologica* 60(4), 342–57.

Yle (2019). "The election compass".

Yle Uutiset (2015). "Kuka on oikeistolaisin, kuka liberaalein? Katso, miten ehdokkaasi asettuu poliittiselle nelikentälle" [Who is the right-wing, who is the liberal? See how your candidate fits into the political dual axis chart]. 13 April.

Yle Uutiset (2018a). "Natural resources institute blasts gold diggers over Lapland mining". 18 September.

Yle Uutiset (2018b). "Civil war still divides Finland after 100 years, poll suggests". 18 January.

Yle Uutiset (2018c). "Ombudsman: Urgent action needed to tackle child poverty in Finland". 6 April.

Yle Uutiset (2018d). "Wealth gap widens as richest 10 per cent owns nearly half of all wealth in Finland". 5 June.

Yle Uutiset (2018e). "Study: Finland's health care system among the best in the world". 28 June.

Yle Uutiset (2019a). "Finland: still the happiest country in the world (says UN report): The UN's seventh annual World Happiness Report ranks the countries of the world on 'how happy their citizens perceive themselves to be'". 20 March.

Yle Uutiset (2019b). "Gambling monopoly Veikkaus on new strategy: 'We haven't done enough to reduce addiction'". 31 October.

Yle Uutiset (2019c). "Minister backtracks over Posti outsourcing, sets up working group". 21 November.

Yle Uutiset (2019d). "Embattled CEO of elder care home quits over negligence reports". 19 January.

Yle Uutiset (2019e). "Multiple cities ditch Esperi Care nursing services – gross neglect reported". 27 January.

Yle Uutiset (2019f). "Archbishop responds to Pride dust-up: 'Same sex couples are welcome at all church activities'". 20 June.

Yle Uutiset (2019g). "Finland ranked second on press freedom index, behind Norway". 18 April.

Yle Uutiset (2019h). "Kjell Westö: 'Finns wouldn't have survived 20th century without pragmatism'". 5 December.

Yue, M. (2014). "Finland education system based on flexibility". *Shanghai Daily*, 30 December.

Zetterberg, S. & P. Pulma (2003). "Autonominen suuriruhtinaskunta" [The autonomous grand duchy]. In S. Zetterberg (ed.) *Suomen historian pikkujättiläinen* [The small giant of Finnish history]. Porvoo: WSOY.

Zhang, P. *et al.* (2019). "Cold weather conditions and risk of hypothermia among people experiencing homelessness: implications for prevention strategies". *International Journal of Environmental Research and Public Health* 16(18), 3259.

Zyskowicz, B. (2018). "Soten Valinnanvapaus" [Freedom of choice in *Sote*]. 27 November.

Index

Page numbers in *italics* indicate illustrations and page numbers in **bold** indicate tables